Praise for Sid James ... from those who know him best

"Sid really shot the moon on this one!"
—Geneva and Dorothy Gaston, grandchildren

"This is better than rotten eggs!"
—Leslie Hunt, daughter

"Surprising and entertaining! I couldn't put it down!"
—Deena Trimble, sister

"The author deftly intertwines his thoughts, ideas and concepts in genuine anticipation of the reader's enjoyment. A literary masterpiece of unknown proportions!"
—Joe James, brother

"Andy Griffith meets Aristotle; a dazzling tale of humor and triumph. Five Stars!"
—Bryan Gaston, son-in-law

"Sid is a master of getting the idea and cooking with gas. I recommend this book to everyone who appreciates an unequaled perspective on life!"
—Jim Parkes, brother-in-law

"An absolutely entertaining book by someone who stumbled and laughed his way through life's ups and downs!"
—Chris and Glenda James, brother- and sister-in-law

"Wow! An unbelievable story by an extraordinary person!"
—Judy and Leroy Voss, life-long friends

"This book is a funny and unique account of a boy-to-man's odyssey in the heartland of Tennessee. A must read!"
—Sandy Lisnak, companion at First United Methodist Church, Lawrenceburg, Tennessee

I was spellbound over the author's lack of using spellcheck.
—James Sewell, former pastor and confidant

This is the best book I never read.
—Marian Parkes: Sister-In-Law

Warming By The Fire is a page turning experience limited only to one's imagination. Definitely "Illigitimus non-caeborundum."
—Chris James, Brother

WARMING BY THE FIRE

WARMING BY THE FIRE

A MEMOIR

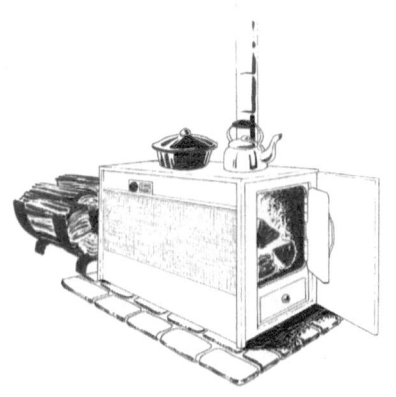

SID JAMES

MISSION POINT PRESS

© Copyright Sid James, 2021

No parts of this book may be reproduced, stored in a retrieval system, or transmitted by any means without written permission from the publisher except in the case of brief quotations for the purpose of critical articles or reviews. For information or permission, contact:

Mission Point Press
2554 Chandler Road
Traverse City, Michigan 49696
www.MissionPointPress.com
231-421-9513

Printed in the United States of America

ISBN: 978-1-954786-25-7
Library of Congress Control Number: 2021910451

TABLE OF CONTENTS

Preface	vii
Childhood Memories	1
College	118
Army Experiences	148
After the Army	232
Lawrenceburg	272
Retirement	312
Denouement	322
Friends	326
Listen	330
Laugh	332
Commonality	336
Synergy	339
The James Code of Conduct	341
Encouragement	343
Build the Fort Today	345
Politics	350
Patriotism	353
The Privilege of Growing Old	357
Faith	360
Being a Good Steward of Mother Earth	362
Legacy	364
About the Author	366

PREFACE

When speaking to an assembly about the significance of the United Negro College Fund in 1989, Vice President Dan Quayle misquoted the slogan, "The mind is a terrible thing to waste," in an infamous, but very humorous, gaffe when he said, "What a waste it is to lose one's mind." Dan's misstatement makes me realize I have also reached the benchmark of human growth and development I call mental pause. I have a relatively clear memory of events that occurred in my childhood and yet many times I fail to remember what happened just a few moments ago.

Pop was a classroom teacher at Summertown High School for thirty-five-plus years. During that time, he distinguished himself by reeling off witty aphorisms which his children called Elmerisms. Among his favorite Elmerisms was, "When I gaze into a mirror, I see a perfect reflection of an over-the-hill life represented by gray hair, warts, and sagging skin." As your writer, I have exerted a tremendous effort to detail chronological events in my life by weaving authentic memories and stories on which my character has been built. Unfortunately, every passing day brings more fog and less perspicuity. Recent hikes to the back of my mind reveal many memories have moved into rusty cerebral filing cabinets, making recollection of factual accounts challenging. However, this is only a small inconvenience since I have vowed to never allow the facts to interfere with telling a good story.

Among my favorite memories is warming by the fire at home in Summertown, Tennessee. Pop purchased the largest Ashley woodstove available because it heated the house most efficiently and also held the fire overnight. He liked to burn large chunks of red oak firewood that were specifically cut to the stove's specifications, maximizing the use of the large firebox of the stove. A frequent Elmerism would follow after he placed a large stick of wood in the stove. "That stick is loaded with BTUs." Pop would watch a thermometer placed about fifteen feet from the stove. When it reached eighty degrees Fahrenheit, he said the temperature was "just right." Mom never required as much heat as Pop. Although she never complained about the roaring fire, she quietly slipped around and opened the windows when Pop wasn't watching, which earned her nickname as Pop's thermostat. Usually a black cast-iron Dutch oven sat on top of the stove filled with beans or turnip greens, standing ready for anyone who needed a quick snack between meals. Granny James's trusty kettle was also a mainstay on the stove top. The kettle provided a low-tech humidifier as well as hot water for a cup of tea or hot chocolate. Most evenings a jigsaw puzzle would be placed on the large kitchen table, inviting family interaction. A card table placed in front of Pop's easy chair was a permanent fixture for playing solitaire, and when a crowd gathered, he would offer a lesson to anyone who wished to challenge him in a game of cards.

WARMING BY THE FIRE

"Warming by the fire" has been a reference point for many of my boyhood memories, and this notion continued to comfort me while I was away from home throughout my life. I recall many occasions I longed for the comfort of Pop's big Ashley woodstove while I was in the army stationed in Fort Lewis, Washington. While completing my advanced infantry training there, I found the continuous rain of Washington's temperate rain forest most unpleasant. Not only was I wet most of the time, but it was downright cold. In my estimation, nothing was worse than a bone-chilling December cold combined with the pouring rain funneling down the back of my field jacket. Wet and chilled to the bone, I shook myself to sleep many a night on the bivouac, and in order to cope with the elements, I imagined myself warming by the fire at home. That mental picture has been my constant companion, providing warmth and security in situations I found cold and insecure.

Mom was an excellent role model for her children. She chose to live on the sunny side of life, facing her many challenges with a smile on her face. Mom's great desideratum for her children was for them to be kind, loving, and generous (like her) because she was convinced that true happiness came from generosity. I confess that I have not always lived up to Mom's philosophy. I was probably Mom's greatest challenge. When her sweet encouragement did not properly take hold of my character, her flyswatter was close at hand, and I felt its sting on my britches many times. Mom's constant reminder for me to strive to be a blessing to others has followed me all the days of my life. She often said, "Be something, do something, and leave something." So, Mom, I dedicate this book to you. I have been there, done

SID JAMES

that, and I leave the story of my life to my family and closest friends. The comfort of the blazing fire in the Ashley woodstove at home has jolted a deluge of memories I wish to share.

WARMING BY THE FIRE

CHILDHOOD MEMORIES

I was blessed to be a member of a family whose vivid imagination made a lasting imprint on my character. When I was a little boy, I would beg my folks to tell me stories. The best storyteller was Grandmother Emmons. She was the proverbial raconteur who could spin an amusing yarn for every occasion. I can remember sitting in her room at the Bud James homeplace listening to Grandmother's stories for hours on end. Grandmother was an expert on the stories surrounding the Civil War battle at Shiloh in western Tennessee. While her husband served as assistant superintendent at the park, she became a tour guide offering visitors a very colorful detailed account of behind-the-scenes anecdotes. She also liked to tell about how she met her husband in the general store where she worked in New Albany, Mississippi. I would sit spellbound as Grandmother weaved euphony into her delightful narratives and comical stories.

Besides being a superb storyteller, she was a skilled artist. Her favorite medium was needle and thread. Whether it was sewing, tatting, crocheting, or knitting, she could make fabric come alive with her artistic flair. As soon as the household chores for the day were finished, Grandmother picked up her crochet needle and began spinning beautiful doilies. It seemed that Grandmother's hands were always busy. Grandmother knew how to stretch a budget by patching our jeans when we wore out the knees and the seats. The jeans were just getting broken in when the frayed areas began to appear. The improved knee patches were ideal for rambunctious play outside. I could zip through a briar patch in nothing flat with those patched pants and not feel a thing. Her prized possession was her Singer treadle sewing machine. She explained how the sewing machine kept her from starving to death after her husband lost his job as park superintendent at the Shiloh National Military Park. When a garment appeared to be past wearing, it put on new life in a quilt pattern or as a last resort as a dusting rag. Buttons were always saved for future projects. A larger sized garment was often made into clothing for my three younger siblings. Grandmother and Mom spent many hours making Deena and Becky dresses out of garment scraps. All of the children's Halloween costumes came from rummaging through fabric scraps. Also, in the lower right drawer of her sewing machine, she tucked away a large ball of twine. Most of the twine was retrieved from packages received in the mail. Anytime we needed a piece of string for a project we knew exactly where to look. Grandmother always kept her room neat and orderly. Everything in her room had a purpose and a special place so that no lost time would be dedicated to a search. She loved potted plants. Even her plants were meticulously rotated in the window so that each one received the proper amount of sunlight. One of her favorite creative pastimes was to cut out pretty pictures from magazines and old greeting cards and cleverly arrange them into murals and shadow boxes. One day when Chris, Jerry, and I came in from school, she gave us a big surprise. She had made each of us an impressive scrapbook containing elaborate murals she had made from old magazines and greeting cards she had saved for this specific purpose. I thought those were the most beautiful paragons I had ever seen.

One year around November she surprised us again with a unique set of dolls she had constructed from spent corn shucks. Each female doll wore a bonnet and a matching long dress with a clever face drawn on the front. The male dolls wore hats fashioned from the shuck material, along with a coat and pants. It was amazing how precise each of her creations were. She also made accoutrements for each doll that included a broom and a basket for the female dolls, and an axe and a plow for the male dolls. When we began to quiz her about her creative genius, she confessed she had been making and playing with shuck dolls since she was a young girl. Shuck dolls were born out of necessity since there was no extra money to spend on store-bought toys. Her mother had coached her enough in the craft so that the art of shuck dolls could be passed forward to her children and her grandchildren. (*Grandmother's corn shuck dolls have come to abide in my family heirloom museum.*)

Grandmother was a great humorist and practical joker. She could turn boring and humdrum situations into fun games. Whether we were shelling peas, shucking corn, canning tomato juice, or making apple butter, she had a knack of making the activity entertaining. She often said, "A spoonful of sugar makes the medicine go down" long before the cliché was made famous in *Mary Poppins*. When we were least expecting it, she would slip in one of her practical jokes and bring the house down with laughter. Of all the lentils Pop raised in the garden every year, the butter beans provided the family with the most dreadful shelling chore. The family worked as a team for days on end processing the butter beans. Grandmother and the kids sat in a large circle in the family room at the homeplace shelling the beans. Occasionally an off-colored bean would appear. Grandmother created a game to see who could find the most colored beans while we were shelling. The competition among the siblings became keen as the running tally was amended each afternoon. On the final day of the shelling the siblings engaged in endless bragging, gouging, and heckling. As the all-time champion of the colored bean contest was about to be announced, Grandmother surprised everyone with a hoard of colored beans she had been hiding under her apron during the competition and easily won the coveted title. She was the ultimate optimist, always choosing to live on the sunny side of life. She taught Chris and Jerry how to give someone a short sheet by removing one sheet from the bed and folding the other sheet in half, making it appear as two sheets. Chris and Jerry anxiously watched one night as I reclined in bed. My struggle with the sheet afforded them both a big belly laugh. Not knowing the trick myself, I followed their lead the next night with a trick of my own by shaking salt between their sheets. When they found the worm had turned, they both pounced to beat me up, but the adults prevailed, teaching them a good practical joker must be willing to receive as well as give. Grandmother called it a "dose of their own medicine." Speaking of medicine, Grandmother also taught us how to apply quinine to chewing gum. At the time, quinine was easily accessible (without prescription) at the pharmacy for two cents a capsule.

That nickel pack of gum provided an explosion of fun. Quinine was easily disguised by gently rubbing the white powder into the fresh stick of gum. Jerry and I loved to offer quinine-laced gum to unsuspecting friends, especially at church. The boys would spit it out immediately, uttering loud protests and making all sorts of twisted and gyrated facial expressions, followed by an instant request for water to relieve them of quinine's terrifically bitter taste. Girls, on the other hand, were more polite and subdued in their protests. They would usually excuse themselves to gag in private. One of Grandmother's favorite holidays was April Fools' Day. On April first, we would wake up to gags and practical jokes she had planned the night before. She made certain every day included fun and games.

When I was in second grade, Grandmother gave Chris, Jerry, and me authentic penny books to collect pennies beginning with the first 1909 Lincoln penny and going through the current date. The three of us instantly became avid collectors. Our new hobby had a tremendously enjoyable side effect that was serendipitous. All of a sudden, our relatives were doling out pennies for our new collections. *(Side Note on July 16, 2015: I had continued on the qui vive for 58 years on my quest to complete the Lincoln penny collection beginning with 1909 and continuing with the current date. Many times I convinced myself the task was impossible. Today I secured the final remaining penny for the collection—a 1909 VDB San Francisco rare mint penny! Yeah! I'll mark that off my bucket list.)* On one particular occasion, Mom's brother, Uncle Paul Emmons, came by for a visit. After we hit him up for his spare pennies, he bragged that he had never fooled with collecting pennies, but he did have a nice collection of rare half dimes having a high numismatic value. Neither of the three of us boys had ever seen a half dime and realizing Uncle Paul was famous for stretching the truth far enough to compensate for his humorous imagination, Chris immediately dismissed the notion as pure malarkey. However, Jerry was not going to be outdone by Uncle Paul's half dime collection yarn. Calling me to his aid, Jerry solicited my mercury dime that I had been saving for a special occasion. It seemed Jerry was forever coming up with ideas that would be financed with my money, but through his smooth talk and personal charm, I was soon convinced this investment would be well worth the pleasure. Taking the dime to the garage, he employed Pop's hacksaw to neatly cut the dime in half. Jerry kept one half and handed me the other half. Later that evening at supper, Jerry asked Uncle Paul about his half dime collection again. After Uncle Paul explained the rarity of such a coin, he added that we boys would probably never have the opportunity to stumble upon one in regular circulated currency. Immediately, Jerry countered that he and Sid had just recently found half dimes. We quickly displayed our recent acquisitions to prove the validity of the story. Everyone had a good laugh concerning the half dime story. It was such a hit that Jerry and I shared our half dimes with gloating audiences many times. We also gained mileage out of the coins we smashed by accommodating trains on the railroad track. To this day, I still possess the smashed coins of yesteryear and the extremely rare half dime. *(In 2006, just a few months before Jerry died, I was surprised with a package in the mail from Jerry. In the package I found his collection of smashed coins and his rare half dime. Once again, I own the whole Mercury dime that was neatly cut into two halves.)*

WARMING BY THE FIRE

Grandmother told many hair-raising tales, but being a boy, I was most impressed about the story of how she began to pack heat in her purse (carry a pistol). While her children were small and living at the Shiloh Park, one night two drunkards wandered up on the porch and started banging on the door to get it. Her husband, Jack, was away at the time, and the incident frightened her greatly. She demanded that the family needed to relocate to ensure the safety of the children. The incident brought about a serious discussion for Grandmother's need to be armed with a pistol. The next day Jack brought her a small snub-nosed .38 pistol which easily fit in her purse. After a brief class on safety and target practice her confidence level soared. A few weeks later a hawk visited the henhouse and was preparing to pounce on one of the chickens. She killed the hawk firing only one round. She continued to carry the pistol after Jack died until she and Mom moved to Nashville. She gave the pistol to her son, Paul, for safekeeping. Paul hid it well enough that the pistol has not been seen since it entered his possession.

One day while my brothers and I were watching an oater movie on TV, I asked Grandmother if she had ever taken a nip of whiskey. "As a matter of fact, I most certainly have," she quickly quipped. Grandmother proceeded to tell her experience with the 1918 Spanish Flu pandemic. In the spring of that year, she was pregnant with her fourth child. Anthony was nine, Jim Tom was six, and Mary was three. One afternoon Mr. Emmons came home from work running a fever and was sick as a dog with the flu. She immediately put him to bed and began applying cold compresses to his head to abate the fever. In just a few days her three children also contracted the flu virus. When the county doctor finally made a home visit, he told her she absolutely could not get sick since she was the only caregiver. The doctor gave detailed instructions about containing the virus, and he added it was imperative that she wash her hands every time she administered care to the ill. As the doctor was about to leave, he placed a pint of whiskey on the fireplace mantle. He told Grandmother to take a sip of that whiskey regularly throughout the day and swish it around in her mouth for a few seconds before spitting it out. Grandmother vividly described her experience of tasting whiskey as her face twizzled into a contorted frown. "Whiskey was the most foul-tasting, evil concoction ever created. I could never understand how anyone could develop a liking for such a putrid potion of fire tonic!" The doctor placed a quarantine sign on the door warning the public not to enter the home. Grandmother said working with the sick for the next two or three weeks was the most exhausting work she had ever done in her life. She prayed often for strength and health so that she could continue to care for her family. Miraculously, she did not succumb to the illness. "That was my first and last experience with whiskey," she added with a grin.

Grandmother was the sentimental type, and she managed to keep several cherished items from her childhood. Every artifact was accompanied by a good story about her difficult childhood in Keownville, Mississippi. Her mother had passed away when Grandmother was nine years old. Therefore, she was raised by her sister and her sister-in-law. We called Grandmother's venerable artifact collection that was neatly wrapped in a basket her museum. As Mom aged, she decided to divide all of Grandmother's family treasures among the children. I now have my own museum containing several of Grandmother's most prized possessions I use to entertain my grandchildren. Grandmother would be so proud!

When Pop finished his master's degree at George Peabody College for Teachers in 1950, we moved back to Pop's boyhood home in Summertown. Papa (James Thomas James) had recently died, and before the following winter Granny consented for Pop, Mom, the three boys, and Grandmother Emmons to move in with her. Pop's mom, Mary Elizabeth James, "Granny," made us feel at home. From the beginning, I considered her a very loving and unique lady. She had some interesting mannerisms that I will never forget. She kept her money in a tobacco sack that was pinned to the inside of her bra. Granny wasn't one to show off her money, but occasionally I would get a chance to take a peek. I liked to sit next to Granny at church, especially when the collection basket was passed since it was a good time to take a peek at her bankroll. All of the folding money was kept in a tidy roll with the smaller bills on the outside and the larger ones protected on the inside of the roll. The roll was tightly secured with a rubber band. Granny's habit was to put a dollar bill in the collection plate when it was passed, and she would also remove fifty cents before she passed the plate on down the row. This being a rather uncommon practice, I once courteously asked her why she made change in the collection plate. She said she took out fifty cents each week so she would have snuff money. Fifty cents bought the large glass jar of snuff. Furthermore, Granny had a smaller aluminum can about the size of a jigger glass she carried in her purse. The empty snuff jars were not wasted. The kitchen cabinet was lined with the jars that had a perfect afterlife as drinking glasses in the family's crystal collection. Most of the jars were clear glass with three dots on the bottom. Granny explained the three dots were reserved for the best snuff. Those without the dots represented an inferior brand of snuff. When it came to snuff, Granny wanted nothing but the best. Granny loved holding me in her lap and reading stories to me. I enjoyed every aspect of this activity with one exception. Granny's breath carried a strong aroma that smelled like her Garrett Snuff. After one reading session I secretly complained to Mom about Granny's snuff breath. I was instructed to never mention this to Granny James. It was one of the first kept secrets of my young life.

Granny received most of her money from selling eggs, milk, and homemade butter. I loved to go with her to gather the eggs. She was quite proud of those laying hens and she had given all of them names. There was one old blind hen in which I was particularly fond. Her name was Pet. Granny allowed me to claim Pet as my very own chicken. Pet was gentle and she would let me carry her around the yard on my tricycle and feed her right out of my hand. She never ran away from me like most of the chickens. I suppose being blind may have been part of the reason she was "so loving." As the day ended, I would carry Pet to the chicken house and carefully place her in a specially prepared bed.

The laying stations for the hens were neatly arranged on the west side of the garage. Granny kept the nests lined with fresh straw and she also included a small gourd or white porcelain doorknob in the bottom of the nest. She said her laying hens needed all the encouragement they could get. I suppose that is why she heaped accolades upon them as she gathered the eggs.

If the hen had laid when Granny checked the nest, she would pat the hen on the head and express her pleasure. However, if the hen got out of practice of laying daily, Granny would also offer encouraging words. The hens would announce with a very loud distinctive cackle as they laid. Other hens would join in a rambunctious cacophony to form a chorus of approval. When a hen got in a motherly way and wanted to set, Granny would move the hen to an enclosed, protected area at the back of the garage. The mama hens would be vulnerable to predators while they were setting because they would guard their nest at all costs. I remember one day a snake made his way to the back of the henhouse. All of the other hens in the yard joined into the terrible squawking alarm. In a flash Granny came to their rescue. She immediately flew into the big snake with her hoe, transforming the snake into a good meal of chopped liver. After the excitement I asked Granny what kind of snake was in the henhouse. "Chicken Snake," was her reply.

A mama hen and baby chickens were always a fun treat to watch from a distance. If I ventured too closely to the chicks, the mama hen would ruffle her feathers and mount a vicious unrelenting attack. The mama hen had a special cluck she used to communicate with her chicks. When Granny poured out the chicken scratch feed in the mornings, the hens would respond with an exuberant chorus of cackling enthusiasm. The mama hens and their chicks were fed separately to ensure the young chicks received their allotted meal for the day.

I was forever asking Granny questions about her laying hens. I never understood why some hens would set while others would simply lay. I suppose Granny didn't want to get in a discussion about the birds and the bees. So she simply stated, "The question is not whether my hens are 'sitting' or 'setting' on the nest. I am most interested about when they cackle; whether they are 'lying' or 'laying.'"

On one occasion someone gave Pop a nest of bobwhite quail eggs that had been found while mowing a hay field. Pop exchanged the quail eggs for the chicken eggs under a hen that had begun to set. In a few weeks the hen hatched out twenty quail chicks. She cared for them as if they were her own chickens until the quail were big enough to manage by themselves. The quail eventually returned to the wild, but if they became distressed, they would return to the back porch for safety.

Granny was also a great lover of flowers. She liked walking me around in her yard while explaining the significance of each plant. Her prized plants were the row of white peonies that resided next to the fence in the front yard. She said her grandmother (the Currin family) had brought the peonies along with their family possessions when they moved from North Carolina to the James Holler near Lynnville, Tennessee. In keeping the family tradition, Granny moved part of the flowers with her from Lynnville to Lawrence County, Tennessee, when she and Bud (James Thomas James's nickname) were married, and each consecutive time she moved thereafter, she moved the peonies as well. In 1958, after Granny's death, we moved in front of the Monument on Highway 20; the peonies were meticulously dug up and carried with us to our new home. Since that time Mom has shared a start of the James's heirlooms with many peony admirers over the years. And, when the homeplace was sold in

2008, the James's peonies were carefully dug up and divided again to take on new life with my brothers, sisters, and me.

Granny's house was one of the earliest homes in Summertown equipped with electric lighting. The ceiling fixtures consisted of a single bulb and a copper socket with a pull string or a key twist switch. The wiring was insulated with an asbestos covering with no grounding wires. Where the wiring ran through the attic, an electric ceramic insulator was nailed to every other rafter and wire was attached to the insulator. When it was necessary to go through the timber, a hole was drilled and a ceramic tube was inserted and wire ran through the tube. This type of wiring called knob and tube was used for many years until Romex type insulated wire was invented. (Single conductors were run through cavities between the structural members in walls and ceilings, with ceramic tubes forming protective channels through joists, and ceramic knobs attached to the structural members to provide air between the wire and lumber to support the wires. Since air was free to circulate over the wires, smaller conductors than required in cables could be used. By arranging wires on opposite sides of the building structural members, some protection was afforded against short circuits that can be caused by driving a nail into both conductors simultaneously.) There was a small sixty-amp fuse box mounted in the kitchen. When Mom and Pop moved in with Granny, extra wiring was required for their electric range, refrigerator, and the ringer washing machine that was placed on the back porch. The wiring was modified again when two chest freezers were added to the back porch. The final electric appliance of great importance was Grandmother Emmons's 1939 Philco walnut veneer console radio. The radio was purchased for their father by Mom and her brothers a few months before he died. The agreement between the siblings was for each to pay an equal part on the radio. When her brothers reneged on their agreement, Mom was caught holding the note of about $50 and had to pay off the remainder in $5 monthly installments *(This gagged Elmer to the nth degree since he helped Mom pay off the note. He never had much use for Mom's brothers after that. In fact, when the brothers came for a visit, Elmer would usually dismiss himself to visit the animals in the barn.)* The radio was placed in the kitchen adjacent to Mom's small china cabinet that was used to hold her dishes. One of my earliest memories was listening to the radio. The first song that caught my attention was Hank Williams's hit, *Hey Good Lookin'*. I can still hear my Mother singing along with Hank on the radio when I hear that song.

The old homeplace was located on Highway 20 in Summertown, Tennessee, beneath the canopy of several majestic oak trees that towered roughly seventy-five feet in the air. Wide porches stretched the entire length of the front and back house. It was a very modern house when it was built in the 1920s. Granny and Papa laid down $1000 cash money for its construction, a tidy sum back in the day. The house was even equipped with an electrical outlet in each room and an overhead light bulb. The front porch also sported a swing. Granny planted tame honeysuckle which bore beautifully fragrant red blossoms. The plant was also a great attraction to hummingbirds, happily obliging curious children with their agile flying skills. The large windows provided cross ventilation, and a large attic aided in trapping the summer heat away from the main floor of the house. In the summertime when the heat became unbearable, we simply moved outside and sat on the porch until the house naturally cooled.

The big wooden swing on the front porch was a favorite summertime gathering place. We used to snuggle in the swing and hear Mom read from the *Children's Bible Stories* book. The only other permanent furnishing on the front porch was a ship thermometer that Aunt Era (Grandmother Emmons's sister-in-law) had given us that advertised life and casualty insurance (Aunt Era's place of employment). There were many occasions that Chris, Jerry, and I would slip the thermometer off the wall and place it under a piece of tin in the sun. This would make the thermometer read at least ten to fifteen degrees higher than the actual temperature. When the maximum temperature was achieved, we would sneak the thermometer back to its proper place and plead with Mom to come look. This devious inveiglement was very helpful in our effort to convince Mom to carry us to the swimming hole.

One summer evening as we were enjoying the porch swing, an automobile pulled into the driveway across the street to the home of Henry Bishop. Mr. Bishop had recently killed a man in a hostile dispute, and he was on trial for murder. Mr. Bishop's evening guest was his attorney, Howard Freeman. The sound of their voices carried over to our front porch that evening. "Henry," Howard began, "we have a real problem with your murder trial. We need witnesses to substantiate your side of the story. Without witnesses I am afraid we are going to lose. Either I will provide the witnesses, or you will need to find the witnesses. What do you want me to do?" Mr. Bishop spoke with a long southern drawl. "Don't worry, Howard. I will be certain I will have the finest witnesses money can buy." Later at the trial, Mr. Bishop was acquitted of all charges. He had manufactured some very fine witnesses indeed.

Granny's house was covered in white clapboard siding, and the interior walls and ceilings were also covered in a beaded wood siding. There was no inside plumbing. Drinking water was provided with a bucket and dipper that sat on a table in the kitchen next to the back door. Adjoining the back porch was a bed of canna lilies. I loved to sit on the little white potty on the back porch and admire the big, beautiful flowers. One of my earliest recollections was being pushed off the porch while sitting on the potty into the lily bed by my mischievous brother, Jerry. I wear a scar above my left eye as a constant reminder of the incident. I remember drawing water from the hand-dug well. The water had a funny taste like "toady frogs" as Mom put it. Nevertheless, we drew water from the well to do the washing and for the baths on Saturday night. We heated the water on the cook stove and poured it into a big #2 washtub in the kitchen. Since I was the least of three boys, I received the third bath in the same dirty water. When my bath was finished, we poured the bath water on the flowers. Mom's ringer washer resided on the back porch. Saturday was always wash day. After Mom finished washing, we hung the clothes on the lines in the backyard. This job was saved for the boys.

About twice a week we would load up eight or ten glass gallon jugs and head to the Summertown spring on the other end of town. We filled up the jugs with cool, tasty spring water used for drinking and cooking. After the jugs were filled, we lined them up on the edge of the porch for future use. One day we came home from church to discover a hole had been burned into the back porch. Apparently the sun had shown through the glass jug like a prism onto a feed sack used for a foot-wiping rug in front of the back door. The sack caught on fire and set the wooden porch on fire underneath it. Luckily the fire extinguished itself after the feed sack was burned. After that scary incident we found another location for the water jugs.

The attic was a great place of discovery for the boys. It was crammed full of Granny and Papa's treasures they had collected at auction sales over the years. They were both big collectors, and there was an interesting assortment of great junk with which to play upstairs. Among their treasures was a stereoscope that provided three-dimensional photographs. Most of the photographs were scenes of important European landmarks. Another great plaything was an oriental hat that was a souvenir they had received from friends from the Spanish-American War. Granny also owned a great collection of kitchen gadgets and baskets. She owned two pressure cookers and a large assortment of blue fruit jars for canning food. There were also two or three camelback trunks filled with old clothing. On Halloween we frequented the trunks to find the perfect Halloween costume. The term thunderstorms took on new meaning in the attic because as the hard rain peppered the tin roof, it made a thundering and almost deafening sound. I actually found the sound very relaxing. The sound of raindrops hitting the tin roof would put me to sleep. Next to the attic steps lay an old feather bed. I once received permission to spend the night in the attic on the feather bed. During the night I rolled off the mattress and tumbled downstairs.

Mom and Pop said I yelped like an Indian carrying on dramatically a good while until I settled down. The next morning, since I couldn't recall what happened, I concluded that I had slept through the whole ordeal.

The house was heated by two woodstoves in the wintertime. When we jumped out of bed and the fire had died down, it was freezing cold to our bare feet since the house was neither underpinned nor had any insulation. I remember on several occasions that the dipper would be frozen to the water bucket in the kitchen. It wasn't hard to get moving on those cold mornings. The blazing fire was a welcome relief, and the whole family would back up to the stove to get warm. Heating with wood provided many chores for the boys. Around the first week in September, Pop would order two large truckloads of wood that needed stacking. Pop wanted the wood stacked neatly in sections exactly four feet high and eight feet long. This was necessary to guarantee that Pop was getting his money's worth from the wood purchase. Stacking wood was an art form that we boys had to learn. If the pieces were placed in the pile the wrong way, the stack would fall over before we reached the ideal height of four feet. One day while we were stacking wood, Jerry uncovered a large red millipede which he promptly carried into the house to show Grandmother Emmons. Upon inspecting the large rambunctious creature, she declared, "Oh no, you have cornered a 'Gallinipper'! This is one of the meanest insects known to man. Be ever so careful and keep your mouths tightly closed in his presence, because if he looks into your mouth and counts your teeth, you will surely die!" Being the youngest of the three boys and most gullible, Grandmother's declaration about the dangerous Gallinipper scared the dickens out of me. Not only did I keep my mouth tightly closed, I also placed my hand over my mouth for good measure. When we returned to the woodpile, Jerry announced, "Watch this, y'all!" He opened his mouth as wide as possible and held the Gallinipper up to his mouth so that it could get a good long look. "See! There's nothing to the old superstitious folklore." (*Although it took a while, Grandmother's prediction was correct. Jerry was the first to die on August 14, 2007.*)

Since there was no inside plumbing, Pop said the house had five rooms and a path. The path to the outhouse was about fifty yards from the back porch behind the chicken house. Pop said that was about fifty yards too close in the summertime (because of the smell), and fifty yards too far in the wintertime (because of the cold weather). The outhouse was equipped with a box in one corner that contained old newspapers (for wiping), and a fifty-pound sack of lime (that helped control the mawkish odor). There was also a stick about three feet long resting on the floor in the corner. The stick was used to move the spiderwebs out of the hole. The outhouse also attracted dirt dobbers in prolific proportions. I assumed that was because the poo poo was a great attraction for the flies, which attracted the spiders, which attracted the dirt dobbers.

Grandmother did a marvelous job enhancing my awareness of Mother Nature. As winter gave way to early spring Grandmother would beckon me to stop, listen, and pay close attention to God's marvelous handiwork. The multitude of dozens of species of birds simultaneously chirping their trademark songs produced a cacophony to my untrained ears. Grandmother would very carefully point to the distinctively melodic songs as she would direct my attention to the unique sound of each bird family. Sometimes she would have me count the different bird species in the yard. The count could easily be enhanced by placing a few bread crumbs on the ground, and the company of birds would quickly file in for a quick snack. With her tutelage I learned to focus on the wind as it rustled through the tree leaves. As I felt the warm sun upon my back, I also learned the new plants would not be able to grow without the nourishment of the radiant sun, the magical moisture of the rain, and the array of elements hidden within the soil. She invited my nose to distinguish the bouquet of sweet spring aromas produced by the exquisite flowers, and petrichor of rain falling upon the dry ground, and to appreciate the musky scent emitted by the barnyard animals. The honeysuckle soon became my very favorite plant as Grandmother invited me to open the blossoms and smell and taste the sweet nectar hidden inside. The spring rains also brought the deafening nocturnal songs of the spring peepers, the chorus frogs, the leopard frogs, and the American toads. She also gave countless insects proper scrutiny because she explained that everything in the balance of our ecosystem depended upon the presence of another species. Grandmother's invitation to truly experience spring made me a tree hugger for life. My thrilling experience has made me yearn for the tutelage of Grandmother Emmons. On numerous occasions I have wished Grandmother Emmons to be present in the lives of my children and grandchildren so that they could also sit mesmerized as she enthusiastically proclaimed the magic of spring. *(Unfortunately, the overuse of chemicals and global warming have silenced the spring*

I remember from my childhood. We have become poor stewards of God's beautiful green earth.)

It was always an exciting time in the spring when the weather warmed enough for the boys to pull off their shirts and start their summer tan. Mom warned us to take the sun in small doses on our bare backs until we were inured to the sun's rays. It would take several weeks before we had a tan good enough to keep from blistering in the sun. In our haste to sport the best tan, we usually blistered anyway. As summer rolled along our tans became progressively darker. The dark bare-backed tan was a fashion statement and trendy for all the boys in the neighborhood. The kids who were not worshipers of the summer Sun God were teased and ridiculed.

Our favorite swimming hole was at the Pleasant Garden Bridge on the Buffalo River located about two-and-a-half miles from home. The bridge provided a high platform about twelve feet high for jumping into the river, and there was usually a tire swing somewhere in the vicinity that beckoned thrill seekers and fools alike. Reaching the stage in life where one finally mustered the nerve to jump off the Pleasant Garden Bridge was considered a rite of passing to manhood among the boys in the community. Unfortunately, there were big rocks on the bottom that provided many skinned shins and cut feet. I recall that once on a dare one foolhardy boy rode his bicycle off the bridge into the river. A few seconds later he emerged still riding the bicycle which landed him a round of applause from the congregation of swimmers. The enthusiasm waned when we realized the fall into the river had crushed both rims on the bicycle. It was a good idea while it lasted.

On another afternoon at the bridge, Chris had sneaked Pop's college class ring from Pop's chest of drawers. Being the oldest, he was wearing the ring to show off. After one jump off the bridge, Chris surfaced with an especially long face. He discovered the ring had slipped off his finger during the jump in an area of the creek where the water was about ten feet deep. Without hesitation Jerry jumped in, and within about twenty seconds he emerged with the ring. The ring was quickly returned to Pop's chest of drawers for safekeeping, and no one mentioned the incident to Pop for fear of reprisal.

Before I started to school at age four, Mom often sent me to the store to pick up odds and ends about a half mile from the house. There was always a gathering of men loafing on the porches of Bucket Holloway's General Merchandise, the U.S. Post Office, and Jimmy Henson's Shoe Shop. They usually sat on empty nail kegs or wooden pop bottle crates. Some would be whittling on red cedar sticks while others would just be chewing the fat. The men left the gossiping to the women; they just chewed the fat. Most everybody either chewed tobacco or smoked. It was a treat to go into the shoe shop. As I entered the shop I could observe about a dozen or more windup clocks on the wall. The most exciting time to be there was at twelve noon to hear the chorus of clocks chime in synchronized harmony. The deafening cacophony of clock bells, gongs, and chimes would perform a short eerie symphony that would give the startled listener goose bumps. On the opposite wall of the shop Jimmy had a series of old railroad calendars hanging in chronological order stretching back for fifteen or twenty years. The shop reeked with heavy smells of leather, dye, and tobacco juice. Jimmy repaired everything. Clocks and shoes were his specialty, but he also repaired watches and guns—even our BB gun on several occasions. His normal charge was ten cents for small jobs and a quarter for larger ones. Jimmy was most always accompanied by his trusty squirrel dog. Jimmy did not pay much attention to hunting season because he normally ate squirrels the year round. Squirrels were his staple meal. However, on the first day of the month when Jimmy received his veteran's check, he would go to Bucket's store to cash the check. Jimmy would buy a coke, a pound of bologna, and a sleeve of crackers. He would immediately go outside and while sitting on a soda crate, he and the dog would enjoy the bologna and crackers—together.

One autumn day before I started to school (I was 4 years old), Mom was outside burning leaves in the yard. The wind picked up and the yard caught on fire. She quickly sent me to the store to enlist volunteers to help put out the fire. There were plenty of idle men sitting around, but I only convinced Charlie Parker to come to our aid. He was at least ninety years old at the time. I begged him to hurry back home with me, but he said he had only one speed—*slow!* When we eventually arrived on the scene, Mom had the fire under control. Mr. Parker insisted on tarrying awhile anyway, "Just in case the fire tindered," he warned.

That same autumn I was outside playing and saw a big black cloud of smoke billowing on the horizon. The Summertown Elementary School was on fire and burned to the ground while school was in session. Luckily, no one was hurt in the fire. The school year continued while a new building was hastily constructed. Classes resumed at churches, stores, and any empty building that had a roof and electricity. I started school the following term going to the first grade at age five. Having a late birthday (November 27) made me the youngest child in the class.

I entered Summertown Elementary School in July of 1954. School began about two weeks after the Fourth of July. It was necessary to commence the term early in anticipation of the cotton-picking vacation. Around the first week of September schools were closed so that all of the children would be on hand to assist the farmers in picking cotton. Roy Bishop was our across-the-street neighbor. Elmer asked if he minded the three older boys coming to his cotton patch to help with the harvest. Elmer gave Chris and Jerry burlap feed sacks, and he handed me a pillowcase. The three of us walked to the field to begin our employment. I remember that I began the journey with great anticipation of working my first job. Roy was paying three cents a pound to the pickers. Much to my dismay I found that making the cotton release from the boll was a menacing task. Each boll had sharp barbs jutting from the opened end. A picker had to navigate around the barbs and carefully remove the cotton from the boll. A wrong turn at the exit point of the boll would cause some of the cotton to remain in the boll, causing the picker extra time to redo the removal process. Cotton pickers who failed to get all of the cotton out of the bolls were scorned by the farmers as "goose pickers." The cotton required a small twist upon exiting the boll to keep all of the cotton intact upon exit. It didn't take me long to realize what the adage "light as cotton" meant. I kept stuffing cotton down in my pillowcase and began to think I would never get it full. I was happy when my bag was stuffed full and I could weigh in. That afternoon I picked ten pounds in the pillowcase. I was happy to walk home once my bag had been filled and leave my cotton-picking experience behind. When I returned to the house Mom started quizzing me as to why I left the cotton patch. "My bag was completely full," I explained. "Why didn't you return and fill your bag again?" Mom inquired. "Oh! I didn't know I was supposed to do that." A few weeks later Roy Bishop came to the house to pay the James boys for their cotton-picking adventure. Roy paid me with three silver Mercury dimes for my contribution. I was so proud!

Sometimes school would be closed for up to six weeks for cotton-picking vacation. Kids returned to school sporting new Levi jeans and flannel shirts. Back in the day, new jeans were purchased at least a size too large in anticipation of the kids' growth spurts. Therefore, it was quite stylish for the new jeans to be turned up in a large cuff around the ankles. The school term was five days shorter than today. Sometimes part of the term would be forgiven if a large amount of the term had been interrupted by cotton-picking vacation and snow days. The Lawrence County Fair was always held the last month of September which coincided very nicely with the end of the cotton-picking vacation. Kids would save some of their cotton-picking money for the assorted amusements at the fair. The one event that held great wonder for me as a boy was the "Hoochie Koochie Show." The event was slated for adults only. However, the free show offered on the stage for the general public was always enticing. I remember the scantily clad ladies wearing heavy makeup being paraded across the public stage for all of the curious onlookers. The emcee meticulously described the erotic euphony of events that were about to commence in the large tent that sat behind the closed curtain. There was a chorus of cat calls, hoots, and whistles from the pleased crowd. The entrance line quickly formed at the conclusion of the erotic spectacle in anticipation of the best show yet to come. It was a watershed moment for the boys when they appeared mature enough to attend the Hoochie Koochie Show, and they could return to school and describe all of the sensual details to the younger kids.

The legendary cotton pickers could pick as much as 400 pounds of cotton in a day. In order to meet that task, it was necessary to hit the patch at dawn. When wet dew had fallen early that morning, the pickers took advantage of the wet cotton weighing heavier than after the sun had melted the dew away. The experienced hands picked two rows at a time, while the novices were assigned only one row. Older folks with weak backs crawled through the rows using knee pads. Of course the beginners would get sore fingers from the sharp barbs of the cotton boll. Some frosty mornings it was freezing cold in the cotton patch, and it was nearly impossible to use gloves. I was never an accomplished cotton picker. I did enjoy the camaraderie in the field with the other hands. Occasionally a farmer would plant some watermelon seed in the cotton row. A big celebration would commence over the discovered watermelons. Of course, it was always entertaining to tease the girls. Almost every afternoon a cotton boll fight would break out to the displeasure of the farmers. We would break for lunch at noon and head to the local county store for a bologna sandwich and a Coke. By the time I deducted the expense of my lunch from the day's work, I was lucky to clear a couple of bucks. During my childhood there were several active cotton gins in the county, one of which was in Summertown. However, the largest gin was the Gladish Gin in Lawrenceburg. As the farmers carried their harvested cotton to the gin, some of the bolls would blow out of the truck landing on the side of the road. By the end of the cotton-picking vacation, the roadsides would be white with cotton. The cotton gins were colossal and very noisy. The drone of the gin motors could be heard from a mile away. At the end of the season the farmers would hire pickers by the hour to pull bolls and to shirt-tail the leftover cotton. In the later years it became an ominous task for farmers to employ hand cotton pickers, forcing the farmers to invest in mechanized equipment. Word must have spread that picking cotton by hand was a really difficult job.

From my viewpoint as a child, Jerry and Chris were always ganging up on me. It was an exciting day when Pop brought each of the three boys a new Daisy BB gun. Much to my surprise and disappointment, I soon learned that my gun fired only ping pong balls and not BBs. Pop said I was too immature for a BB gun, so I consoled myself by playing with my toy. After a fast flurry of rapid-fire ping pong balls, I was bending over to retrieve my ammo when I felt two sharp stings in the seat of my pants. Chris and Jerry had turned the BB guns on a human target at my expense. Of course, at my young age my best defense was to cry and wail at the top of my lungs in most dramatic fashion. My only consolation was the BB guns were immediately put out of reach for safekeeping for a good while. When they were eventually retrieved, Mom announced she had mis-judged her older boys about BB gun maturity, and that I was certainly old enough to play with the BB guns.

Mom and Pop managed to raise five smart kids and one

smart aleck. Jerry, Deena, and Joe were all valedictorians, Chris was highly intelligent but didn't allow books to interfere with more important matters of life, and Becky was third in her senior class. I was just plain dumb. Looking back on the numerous occasions I was asked to explain my poor marks on my report card, I wish I had been clever enough to explain the poor grades were probably due to my heredity or my environment, but most certainly due to my poor luck of the draw from the gene pool. One of my earliest memories was Pop offering us three boys change for the collection plate on Sunday mornings. Since I was the youngest Pop would let me choose first. Of the two dimes and a nickel, I would always choose the nickel because it was the biggest. Jerry was most definitely the smartest of the six kids. He chided me about my dumbness and called me Twerp most of my childhood. It didn't take me long to recognize that I was not the most likely to succeed, and I tried to live up to my reputation as a smart mouth rarely attempting to rise to the academic level of my siblings.

I still recall my first day at school. About 7:30 a.m. Pop took me by the arm and marched me into Mrs. Alexander's first grade classroom, said goodbye and immediately left. We had discussed this arrangement at home, and I was prepared to stay at school alone on my first day. When we entered the classroom, the walls were aligned by parents holding their crying children. I wondered to myself, "Why is everyone so sad?" I learned the answer the following day. I recall my introduction to books. The teacher demonstrated the proper method to turn the pages, and added, "Anyone not listening, and failing to model correct page-turning method would be paddled." Dang! Now I knew why everyone was so upset the first day! When it came my turn to demonstrate the correct page-turning method, I slipped my hand behind the page and gave it a gentle push so Mrs. Alexander would not notice. She said, "Okay," and moved to the next student. Talking to myself in my reassuring out-loud voice I said, "Phew! She didn't catch me pushing that page forward!" Mrs. Alexander heard my comment and immediately carried me to the hall for my first spanking at school. Hardly a day went by during my year in first grade that I didn't get a spanking. Talking to myself gave me confidence, and I vowed I would not be cowered to reformation.

An event of epic proportions occurred in the fall of 1954 when Pop brought home our first television set. It was a large console model that could receive three channels, all black and white—but mostly white. The reception was terrible (Shorty King called it conception), but that was par for the course for its day. Purchasing the TV was actually Granny's idea. She told Pop if he would bring home the TV, she would spring for half the purchase price of $250 (which was a large hunk of change at that time). Granny's proposal about purchasing a TV was a shock to everyone because this naturally went against the grain of Granny's parsimonious nature. Almost immediately, Granny became the biggest TV fan. She would stay up each night and watch until the programs went off the air usually around midnight. I remember watching Adlai Stevenson winning the Democratic nomination and Dwight Eisenhower winning the Republican nomination and being elected President of the United States. One reason the election made such a large impression on me was because Ben Boles wore a button during the campaign that said, "I Like Ike." He also gave buttons to Chris, Jerry, and me, but I also noticed Pop, being a yellow dog Democrat (he would sooner vote for a yellow dog than a Republican), was not very interested in the "I Like Ike" buttons. This was my first lesson that political arguments had two sides.

Saturday morning TV catered to the kids. We watched *Howdy Doody, Tarzan, the Ape Man, Big Top Circus, Sky King, Mighty Mouse*, and a host of oater westerns with *The Roy Rogers Show* being our favorite. In the afternoons after school, we tuned into *Adventures of Superman*. Chris, being a master of imagination, coaxed Mom into giving him one of her old slips. After an hour or so on the treadle sewing machine, Chris had designed a large cape with an *S* in the middle. Jerry said, "Okay who are you? We give up. AH HA! You must be 'Super Slip!' Can you fly faster than a speeding bullet; change the course of mighty rivers; bend steel with your bare hands? No, because it is only Chris James disguised in a mildly altered lady's slip." Chris discarded the slip soon afterwards as the barrage of teasing increased.

Among the selection of oater movies (which Grandmother Emmons called "shoot-um-up-tonies") were Hopalong Cassidy, The Lone Ranger, Bob Steele, Red Ryder, and Roy Rogers. Roy Rogers was probably our favorite cowboy on TV. When we played Cowboys and Indians, an argument would soon erupt about who would portray Roy Rogers. Roy had the whitest hat, the slickest guns, the greatest horse named Trigger and a German shepherd dog named Bullet. Roy Rogers was the first cowboy who cleverly marketed his wares making his own television commercials. Local dry goods stores carried a full collection of official Roy Rogers side guns with holsters, white hats, and cowboy suits. The suits were especially desirable; they came equipped with suede vests and black chaps trimmed with leather fringe, and silver spurs that would artfully mount on a full array of colorful leather cowboy boots. One afternoon Mom and Pop announced that it was time for the three boys to have suits to wear to church. Wow! That was excitement to our ears, since suits could only mean one thing—cowboy suits! At last we would be the proud owners of an official Roy Rogers cowboy suit! Unbeknownst to the three boys, Pop had instructed the store merchant to tell the kids the Roy Rogers cowboy suits were no longer available. Upon entering the store our bubbles were soon burst with the distressing news about the Roy Rogers clothing line. However, Jerry was insistent that the line was still available. He thoroughly questioned the clerk about his mistake, but the clerk didn't budge an inch about the cowboy suits. We were then marched to the back of the store to try on adult-type suits. What a shock! Never in my wildest imagination would I have guessed that dress suits were made in children's sizes. As I tried on the pants Mom instructed the clerk to put me in a larger size so the suit could be altered when I began to outgrow it. This meant the suit actually fit in one place—around the chest—as long as I had the pants securely fastened with a belt to keep them from slipping around my ankles. I was also astonished how the wool pants itched. It reminded me of a line from a Tarzan movie when Jane was dressing Tarzan for his first trip out of the jungle to New York City. Tarzan said, "Clothes itch. Will put on clothes in New York." Meanwhile, Jerry had broken free from Mom, Pop, and the store clerk to do some exploring on his own. A few moments later, he appeared dressed in an official Roy

Rogers cowboy suit, and announced he had found the perfect size making it unnecessary for the store clerk to help him with any alteration need. For a fleeting moment, I actually thought Jerry had saved the day, but I soon realized (for the first time) we had been deceived by adults. I couldn't understand how that fit with Mom and Pop's instructions to always tell the truth. Licking our sores, we wore the shitty clothes home, and being the smallest of the three boys, it was my privilege to wear each of the three suits as I grew up. In keeping with the 1950s style, the suit pants had an extremely long stride causing the pants to ride upward toward my arm pits. I still hate the sight of a dress suit to this day. Since retiring from a life as a school official, I gladly hung my suit in the closet. I tell my friends if they see me in a suit, they will know somebody's dead.

I thought Granny James had an uncommon fear of a phenomenon she called "falling dead." She explained that it was a great mystery how a person could be in relatively good health one moment and dead as a doornail the next. Of course, this was a time before regular checkups at the doctor's office where one's blood would be analyzed and before any credence was given to special low-fat or low-cholesterol diets. None of the doctors were performing heart surgeries or "rotorootering" carotid arteries. The most common treatment for heart disease was rest. Blood pressure could indicate a problem, but few remedies were available to counteract the problem. Occasionally a relatively young person would succumb to a debilitating stroke or a massive heart attack. When I was a young child, anyone over the age of twenty appeared to be really old to me. I counted my lucky stars because falling dead was a problem that only plagued old people.

A death in the family brought on another curious tradition that was the sign of the times in the 1950s. When a person died, it was not unusual for the undertaker to come to the family's home to prepare the body for burial. The casket would be placed in the corner of the sitting room of the house where visitors would come and pay their respects to the grieving family. At night it was necessary for someone to be present with the corpse to make certain rats would not come and feast on the dead body. Neighbors and friends would volunteer to take a shift at night to watch over the corpse to keep the rats at bay.

Grandmother Emmons worked for the Shackelford Morticians for several years in Savannah, Tennessee. She told a funny story about a lady who had died and the family came to them to help with the body. However, there was a big problem with the corpse. The lady had suffered with crippling arthritis for many years and the body had frozen in the sitting position. The morticians decided to strap the body down to the bottom of the casket to make certain the body would remain in the prone position. It appeared to be an excellent plan until late one night while someone was sitting with the corpse, the straps broke and the body sat up in the casket, scaring the female sitter half to death. She screamed to the top of her lungs, waking the sleeping family in the house.

Ben Boles ran the garage next to the railroad tracks in Summertown. He was crippled from polio and walked with a crutch. He drove a red 1950 Chevrolet truck equipped with a spotlight, and he wore bib overalls always donning a policeman-style cap. In the bib of his overalls, he carried a tobacco sack and his money roll. Ben rolled his own cigarettes, and he kept one dangling from his mouth at all times. When he talked, the saliva-soaked cigarette dangled up and down between his lips. He and his wife, Estelle, didn't have children of their own, but they had a special fondness for the James kids. Pop had worked for Ben many years before and they were very close friends. Ben carried Chris, Jerry, and me to the drive-in picture show when were kids. That was my first experience with the silver screen. It made a big impression on me. I don't remember anything about the movie, but I do remember all three of us boys fell asleep before the picture was over. That provided a rare evening for Mom and Pop to be alone. About nine months after our debut with the movies, Becky was born.

Since Ben's disability confined him to his truck a great deal of time, he developed some unusual hobbies. He liked to feed the birds, and he became caretaker of stray dogs that were fortunate enough to happen upon his garage. He fed the dogs bologna. It was easy to pick out the junkyard dogs that hung around Ben's garage. They were fat and covered in grease from the motors that littered the junkyard adjacent to the garage. I once asked Ben why he fed the birds and the stray dogs. Even as a little kid he called me "Mr. James." "Well, Mr. James," he said, "when I die, I want somebody to miss me. I have learned that dogs and birds are more sincere than most people." One of Ben's favorite Sunday afternoon activities was to go to the dump and shoot rats with his pistol. He also kept an eye peeled for possibilities in the junk pile. Ben had a knack in turning others' trash into treasure. All of the tricycles and wagons we played with came to us as compliments from Ben Boles and from the dump. Ben would retrieve the broken toys to the garage and with a combination of his creativity and Yankee ingenuity, he would refurbish the toys and make them like new. His best present of all was a contraption that he made out of a truck hub and axle. He mounted a board about ten feet long on the axle, placed steering wheels about three feet from each end of the board, and mounted the other end of the truck hub in concrete in the ground. He had created the fastest merry-go-round in town. It was a real challenge to hang on when the board was spun at a fast speed. Our backyard became the destination for many kids in the neighborhood that wanted to play on the merry-go-round we called the flying Jenny.

Even though Ben was afflicted with polio, he could manage to drive a straight shift automobile. Ben would start off in high gear by carefully lifting his foot off the clutch and sousing the hand operated accelerator. If he had to start up a steep hill, he would resort to second gear. I never saw Ben drive faster than 30 miles per hour. Every Sunday morning Ben would drive Estelle and Marguerite to church. Ben would sit in the parking lot during church. Someone always carried communion out to him in his automobile. Occasionally, some of the boys would slip out of church and sit with Ben during church services. Ben enjoyed the company, and he would entertain us by telling tall tales about his childhood. To my knowledge he never ratted on any of his visitors who found church boring.

Ben was only one of a handful of staunch, nonconforming, dyed-in-the-wool Republicans who lived in Summertown. He moaned constantly about progressive social programs and how America was going to "hell in a hand basket." He was the only person I have ever known to refuse to participate in daylight saving time. I once questioned why he did not adjust his pocket watch for the event. "Well, Mr. James, the government interferes too much already. I will be darned if I allow the government to take charge of my pocket watch."

One of my earliest memories occurred before I began school. One winter day after our supper Pop announced he was going down to the garage to visit Ben for a while. Very quickly I chimed in, "Please let me go with you." To my astonishment, Pop agreed to take me with him. Before we arrived at the garage Pop instructed me to find a seat and stay quiet. When we entered the rear of the garage, there were about a dozen men sitting round the homemade heater. Ben had designed a fifty-five-gallon drum with a lid and a front door for stoking the fire. He also ingeniously added a copper tub and a valve that added burnt motor oil to the fire to help the wood burn at a high temperature. All of the men sat silently as Ben reeled off a series of funny stories about his life. I marveled at Ben's ability to speak for a long time and keep his guests entertained with his personal collection of amusing anecdotes. I became inspired at that very moment to live a memorable life so that my personal collection of stories would also come to fruition.

I also remember the last two days of Ben's life. Estelle called one evening around six and beckoned Pop to make an immediate appearance at their home. For some reason I cannot recall, I accompanied Pop to Ben and Estelle's home. Ben was in the bed and had been sick for about a week. Estelle wanted Ben to go to the hospital, but Ben continued to refuse. Estelle wanted Pop to convince Ben that her idea was Ben's only choice. As one could imagine, the friction between Ben and Estelle was escalating when we arrived. Pop and I stood at Ben's bedside, and Pop began to coax Ben to go to the hospital. Very matter-of-factly Ben responded, "I am dying, and I want to be left alone. There is no reason to take me to the hospital. It won't change the fact that I am dying. I don't need the hospital, but very soon I will indeed need the funeral parlor! Elmer, if you truly want to help, drive me to the funeral parlor." Contrary to Ben's wishes and at Estelle's insistence, Pop carried Ben to the hospital. Just as Ben predicted, he died just a few hours after he arrived at the hospital. About two days later, all of the James family visited Ben and his family at the North Funeral Home in Lawrenceburg, Tennessee. Poor Estelle was totally crushed. As Mom began expressing her sympathy, Estelle wanted to know if Mom thought Ben looked natural. Estelle had Ben dressed in a beautiful blue suit and a new tie to match. Ben was scrubbed and polished like a new penny, and his bald head shined like a bowling ball under the aura of the pink-tinted funeral parlor lighting. Mom responded, "Ben certainly looks good, Estelle." Estelle countered, "Alice Lou, don't you think Ben looks natural?" Mom reworded her response in a most complimentary manner. "I have never seen Ben dressed nicer in my life. The blue suit fits him to a tee." Estelle countered again, "Yes, but don't you think Ben looks natural?" Mom smiled and hugged Estelle tightly and responded at Estelle's insistence, "Yes, he looks natural." I had known Ben Boles since childhood, and I rarely had seen Ben dressed in anything but bib overalls and a policeman's hat. He was also missing his trademark saliva-soaked cigarette precariously dangling from his lower lip. He certainly did not look natural to me. I don't think I would have recognized Ben in the casket without his entourage of family and friends. Ben was right. Estelle could have avoided a hospital bill if she had honored his request and allowed him to die at home.

Mom and Pop's most frequent house guests were Howard and Willer (Willodean), and son, Charlie Mabry. They would come over after church on Sunday and Wednesday nights to enjoy some fresh-cranked ice cream. Mom made a variety of flavors depending upon the availability of the fruit. After about the third bowl Howard would say to Pop, "Now, Preacher, what flavor is this we are eating?" Howard was Pop's best friend. They loved to hunt and fish together and play Ping-Pong. I remember one occasion our families went to Napier Lake (about 20 miles from home in Lewis County) to fish and picnic. Everyone had a fishing pole but me. This didn't set too well with me and I expressed my displeasure with the situation. Pop rigged me a cane pole he had found in a nearby canebrake. He fixed it up like a real fishing pole and I was pleased as punch. After he baited my hook, I threw the line in the water. Almost immediately the float sank out of sight. Jerry told me to pull because I had a fish. I pulled with all my might, and the cane pole bent double. Luckily the fish stayed on the hook as I wrestled the fish to dry land. It was my first fishing trip and I caught the largest fish of the day. We had a fish fry over at Howard and Willer's the next evening. They served me a piece of the fish I had caught. Boy, was I ever proud!

After that fishing experience, we bugged Pop to carry us fishing with him, but it was only on rare occasions he would concede to being lord and master of the Chinese fire drill of trying to bait and untangle three fishing poles simultaneously. As a result, he made the rule the three boys would have to take turns because there was no way he could make three boys happy at the same time. Pop was very picky about his fishing equipment. He owned two Pflueger casting reels: the Akron he purchased after graduating from high school, and the Summit he purchased after graduating from college. He also owned about five choice lures: The Pflueger Tandem Spinner (which he called the Guinea Tail), the Arbogast Hawaiian Wiggler, the Creek Chub Bait Company Jointed Minnow, the Arbogast Jitterbug, and the Heddon Wounded Minnow. The largest lure of them all was the Jointed Minnow (which he called the Broken Back) that weighed in at almost an ounce. The lure was actually three pieces containing four sets of treble hooks. The lure also contained glass eyes and was painted to match the skin of a chub minnow from the creek. Because of its massive weight, Pop could throw that lure a country mile. On one occasion we were fishing in early spring and Pop cast the Broken Back in a tree on the other side of the creek. I watched him peel off all his clothes and swim across the creek to retrieve his prized lure. He later commented to me that he paid $3.50 for that lure, and there was no way he was going to leave it in a tree.

At the conclusion of one fishing trip Jerry accidently stepped on Pop's metal casting rod and broke off the tip. On the way home Pop lectured us on the importance of caring for our gear. To make up for the loss that summer, Chris, Jerry, and I saved our allowance and vegetable money and bought Pop a Pflueger Supreme casting reel for Father's Day. I remember the reel sold for over $20 at the time. That was a tidy sum of money in the 1950s. We had heard Pop mention several times that he would really like to own that reel. He was very surprised when we presented the reel to him. The gift made everyone feel especially proud.

Using a casting reel required a unique skill, especially while fishing in a creek where a canopy of tree limbs usually covered the best fishing holes. If the tension on the reel was set too tight, the lure could not be cast very far. If the tension on the reel was set too loose, a backlash would occur in the line that we called a bird's nest. The line we often used was a heavy nylon camouflaged line that required a clear lead close to the lure. Special knowledge of tying fishermen's knots was necessary to adequately attach everything in its proper place. I spent many an afternoon in the backyard practicing my casting skill using a sinker as a lure and a bushel basket as the cast target.

One beautiful spring Sunday afternoon, our family boarded the 1949 Chevrolet and drove to Meriwether Lewis Park for a picnic dinner. We rendezvoused there with Howard, Willer, and Charlie. The adults spread the fixings on one of the picnic tables while the boys played in the nearby stream. Picnics were always among my favorite childhood dinners. We were traditionally served fried chicken, stuffed eggs, potato chips, and soda pop. For dessert, apple pie and chocolate chip cookies topped off the award-winning meal, and it was not unusual for the picnickers to hand crank a churn of homemade ice cream. Wow! For kids, this was a heavenly treat! After we finished our meal, the boys returned to play in the stream. After the adults packed up, Elmer and Granny began searching for four-leaf clovers. Much to everyone's surprise, Granny found three nickels and a dime while looking for the clovers. Soon all the adults joined in for the new search for the loose change bonanza. Unbeknownst to Granny, Mom and Willer began to drop coins on the ground to sweeten Granny's search. Occasionally Mom and Willer would announce they had also found some loose change in an effort to lure Granny closer to their planted stash. As the coins continued to appear, Granny began searching faster and more furiously, much to the amusement of Mom and Willer. All of the commotion caught Charlie's eye who beckoned the James boys to investigate the foofaraw! Willer had just planted a silver half dollar before the hellions arrived. She very quickly covered it with her shoe so that the big prize could be saved for Granny's discovery. Very soon the boys became bored with the search and returned to the stream. Granny blurted a jubilant squeal when she retrieved the half dollar. On the way home Granny told Pop she had experienced one of the most exciting days of her life because she had found more than a dollar in loose change.

The congregation of automobiles and farm trucks assembled in the church parking lot were much more entertaining for me than the service being held inside the building. Before and after church I noticed the adult conversations usually centered on their automobiles. Gas mileage was of major importance; it transformed some of the congregants into braggers and/or liars as they related their automobile's mpg statistics. Ninety percent of the vehicles had a straight shift transmission and a six-volt battery. In the wintertime the six-volt battery was strained to its maximum limit when cranking the automobile. Depending upon the season of the year, car bodies were coated in a thick layer of mud or dust since all the rural roads were unpaved. Bumpers were also very important to give cold collared vehicles a gentle push to get going. No one owned jumper cables. If there was not another auto available to give the stranded car a push, five or six volunteers would team up to get the old jalopies moving. A slow push and a pop of the clutch in low gear would usually fire off the vehicle. Most autos were equipped with a manual choke and throttle to help get the engine started and to keep it running. In the summertime it was also interesting to note the flat tires in the parking lot. Hardly anybody purchased new tires for their cars. Retreads were popular because they were about half the price of a new tire. The big automobile trunks carried a large jack and often two spare tires in anticipation of flats. Many of the vehicles were equipped with malfunctioning clocks and radios (which Elmer said were only useful to entice the prospective buyers). Emergency brakes also aided in keeping a cold collared engine running on a cold day. One foot operated the clutch, the other foot would be on the accelerator, and the emergency brake would be used to stop. Also, it was not uncommon to see an automobile arrive in a heavy cloud of engine smoke since auto engines wore quickly and needed an expensive ring job that was called an overhaul. The oil dip stick required frequent monitoring since most vehicle engines at that time burned oil quickly. Car engines were considered "wore out" when the odometer reached eighty thousand to one hundred thousand miles.

    A few weeks before Thanksgiving Pop would carry the family out to the woods to hunt hickory nuts. The scalybark hickory trees were rare in the Summertown area, but they bore the largest nuts. We eventually found a dandy mature tree on the Sam Lentz farm at Henryville where we could easily gather several buckets full of nuts. The nuts were especially hard making it difficult to remove the kernel. With years of practice Pop had derived a special technique making the kernel easier to remove. He would crack the nuts, and the kids would dig out the kernels. Pop wanted enough nuts to make a hickory nut pie or a cake for Thanksgiving. After years of trial and error, Mom became an excellent confectioner. She eventually hit upon a prune cake recipe that included a sugary glaze of hickory nuts or locally grown walnuts. The cake became a regular attraction at Thanksgiving and Christmas. Walnuts were gathered in October. The walnuts would be covered in a thick green husk. Pop would place the walnuts in the driveway and run over them with the automobile to remove the husk.

The family's primary social event was attending church services. Besides going the two usual trips on Sunday, and the Wednesday night Bible study, we also made every gospel meeting and special monthly singing in driving distance. As a child I had not developed an appreciation for religious activities. In fact, church literally bored me to death. I could usually live through a singing without much problem, but preaching seemed to go on forever. I would always cringe when Gilbert Gibbs was called on for a word of prayer. Gilbert was a man who was carried away with the sound of his own voice, and on many occasions, I timed his prayers going past five minutes. He didn't pay any attention to the short prayer Jesus taught his disciples to pray; instead, I guess he figured God needed a little preaching as well as everyone else.

On the other hand, it was always entertaining to hear Burton Crosthwaite (Estelle Boles's brother) lift his voice to God. He too would pray for quite a while, but substance was substituted for his stuttering. When we played church at home, Jerry and I loved to imitate Burton. Each of his prayers began with "Mo Mo Mo Mo Umhum, Most Righteous Heavenly Fa Fa Fa Fa Father." Burton served as the church treasurer for years. We enjoyed putting play money in the offering plate or wrapping and tying a dollar bill in a tight knot to see him later struggle with the untying. Being a cheerful giver took on new meaning with Burton counting the money. Jerry, Roy Martin, and I once discovered a cache of Summertown Banking Company checks. Most of the checks were canceled, dating to the early 1900s. However, we found two or three unspent checkbooks. The Summertown Banking Company closed its doors after the stock market crash in 1929. We soon found the old checks to be useful. On Sundays we would secretly drop them in the collection plate at church. We made them out for large amounts of money ($20, $50, and $100) payable to the Summertown Church of Christ, and we would forge celebrities' names (John Wayne, Mickey Mantle, Elvis Presley) to the checks. The best fun was yet to come. After church we would hide and watch Burton very slowly and deliberately examine the bogus checks. It was highly entertaining to watch Burton scratch his head, and then shuffle around to some of the elders inquiring about the proper method to dispose of the contribution. Bah!

The reason Jerry and I felt Burton was fair game for a good teasing resulted in the humorous stories Pop told on Burton when he and Marvin Crosthwaite (Burton's brother) used to kid him when they were in high school. Pop and Marvin were best friends. Ben Boles was married to Marvin's sister, Estelle.

On many Sunday afternoons, Estelle and her sister, Marguerite, would prepare Sunday dinner for the family. Estelle would often invite her brother, Burton, and wife, Anne Tate, Estelle's brother, Marvin, and Pop to join them in a fabulous meal and reunion of family. Quite often after the meal the family would play amusing games. Marvin loved to suggest the fruit basket turnover game, because he always wanted to name his older brother, Burton, "plum." After all contestants were named a fruit, the object of the game was the person in the middle would have to say the fruit three times before the contestant would say their fruity name only once. If they failed, they became the person in the middle. Plum was a most appropriate fruit for Burton because Marvin knew Burton would not be able to say "Plum" without stuttering. Poor Burton could only mutter "pl, pl, pl, pl" when his fruit was announced by the person in the center of the ring. Pop's other childhood friend was Bucket Holloway. Bucket loved to tell the tale on Burton on the day his son, Tommy, was born. The doctor came into the waiting room and announced to Burton that he and Anne Tate were parents to a baby boy. Burton quickly responded to the doctor stating, "Only one child? Anne Tate and I were naught twice." On another occasion Marvin came home sporting a slick new Cadillac sedan. He managed to help Ben and Burton into the back seat to take a quick ride around town. They stopped momentarily at the post office, and one of the loafers approached the automobile and began to chide Burton rather harshly. Ben immediately took offense to the loafer's imposition and hit the guy in the head with his cane. Ben jeered, "Put that in your pipe and smoke it!"

 Burton and Anne Tate had only one son named Thomas.

Everyone called him Tommy. Tommy was twelve years older than me, but I recall how everyone in the Crosthwaite family gave in to Tommy's every desire. On one hot summer day the Crosthwaite family visited us at the Bud James house. As we assembled in the living room Tommy took off his shoes, put his feet in his mother's lap, and commanded her to fan his feet. Tommy never outgrew his severe speech impediment. He had few friends and spent most of his time in the house. He rarely went outside because he disliked being in the sun. When Tommy graduated from high school, he was the featured pianist for the commencement ceremony. After Tommy's failed attempt at college, he began looking for a job. Walking in his father's footsteps he worked for a short while as a Watkins door-to-door salesman. Later he became a licensed barber. D.W. Shelton gave Tommy an opportunity to work in his shop in Summertown, but Tommy's demeanor did not attract very many customers. Pop approached Chris, Jerry, and me to give Tommy an opportunity to cut our hair. I remember vividly that my visit to Tommy's barber chair set an all-time record for the longest haircut in my life. When he finished, I had been in his chair for well over an hour. We three boys were reluctant about going back to Tommy for another haircut. Unfortunately for Tommy, he managed to get an infected eye from a small piece of hair in the barbershop. We boys were relieved when Tommy did not return to the barber profession. Tommy decided to sell me his 1955 Studebaker for $125 when I was a senior in high school. To everyone's surprise he packed his suitcase and moved to Chicago where he worked as a taxi driver for many years.

When I was a small boy about four years old, some of the men in the Summertown church congregation began calling me "little preacher." I was always talking. If I didn't have an audience, I talked out loud to myself. This amused many people at church, but it was not amusing to my mom. She used to pinch me on the ear to get me to shut up for a bit. Everything about church was boring to me but singing. I really loved to sing. One summer, Gilbert Gibbs came to church and directed a song leading class for the menfolk. Lawrence County, Tennessee, earned notoriety through James Vaughan, the father of Southern gospel music. He ran the first radio station in the county for the sole purpose of broadcasting his brand of gospel music and advertising his published music books. He distributed them all over the country and formed special gospel quartets that would hold singing exhibitions, and music schools. Gilbert had been trained in one of the Vaughan singing schools, and he was eager to pass on his newfound knowledge. Vaughan's gospel singing style was based on a ramped-up version of the old "Sacred Harp" shape note music. Vaughan used all eight notes in the scale that were represented by a special shape, and were named "do, re, me, fa, sol, la, ti, do." Song books included the shape notes, and the instructor would cue the class to sing the notes before they sang the song. During the final classes, young men were encouraged in leading a song, starting with the notes. The singing school was very intriguing to me. When the song leading portion of the class began, I told Mom I wanted to lead a song. We practiced at home until I had the notes and words down perfectly. When I requested to lead a song, everyone was amused at a little tyke volunteering. I announced the number of the song, sang the notes first, and then sang the words perfectly—all the while, I held my songbook upside down.

One of Pop's all-time favorite dishes was Mom's blackberry cobbler. Mom used a deep casserole dish especially reserved for her cobbler. With nine hungry mouths sitting around the table, it took at least a quart of berries to make a pie large enough to feed everyone. The handmade crust made a bed for the berries, and Mom would cut the dough in strips and lace it on the top of the pie. Pop called the top crust "galluses" (a colloquial expression for suspenders). As if Mom wouldn't remember, Pop regularly reminded Mom to add a stick of butter to the top of the pie for extra flavor. Those blackberry pies were extremely popular with every family member. As a result, at 5:00 a.m. on beautiful July mornings, Pop beckoned Chris, Jerry, and me to accompany him to the blackberry patch. There was not much about picking berries the boys liked. Just the thought of rising at dawn and braving the elements made my stomach hurt. Of course, there were the briars and heavy dew to greet us, but there were also chiggers. Chiggers knew how to move into the crotch of my pants and camp out for a week of itching before they moved on. In preparation for the trip, Mom would tie kerosene-soaked rags around the cuffs of our britches to keep the chiggers at bay. One summer, the blackberry crop was especially good. We had already picked enough for several pies when Mom and Pop decided to put up juice and make jellies. On one particular occasion, Jerry coached me to ask Pop if we could have permission to go home. Pop was a rather accomplished blackberry picker. He could pick circles around the three of us. Pop explained we could go home when each of us had filled our buckets. Upon learning Pop's proposition to go home, Jerry had an idea. Pop had already carried one full bucket to the car, and he was working on his second bucket. Jerry sneaked back to the car, retrieved Pop's first full bucket, and neatly filled each of our buckets with Pop's berries. After everyone returned to their post in the berry patch, we announced that our buckets were full. Pop kept his bargain and we went home. Upon arriving at home, Pop soon discovered he had been snookered by his kids. To our enjoyment Pop found the whole episode to be amusing. He retold the blackberry picking story many times from the pulpit about how his boys had snookered him in the blackberry patch.

About the same time Pop was preaching for the Leoma Church of Christ (five miles south of Lawrenceburg on U.S. Highway 43). Jerry and I soon became buddies with David and Don Woodward. We really enjoyed going home with them to spend Sunday afternoons at the Woodward home. The best part was Sunday dinner. David and Don's mother would make us peanut butter and banana sandwiches, and she usually offered potato chips and sodas. Wow! This was a special treat for Jerry and me. David and Don's dad operated a donkey basketball business. After the splendid Sunday dinner, we would often go outside to the barnyard and attempt to ride the bucking donkeys. This greatly displeased Mom because we came to church that evening with soiled clothing that carried a strong scent of donkey sweat. One Sunday afternoon Jerry went home with David and Don, and I went home with my friend, Larry Belew. The following morning after Jerry had sworn me to secrecy, he carried me to the barn. There in the barn was a gift from

David and Don, a gray speckled baby kitten that was just barely weaned. Jerry had managed to hide the kitten in the toe of his everyday shoes and his play clothes. Jerry and I had recently asked Mom and Pop for a kitten, but we were refused. Pop said the last thing he needed was to have more mouths to feed. A cat to kick out of the doorway every time it opened would be a nuisance—absolutely not! For the next few days, Jerry and I were able to sneak food out to the kitten unnoticed. Eventually, the parents wised up and we were called on the carpet to fess up. I was very willing to lay all the blame on Jerry. However, fessing up ended up being a good thing. We were allowed to keep the kitten, and we didn't have to be sneaky anymore. Jerry named the kitten Spittoon. Spittoon ended up being a very loving and dependable kitty. She was a great mouser, and she regularly brought her prey to the back porch so we all could brag on her. She was also a fertile kitty. She would have two litters of kittens each year, one in the spring and one in the fall. Spittoon moved with us from the old homeplace to the new house on the corner by the monument on Highway 20, and she continued having babies. In her older years, she quit having the babies on the back porch and began hiding them under the house. These babies did not receive the regular TLC and returned to their feral nature. The later litters were more like varmints than pets. Eventually, Jerry and I were required to gather up all the wild felines and give them a proper baptism. While Deena and Becky were young, Chico (one of Spittoon's offspring) had a litter of kittens on the back porch. The girls promptly named all of the kittens. Deena named one kitten Mountain Climber because of the kitten's exceptional climbing skills. To reinforce Mountain

Climber's legend, Jerry and I would throw the cat upon the roof of the house when no one was watching. Then we would beckon our sisters to see Mountain Climber gaining new heights. There was a maple tree close to the roof, and Mountain Climber had no problem exiting the rooftop.

I recall my first lesson in sex education came one Sunday evening as we were driving home from Leoma Church of Christ. When we arrived at Lawrenceburg, Mom announced that she and Pop were going to swing by the hospital and check on Sue Gibbs, who was recovering from a minor operation. She and Johnny had recently gotten married, and she was now in the Lawrence County Hospital. Of course, we three boys were ordered to remain in the car during the visit. When Mom and Pop returned from the visit, I innocently asked what was wrong with Sue. "She is sick," Mom replied. "I know she's sick, but what is wrong with her?" I countered. "She is just sick," Mom replied. These answers were mysteriously unsatisfactory, so I pressed ahead with another set of questions. "Is it her stomach, or her head, or could it be her heart?" I wondered. Exasperated with my questions, Pop sternly replied, "She is just sick, now cease your questioning, and I mean now!" At that point, Chris, being the oldest and most experienced in the ways of the world, motioned for the three of us to secretly put our heads together in the back seat. Then he lightly whispered, "Johnny's pecker was too big for Sue." Shazam! This explanation left me awestruck. I pondered my older brother's knowledge of such things, and spent many hours asking myself, "What was Sue doing with Johnny's pecker in the first place?"

One Saturday evening, Pop announced we were driving to

Lawrenceburg to attend a tent meeting being held by Marshall Keeble, a dynamic black minister of the Gospel. This was my first experience to be in the midst of folks from the black community. A large crowd had gathered for the meeting, and much to my surprise, the crowd was about an even mix of black and white. The songs were directed by multiple leaders, and I was impressed with the enthusiasm which the leaders embraced each song. When Brother Keeble took the stage, the audience broke out in applause. I had never heard applause at church before. Brother Keeble began with this illustration: "I like to hear the 'amens' out in the audience. If you go to a football game and don't yell, then the man next to you asks, 'Don't you like football?' We need to let all our neighbors know we like God and his Gospel." That introduction began a lively exchange of conversation between Brother Keeble and the parishioners. I was convinced this was the most interesting church meeting I had ever attended. Brother Keeble talked about keeping the cows out of the ditch. He said you have to help your brother because sometimes he doesn't know his cow is in the ditch. He added, "I know the Bible says not to judge, but we can be fruit inspectors. The Bible also says, 'By their fruits you shall know them.' If you see a brother fooling around with someone else's wife, tell him to stop! It might feel good in the beginning, but all sin is bad."

On Sunday afternoons while Pop was preaching at Leoma, the entire James family would be invited to Sunday dinner and an afternoon visit. This was a regular part of southern hospitality shown to the preacher and his family during the fifties. Chris, Jerry, and I really liked going to the Rinks house for Sunday dinner. The Rinks family had about as many kids as the James family, and most of them were girls that mirrored our ages. The girls were great entertainers. They carried us to see their special playhouse under the big oak tree that shaded the far end of their backyard. The rooms of the playhouse were lined rocks, and each room came with make-believe furniture fabricated out of slab wood they had adorned with flowers and colored glass. The three James boys actually had a swell time playing with the girls. On another Sunday afternoon the girls carried us to the barn to show us how to catch carpenter bees. The male carpenter bees had yellow spots on their faces. We would swat them down with a board and tie a string around their legs. When two or three were tied together, the bees would fly in circles that simulated the flight of a helicopter. The carpenter bee experience proved to be enormously exciting. However, given our ages, Chris and Jerry began to worry what the other boys might think if they knew we had spent the afternoon playing with the Rinks girls. Therefore, we took a vow of secrecy, and never tell any of the boys we had stooped so low to play with girls. I remember I was coerced into taking my vow of secrecy. Chris and Jerry warned me that I would be fed a knuckle sandwich if I ever told.

On Sunday nights at the Leoma Church of Christ, all the boys were invited to lead the congregation in a hymn. At the conclusion, Brother Rinks, the regular Sunday night song leader, would take requests from the audience. Jerry and I always requested *When the Roll is Called Up Yonder*. Brother Rinks was a homegrown Southerner who had a distinctive nasal drawl. He pronounced yonder as "yannnnder." As the congregation joined in the song, most of the boys would chime in with a loud "yannnder" mimicking Brother Rinks's nasal tone. Such entertainment almost made the Sunday night service worth attending.

Excluding school and Saturday morning TV, the kids spent most of their daylight hours playing outside. Our favorite place to play was out in the barnyard. We all had homemade bows, and there were plenty of milkweeds that would make perfect arrows. A crimped bottle cap from a soda bottle added the perfect weight to make the arrow travel faster with less yaw. We frequently engaged in corncob battles. Occasionally, James Allen Martin and his younger brother Roy would come over to play. James was the age of Chris and Roy was between Jerry and me. James had a peculiar habit of rocking back and forth as a child. He also stuttered when he became agitated or excited. We nicknamed him Speedy and spent a great deal of time trying to get Speedy excited. One afternoon we chose up for a corncob battle. Chris and Speedy challenged Roy, Jerry, and me to a battle provided they could have the advantage of the hay fort opening to the door of the barn loft. Chris and Speedy were getting the better end of the battle when the three smaller boys retreated to plan a new battle strategy. Jerry, being the oldest and savviest, came up with a foolproof plan for victory. There was a walnut tree on the end of the orchard. Roy and Jerry would gather nuts while I would provide a one-man assault on the fort. Doing so would bring Chris and Speedy out into the open. The plan was a great success! Of course, I fell prey to a barrage of corncobs, but the distraction was enough to allow Roy and Jerry to pepper the Axis Regime with the secret weapon—walnuts. Walnuts, being heavier and denser than corncobs, provided superior firepower. Suddenly, one walnut hit Speedy in the eye. This prompted

Chris to pick up his bow and arrow, and taking dead aim, one of the special arrows equipped with the bottle cap end caught Roy in the back of the head. Speedy, being the emotional type, ran crying to Mama. By the time he arrived in the kitchen, his eye had almost swollen shut. Speedy said, "Ma Ma Ma Ma Ma, th th th th those James boys cheated. They hit m m me in the eye wi wi wi wi with a wal wal wal nut." That seemed funny to the Allied Forces at the time, but Speedy's mother took great objection when she soon discovered that Roy was also wounded. She gathered up Speedy and Roy and carried them to the car vowing not to bring her children back to be harassed by those mean old James boys.

After visiting with Millard Benson one afternoon, Pop decided to get into the sheep business. Millard gave Pop an orphan lamb that required bottle feeding. It was an unusually cold winter, so the lamb had to spend some time in the house. The lamb kept jumping out of her box behind the stove, so we named the lamb Leaping Lena. Lena became an instant pet and tolerated all the attention and affection bestowed upon her by the kids. Years later Lena became a mama giving birth to twin lambs—a boy and a girl. Jerry immediately claimed the boy lamb for himself which he named Bill. Bill had a much different disposition than Lena. While Lena was docile, Bill was domineering. One afternoon Jerry invited me to the barn to see Bill's new trick. Rubbing Bill's head and pushing him backward would make Bill butt our hands. Fascinated by Bill's new trick, we spent many afternoons reinforcing the trick. As Bill grew larger, he butted harder and without provocation until butting became no fun. In Bill's barn lot was an apple orchard. One afternoon a cousin came over to pick apples. Unaware of Bill's unsavory reputation, when she bent over to pick the apples, Bill scored a bull's eye on her nice, round derriere. As Bill prepared to butt again, the frightened lady bolted into a fast sprint and jumped the fence without breaking her stride.

Pop also raised hogs in another section of the barn lot. One remarkably stubborn sow was hell-bent on getting out of the lot. After Pop tired of chasing the old sow, he installed an electric fence. The first time the old sow put her wet nose to the fence we were treated with the sow's startled squeal. It was really entertaining to see all the pigs come out and investigate the electric fence, but that was just the beginning of the fun. Pop showed us a trick with the electric fence. He demonstrated how we could harmlessly touch the fence while standing on a board. The board kept us from receiving the proper ground necessary to receive the electrical shock. Excited about the trick, we invited the three McMullin neighbor boys to investigate the electric fence the next afternoon after school. There were three boys about the same age as Chris, Jerry, and me. Their names were Doris (pronounced Darce), Larry, and Bill. Unlike the Martin boys, the McMullins were rough as sandpaper and were not afraid of the Devil himself. The McMullins enjoyed profanity and tobacco, and they usually brought smokes with them. However, they wouldn't let me smoke much because they said I didn't use the proper form and wouldn't inhale. This would be the day we would level the playing field with the rough-necked McMullins. First Chris dared Doris to touch the fence. Doris said, "I will touch it if you will touch it." Chris stepped up to the fence, and while standing on the board, grasped the fence and made a grunt as if he had received a mild shock. Not to be outdone, Doris grasped the fence to receive the shock of his life. The feat was repeated by Jerry and Larry, and Bill and me. The McMullin boys were impressed how the James boys could repeatedly take a shock and left our presence that afternoon more humble. One afternoon after a good soaking rain, Chris and Jerry invited me back to the board and the fence. I found out the hard way the board held no protective insulation from the shock when the board was wet.

One cold winter day Pop announced he had planned a hog killing in the backyard. The hogs were killed, gutted, and quartered the following Friday afternoon after school. I was introduced to a new and peculiar odor when the hog guts fell into a wheelbarrow. When the intestines and livers were removed from the carcasses, the mawkish sickening odor leached through the backyard. The unused guts were carried to a hole for burial. The quarters were placed in the garage on meat hooks to chill through the night. The idiom, "It's cold enough for a hog killing," comes from the evening temperatures falling well below freezing. The cold quarters of meat are much easier prepared after an overnight chilling. Pop said warm flabby meat was hard to process.

Pop worked out a deal with three Amish men to help with the hog killing the following day. For their labor, they would receive the hog heads, feet, intestines (for chitlings), and half the lard, cracklings, brains, and livers. Pop also had jobs for Mom, Grandmother, and the three oldest boys. Mom was wrapping the meat in the house for the freezer and Grandmother was in charge of rendering the lard. Chris, Jerry, and I were the gofers.

Chris and Jerry helped Pop move the heavy quarters of pork onto the meat table. Pop inherited most of the equipment necessary to process the pork from his father, with the exception of a few knives and a meat saw he absconded from his WWII service as an army cook. The meat table was made from a cross section of a large oak tree. The tabletop was about three feet in diameter and a foot thick. It was balanced on three legs about twenty-eight inches long. The top of the table was riddled with numerous knife and saw marks from previous use, and it was permeated with fat drippings from the many hogs and cattle that had been processed on its top.

While Jerry and Chris were helping Pop, he gave me a hog's head and a special razor used to give the heads a close shave. "You stay with this job until the head is completely clean and hairless," Pop instructed. The head was heavy and cumbersome for a novice like me. A medium wash kettle was atop a fire for boiling water. I dunked the head in the boiling water for cleaning as I shaved the head. At my young age, this was probably the most repulsive job I had encountered. The hog's ears had been removed, making the hog's head a hideous sight to behold. I carried my head into the garage several times for Pop's evaluation, and he continued to point out areas on which I needed to improve. When the head passed Pop's final inspection, he used a meat saw to cut the head in half to remove the hog brains. I was a dreadfully slow worker and was very happy when Jerry and Chris came to assist me.

Grandmother gave our largest wash kettle a thorough cleaning and placed it on another fire she had prepared. With the help of the Amish men, the hog fat was cut into strips and pieces three-quarters of an inch wide and two inches long called cracklings. The cracklings were placed into Grandmother's kettle. Grandmother would occasionally stir the fat with a long wooden paddle as the heat from the fire melted the fat. The excess liquid was carefully ladled out of the kettle with a large coffee can Pop had fastened to a long stick. The hot fat was then transferred to lard stands. When the cracklings turned golden brown, Grandmother would place them in a flour sack hanging over another lard stand so that the hot fat would drain from the cracklings.

As Pop cut the pork into slices, he placed the processed meat on large metal trays for transport into the house. Mom wrapped the meat in white butcher paper and labeled the meat by its proper name with a black wax pencil. Pop had purchased two large deep freezers that sat on the back porch of the house. By late afternoon, all of the meat had been processed and placed into the freezers. While cutting the pork, Pop moved meat scraps into a special pile for making sausage.

By late afternoon with the extra help from the Amish men, the long tedious job was mostly finished. That evening for supper, Grandmother made delicious crackling cornbread. Early that morning Mom prepared a large pot of white beans which had simmered on the woodstove throughout the day. After a hard day's labor, everyone especially enjoyed their supper that evening. The following morning, I was introduced to a meal Elmer called a special delicacy, fried hog brains and scrambled eggs. That was one dish I never could get my head around, because the image of the hog brains swimming around in the large dishpan was freshly imbedded in my mind.

In anticipation of the hog killing, Pop prepared a small 8 ×

8-feet smokehouse in the corner of the chicken house behind the garage. He built a large box that was four feet long, three feet wide, and three feet high equipped with a hinged wooden lid. He had purchased one hundred pounds of salt from the farmer's cooperative. As the pork hams, shoulders, and bacon slabs were placed in the box, Pop carefully rubbed as much salt into the meat as possible. The rest of the salt was neatly poured on top of the meat so that all the meat would be completely inundated with the salt. Pop inspected and rotated all of the pork in the salt box every few days making sure all the meat was properly soaking up the salt. After about three weeks, he removed the pork from the box and placed it on meat hooks in the top of the little room.

Pop knocked a few holes in the side of an old fifty-five-gallon drum to serve as a fire box. Green, water-soaked hickory wood would provide the necessary smoke for the meat. Once the fire was started, Pop would adjust the top of the barrel so that the fire would only smolder to provide an abundance of smoke. Pop checked the smoke house regularly to make sure the smoldering fire continued. The smoking continued for a few weeks until the pork turned a beautiful amber color.

Pop sliced the bacon first. We boys carried the sliced bacon to the house on the large metal trays where Mom and Grandmother would wrap and label the bacon for the deep freezer. Mom could coax Pop into removing the pork shoulders first for Sunday dinners. However, Pop was especially stubborn about cutting the hams too early. Folklore dictated the tradition of allowing hams to hang in the smokehouse for about a year. During that time frequent inspection of the hams was necessary to ensure the skippers had not gotten into the meat. On one inspection Pop found a cat sitting atop one of the hams enjoying a quick lunch. Pop removed the ham and quickly sliced it for an enjoyable meal. As a ham aged, a blue-green mold would cover the carcass. Before slicing the ham, Pop would soak the ham in vinegar and brush away the mold. The aged ham was accompanied by an especially thick, dark rime that was tough as whitleather. Pop insisted the tough rime must remain on the ham so that there would be little waste.

I personally never cared for the tough dark coating of a country ham. Years later after Carol and I married, I would traditionally prepare a country ham every Christmas. One particular Christmas, Carol and I invited our parents to join us in eating a country ham breakfast on Christmas morning. A day earlier Pop happened to be visiting at our house while I was preparing the ham. Pop flew into a frenzy when he saw me removing the tough rime from the ham. "You are just wasting it," he bellowed like a cow in heat! Finding his protest amusing, I simply ignored his comment. The next morning while eating breakfast, Pop admitted, "I believe that was the best country ham I have ever eaten."

One afternoon, my brothers and I were playing in the big oak tree in the corner of the backyard. After seeing an exciting episode of Roy Rogers, Chris made a hangman's noose. I reluctantly played the role of a rustler. Mom just happened to look up from her household chores when she noticed Jerry was about to kick the table out from under me with my head in the noose. It seemed our child play always had a flair for the dramatic comedy, and if there were a need for a stooge, an Igor, or a guinea pig, I was chosen. Jerry was always the buffo, and I played the buffoon.

On another occasion Chris had traded for a two-cylinder gasoline motor that mounted on a washing machine. He had imagined the motor could provide power for his homemade go-kart. The motor had a kick starter similar to a motorcycle. Chris ran into a conundrum with his new invention. Try as he might, he couldn't start the motor. I was curiously watching when Chris suggested that I should hold on to the spark plugs to make sure the motor was getting fire. This was my introduction to internal combustion engines. I gladly grabbed the spark plugs as Chris gave the motor a crank. When the motor cranked, I experienced a new sensation called electrocution. The jolt doubled me over as I fell to the ground. I wanted to cry, but it knocked the breath out of me. Still playing on my naivety, Chris consoled me by thanking me to help him determine the engine was receiving fire.

When I was in seventh grade, I made the best grades of my school career. I suppose it was because Pop was one of my teachers. Growing up under Pop's feet gave me an advantage of being familiar with his mannerisms, and it paid large dividends of knowing what and how to study for an exam. At the close of the final grading period, he planned to review the class for the test the following day. Much to my surprise he announced that any student with an A average in his classes would be excused to go home at around 1:30 p.m. Poochie Scott and I qualified, and we began walking home. When we passed the Baptist church on Highway 20, I suggested we walk down Richardson Lane to see if we could see any snakes in the creek. We stopped and played in the creek for a few minutes when we spotted an old, abandoned house in the woods. The yard had grown up in brambles, some of the windows were missing from the house, and the front door was ajar. We stepped up on the front porch to discover some of the roof was missing as well. This was too exciting an adventure to pass up, so with a wink and a nod, Poochie and I entered the abandoned house to see what may have been left behind. We discovered broken-down furniture, lots of old newspapers and magazines, and outdated cans of food left in the kitchen pantry. We very carefully walked up a set of rickety stairs leading to the attic. Much to our surprise, we found a WWII German machine gun that was heavily coated in Cosmoline wax and treated paper to prevent rust. We could tell the machine gun had never been removed from its original wooden box.

The following Sunday Tommy Dye visited me after church services. While we were playing, I told Tommy about Friday's discovery. Tommy was anxious to see the machine gun, and we left it in the attic. I didn't think too much about the machine gun again until about two weeks later when Billy McMullin and Larry Chapman stopped me one afternoon in the road as I was finishing my paper route. I could tell both of the boys were frightened. Bill told me he had been questioned by the ATF (Bureau of Alcohol, Tobacco and Firearms) about a stolen German machine gun, and if they questioned me under no circumstances was I to mention their names or they would beat me to death. Somewhat bewildered about the encounter, I assured them I would remain mum. I didn't rest well the next few weeks thinking I would be brought in for questioning. I had no idea what Bill and Larry were talking about until I went back to the abandoned house to discover the German machine gun was missing. Tommy must have told Bill and then someone stole the machine gun.

That was the last I heard about the gun until a few weeks later when I was at Bucket Holloway's store. I overheard Bucket telling another fellow that Zip Zap Reynolds was being paroled from prison. He had served time for dealing with German WWII automatic weapons without a federal firearms license. "Where did this guy live?" I innocently asked. "Right off Richardson Lane with his grandmother," Bucket replied. He quickly added, "Grandmother died while he was in prison." My nightmares returned for a few days until conversations ceased about the German machine gun. I learned a valuable lesson about pilfering through other people's junk.

Jerry and I spent many afternoons playing pitch in the yard. When Jerry was about sixteen, he developed into a pretty good pitcher. He had a really hard fast ball that would make my hand sting when catching it in a regular glove. He also liked working on his curve balls. The balls had plenty of fire, but he wasn't known for his accuracy. After several knocks and bruises, I refused to catch for him anymore. Occasionally a neighbor (Terry Pierce) would come over and Jerry would persuade him to catch for him. Besides being smart, Jerry was a natural-born athlete. Along with being a great pitcher, he was also the best batter on the team. I saw him knock multiple home runs in games as well as pitch the whole game. He was sharp at chess, poker, Monopoly, Hearts, Spades, and Rook. Many times on a Friday night he and Pop would play Mom and me. We only won a Rook game on rare occasions. Jerry was also a great tennis player, but he was probably best at basketball. Our outside basketball court was worn down to the bare dirt with so much activity. Jerry really hated to lose, especially to me. As I grew older, I could give him a challenging game of basketball, and when it became apparent that I was going to win he would quit playing basketball and begin fighting. He was also a great fighter and normally I would end up holding the short end of the stick.

In February of 1956, Granny (Mary Elizabeth James) passed away suddenly at home after a short bout with pneumonia. As a result, Pop and Uncle Paul became heirs of their father and mother's estate. Each son received a farm and each half of the $1600 in cash that Granny had kept in her tobacco sack pinned to her bra. I remember how impressed I was one evening when Pop revealed that he had $800 in his wallet, and for emphasis he added that was the most cash money he had ever held in his hands. Mom immediately had ideas about how to separate Pop from some of that money. The current news flash in Summertown was Mount Pleasant planned to extend their telephone service down Highway 20 in Summertown if there were enough subscribers to the new telephone service to make it profitable. With some arm twisting from Mom, Pop reluctantly agreed to become one of the first subscribers to the new telephone venture.

For the steep price of $7 a month, Mount Pleasant would offer subscribers one black rotary telephone per residence. Telephones could only be purchased from the telephone company, and additional telephones could be purchased for a fee of $2 per telephone per month. The only service provided was an eight-party cooperative line. With no private lines available, each line would be shared with eight separate family subscribers. Our ring would be one long ring. Also ringing at our home would be a long and a short ring, one short ring, and three short rings. When the telephone was installed, Pop built a special shelf in the kitchen just below the seven-day windup clock to hold our telephone. Our telephone number was just four digits: 5682. There was great excitement when the newly installed telephone would ring. When the phone would ring, Chris, Jerry, and I would make a quick dash to the phone to be the one privileged to answer.

It didn't take long for the new to wear off since the call was rarely for the kids. Another unanticipated event followed the installation of the telephone. Almost every evening around suppertime, we would be visited by neighbors who needed to make a phone call. Local calls could be made to Mt. Pleasant and Columbia, but anything further than four miles south of Summertown was considered a long-distance call. Long-distance calls were very expensive because they required operator assistance. Pop was especially annoyed when neighbors "wore out their welcome" by making excessively long calls, especially long-distance ones.

This called for telephone rules. Only local calls could be placed, and Pop put a three-minute limit on the use of the phone. The three-minute rule remained in place for all the James kids for many years to come. Another unanticipated event occurred that Pop found thoroughly disgusting. The telephone allowed disgruntled parents a sounding board away from school. All of a sudden, his school day was extended to evening hours. After one especially annoying occurrence, Pop informed Mom to tell future callers that he was not at home. Mom protested telling a fib, but Pop said if she failed to heed his instructions, he was going to call the telephone company to pick up their telephone in the yard and cancel his subscription.

The eight-party telephone line provided a unique glimpse of the community if anyone just happened to be interested in the news of the neighbors sharing the same line. Grandmother Emmons loved to listen in on the neighbors' conversations to discover the talk of the town. However, it wasn't really necessary to listen in to learn about the neighbors on the party line. One careless act of knocking the telephone off the hook at any home would render all phones useless on the party line until the telephone was replaced on its receiver. Occasionally accidents would happen, but some of the more sinister neighbors would leave the telephone off the hook on purpose if they had felt someone of the party line had been rude to them. There was plenty of rudeness to go around on the party line. If we picked up the phone to make a call, some neighbors felt the need to be melodramatic and would cuss and hiss. Then at other times during our call, a neighbor would demand the line to make an emergency call. There seemed to be an overabundance of emergencies during the days of the party line.

A few years later when we moved to the house by the monument, we had a renter next door named Mrs. McDonald. Mrs. McDonald came over about every afternoon around 1:00 p.m. to borrow an aspirin and use the telephone. Mrs. McDonald was a neurotic type who had a flair for drama. Most of her calls were to her brother explaining the eerie noises, strange lights, and UFO occurrences from the night before. One night about midnight she came over in a panic coaxing Pop out of bed to report a mysterious blinking light in her living room. Pop carried a new light bulb with him and screwed it into the living room light socket, and while he was there, he suggested Mrs. McDonald needed to find another place to live. Not long after Mrs. McDonald moved out, Pop decided to make the rental house next door a woodworking shop. He said, "Renters this close to home were nothing but a nuisance!" Pop liked the word nuisance. He frequently used this word to describe almost anything that didn't fit his paradigm. He used this word many times to describe how he felt about my ideas and antics. It's a wonder how I managed to amount to anything being a nuisance most of my life.

When Chris, Jerry, and I went off to college, we established a signal to let the home team know we had arrived safely at school. We would ask the operator to place a collect person-to-person call to ourselves at home. When Mom would get the call, she would tell the operator the person requested to the phone was not present. Viola! A free long-distance call! If we had an emergency and we had to call home, it cost $1.25 for three minutes on a pay phone.

The eight-party line was replaced with private lines in the 1970s, but it was several years before customers could purchase their own phones and not be charged extra by the phone company for using them in their homes. When Carol and I married in 1973, we were allowed just one phone without an extra fee. However, rotary telephones were available in several colors at no extra charge. We chose a racy red color to match our seventies home décor.

When Jerry was about eleven a hepatitis epidemic hit

Tennessee. Jerry was the unlucky one in the family to contract the disease. At least school was not in session at the time. The bad news was Jerry was confined to the bed for about six weeks. Pop bought Jerry a BB pistol to pass his time in bed. The pistol did not shoot very hard, so with guidance, Jerry was allowed to shoot it from his bed in the house. Jerry owned an incredibly large collection of miniature plastic army men. At Christmas and on birthdays for several years, Jerry requested army men as gifts. As a backdrop for the army men, we used a large cardboard box. The box would trap the BBs and it was my job to set up the firing range and gather the ammo. I spent countless hours entertaining Jerry from his sick bed. The experience gave each of us a greater appreciation for each other.

One of our favorite activities was developing our Pig Latin skill. The conlang was produced by taking the first letter of a word and inserting it at the end of the word followed by the letter *a*. Thus, the conlang for pig would be igpa. Jerry and I practiced until we became fluent practitioners, reeling off the archaic sounds a mile a minute. My only claim to fame as a polyglot was my mastery of Pig Latin. Elmer and Alice Lou were not very fond of our effort. I was often chastised by Elmer as he invited me to spend more time on mastering the King's English and less time on foolishness. It was especially gaggy for Elmer because he had no idea what Jerry and I were talking about when we conversed in Pig Latin.

Another activity among the neighborhood boys was trading comic books. Comic books cost about ten cents each, and fifteen cents for the special editions. I hated to read textbooks at school, but I loved reading comic books. By swapping books we could get more mileage out of a dime. We always liked swapping with Speedy and Roy because they seemed to have the largest supply of new books. Reading and swapping comic books was a hobby that actually followed us through high school. To our great delight a new series of comics began called *Classic Comics*. These were super condensed illustrated versions of the classic novels like *The Adventures of Tom Sawyer* and *Treasure Island*. As a result most of my book reports in English and American literature came from the *Classic Comics*.

When I was eight years old, I was given a model car kit for a birthday present. The plastic kit came with a detailed set of step-by-step assembly instructions. In order to master the project, I had to comprehend the instructions. For the first time in my life, reading comprehension was important. I would read and then read again the instructions, being very careful not to flub the project by gluing a part out of sequence. Model car building was very exciting for me. I would work countless hours on a project, giving great attention to detail. One day at school I brought a finished car model for show and tell. A friend asked me if I would assemble a model car for him for $2. Shazam! I enjoyed assembling the models more than collecting them. I quickly agreed. Over the next few years, I assembled dozens of models for my friends, and picked up some cool cash. I am confident there was a direct correlation between my improvement in reading comprehension and my model building hobby.

The late fifties was an uncertain time for our country. We were engaged in what was called the Cold War with the Soviet Union. Soviet Premier Khrushchev was making scary threats toward America. Thus, the nation went on high alert, and Pop became a civil defense instructor, conducting readiness training classes for several years. The big change for the kids was practicing air raids at school. Our Summertown Elementary principal was Ruby O'Rear. She was a large, no-nonsense lady standing six feet seven and weighing about 275 pounds. During an air raid drill, the entire student body was silently marched to the gymnasium where we were lined by classes in a flat, supine position on the gym floor. Miss Ruby would parade around the kids, making sure each child was lying perfectly quiet and still. Those who dared to move during the drill would be taken to the office for further discipline: a paddling. Quiet and still were two things Jerry and I did not do very well. Sometimes the drill would last upwards of five minutes, an eternity for a growing boy. Thus, Jerry the schemer derived a plan for the next drill. We agreed that during the period of perfect silence, the two of us would innocently and periodically cough. The idea of innocent coughs caught on like wildfire with the Summertown student body. Soon there was a steady chorus of coughing that rang out like spring peepers on a summer night. Miss Ruby was not impressed, but there were too many innocent coughers to paddle. From that day forward, the air raid drills were a treat for the boys. We could defy Miss Ruby without consequence. Miss Ruby's discipline philosophy was to swing the paddle and ask questions later. When teachers had disruptions in the classroom, they would send the troublemakers out to the hall to await the ire of the big lady carrying the big stick. The kids called her Ole Lady Big Rear, but never to her face. Being a hyper child, I often found myself awaiting the big stick on numerous occasions. Therefore, as a countermeasure, I would hide behind the door so that I would not be seen. After the paddle swings subsided, I would be beckoned to return to the class by the teacher. My hyperactivity gave me endless opportunity to hone my sneaky tactics.

The boys who had felt the sting of Miss Ruby's paddle would discuss their peril during recess under the big oak tree. We were in agreement that Miss Ruby delivered three stinging retributions with her board of education. If a kid was lucky enough to get the board while guests were present at the school, he would receive the paddy which consisted of three soft licks on the buttocks. Those running in the hall would be surprised by Miss Ruby who would grab them as they were racing around the corner to the buses. She would hold them up by the belt and give them six to ten quick licks in a fast and furious order. That was called the drag. For the unlucky ones who were summoned to the privacy of her office, God rest their souls. They were in for the major operation where she literally tried to beat the hell out of her captors. All who had survived the major operation unanimously agreed they were still mean as ever.

On the school ground, an abundance of rusty nails remained from the school burning a few years back. The boys designed a new game to get the girl's attention. By placing a nail in a mortar joint along the building and walking a few feet while holding the nail steady, the friction would cause the nail to heat. We would chase the girls and apply the heated nail to their arms. Miss O'Rear took exception to this new game right away. She gathered all the boys together and said she would whip the next perpetrator applying the nail technique. It just so happened one of the boys had been absent during the nail game. His friend was more than happy to show his buddy what not to do on the playground. He was spotted by Miss O'Rear giving instruction, and she paddled him.

Almost every Thanksgiving holiday we would be paid a visit from our Nashville kinfolk: Aunt Era, Aunt Lody, and Uncle Byrne. Era and Lora were siblings of Grandmother Emmons's hubby, Elbert. Elbert passed away in 1941, leaving Mom and Grandmother to fend for themselves until Mom married Pop in 1943. Grandmother Emmons lived with us until she passed away in 1971. Byrne (Lora's husband) had recently retired after forty-five years of service as a mail clerk on the Tennessee Central Railroad. It was always a treat to be visited by the rich Nashville kinfolk. Era would generally bring hot dogs, potato chips, and soda pop. This was a rare special treat for the kids. Aunt Era also brought a large camera to make photographs of the occasion—another rarity for the James household. Aunt Lody was a rather large, heavyset woman. She wore thick rouge, dark red lipstick, and heavy perfume. She always wanted to hug each of the children, pulling them tightly to her large bosom and kissing them on the cheek. Of course, this was a very repulsive gesture to young boys. (*As I grew older, I became very fond of being pulled tightly against a woman's bosom.*) However, this tradition had a happy ending. After each captivating embrace, Aunt Lody would instruct Uncle Byrne to give each child a quarter. Uncle Byrne carried a large two-section change purse that budged at the seams from the weight of loose change. With each command from Lody, he reluctantly opened his purse in search of the quarter. At this point in our lives, Chris, Jerry, and I would do anything for a quarter.

For added entertainment, Chris, Jerry, and I gave each other nicknames. Chris was Trapsy, Jerry was Tubby, and I was Twerp. I accepted my nickname simply because I was the smallest. Trapsy and Tubby didn't take kindly to theirs. I was careful not to mention the nicknames unless I was within running distance of Mom's coattail. I suppose the name Tubby was a particularly disparaging name in the fifties. Anyone the slightest bit overweight was ostracized and bullied. Jerry wasn't overweight, but he could always dish out the teasing much better than he could take it. As a result, the Tubby slur became my best strategy to even the score with Jerry.

Chris attracted the admiration of a neighbor girl, Juanice Bonewitz. Juanice began spending unusual amounts of time at our house during one summer vacation, hoping Chris would notice. One afternoon after Juanice went home, Mom and Chris complained about Juanice's long visits, and lamented for a remedy to their dilemma. Eureka! Jerry seemed to always have a solution to a fubar. Chris agreed to lure Juanice outside near the barn where Jerry and I had taken up camouflaged sniper positions with BB guns. As the master plan unfolded, everything developed perfectly, catching Juanice in a cross fire. Then the unexpected happened. Instead of Juanice running for home, she charged our sniper positions. Jerry and I held our ground and kept firing. Then Juanice played the wild card. Instead of running home, she ran back to the kitchen where she thoroughly told on Jerry and me. As Juanice was pointing toward us, Jerry managed to squeeze off one more shot, hitting Juanice in the leg through the screen door. When Juanice promptly went home,

Mom gave Jerry and me a lecture on our poor conduct. However, we reminded Mom that it was her idea—sort of.

Mom and Pop were products of the Great Depression and WWII. Because of those horrifying experiences, they learned to be frugal and save almost everything. After Pop spent five years of service at the convenience of the United States government in the United States Army Infantry, he was very happy to be released as a civilian. Pop reminisced many times about his army experiences and concluded that being chosen as a cook in an infantry unit probably saved his life. The other positive about his service during the war gave him the privilege of receiving the GI Bill, entitling him to a full scholarship to college that included housing for his family. Almost immediately upon his return to civilian life, he enrolled in David Lipscomb College in Nashville, Tennessee, in 1945. He and Mom moved into the veteran apartments adjacent to the college. The small, poorly constructed apartments had been quickly fabricated to accommodate the onslaught of returning soldiers entering college. The first year was a great struggle for the family. Pop was having great difficulty preparing for his classes, but with the help and guidance from a friend, Whitney Watson, he began to adapt. Mom also helped out at home by typing and occasionally writing his papers for class. Frequently Pop said college was an endurance course. He learned that if he arrived early on the first day, sat on the front seat, smiled at the professor, and entered into discussion, he would be rewarded with good grades. More than half the battle was learning how to play the game. Pop played the game well. On the edge of the apartment complex there was a small vacant lot. Pop convinced the dean to allow him to turn the lot into a vegetable garden. Pop found out that bringing his professors fresh produce secured him special status. During one summer class, Pop presented the professor with a box of fresh tomatoes. At the conclusion of the class the professor asked Pop to come by his office. Expressing his gratitude for the tomatoes the professor stated, "Elmer, I can only issue three As for this summer class, but I assure you that you will receive one of them." The GI Bill paid students very generously. Besides paying for books, tuition, and housing, each quarter Pop received an allotment of pencils and paper. After his five years in school, Pop amassed a large collection of #2 yellow pencils. The pencils came out of the boxes many times to construct forts and borders for imaginary highways that stretched across the kitchen floor. At the end of play, they went back into their boxes to be saved for their intended purpose. As a result, there were enough pencils available to service the kids in school until I reached the sixth grade.

In 1950 Pop was hired to work as a teacher at Summertown High School. While attending college at Lipscomb and Peabody, he worked part time as a butcher for H.G. Hills in the Hillsboro Village neighborhood. After receiving his salary for his first year of teaching in Lawrence County in 1950, he discovered he had actually made more money annually working part time from H.G. Hills ($2,500) than he made teaching full time in Lawrence County, Tennessee ($2,000) with a master's degree from George Peabody College for Teachers, the most prominent teacher's college in the Southeast. Therefore, Pop spent every waking hour moonlighting at extra jobs to provide for his family. On the farm he raised hogs and cattle to provide the family with meat on the table. In the spring he prepared a large garden that provided the family with plenty of fresh vegetables. Mom and Grandmother also spent the summers freezing and canning vegetables to provide food year-round. They also canned fruit and tomato juice. In the fall of the year Pop would gather nuts from the walnut and hickory trees and would spend endless hours picking out the goodies for cakes and pies. Almost every summer vacation Pop would build or remodel houses. When a James child was old enough to swing a hammer, Pop would enroll them in the James Construction Company. He also taught adult education and homebound instruction after regular school hours.

In addition, Pop worked part time as a Church of Christ preacher. As a result, all of the members of my family were very well churched. Of course, we made the usual three trips a week to church for regular services. In addition, our summer evenings were spent attending gospel meetings. If Pop wasn't the preacher, he sought out other meetings to attend, making it understood that our family had a regular evening commitment to gospel meetings. For those of you who may not be familiar with a gospel meeting, it's just like a revival, but the Church of Christ doesn't hold revivals—only gospel meetings. Gospel meetings generally meant more hype and longer services. This was my pet peeve as a child. I could handle the singing tolerably well, but the long-winded praying and preaching seemed to never end for a ten-year-old boy.

Pop discovered that attending multiple gospel meetings during the summer would often yield him opportunities to become a guest evangelist. Pop was often called upon to pray at the meetings. Pop inherited his resounding orotund voice from his father. As a result, Pop never needed a microphone to be heard. His thunderous voice was shocking to those who were not accustomed to his oratory manner.

One particular summer gospel meeting stands out as a wonderfully memorable occasion. Pop was asked to be the guest minister at the Long Branch Church of Christ, located on a rural chert road about five miles southwest of Lawrenceburg, Tennessee. The church building was a clapboard-sided, one-room building that sat in the curve of the road about fifty feet away. The small church was equipped with homemade pews, incandescent light bulbs, and four long and narrow windows on each side of the building. The windows were unscreened and provided the only ventilation long before central air conditioning was a consideration.

Pop took pride in arriving early and being one of the last to leave the services. The time beforehand gave my older brothers and me an opportunity to explore a gristmill located across the street. The mill was inside a dilapidated shed with a rusty tin roof that sat on the edge of a natural waterfall about ten feet high. The mill had not been operational in years, but it presented a great challenge to explore the nooks and crannies of the property and enjoy the beautiful falls that were exposed through a gaping hole in the side of the building. Much to our delight and bewilderment, we found an unopened six pack of Schlitz beer and a church key (beer can opener) lying in the corner of the main grinding room. Being from a family of teetotalers (non-drinkers), this was a new experience for the three of us. After much discussion and the ritual daring, I was nominated to open the first can of hot beer. To our great surprise, the beer spewed out of the can with much gusto and enthusiasm and landed in a big puddle that covered my shoes. Next, we wondered what would happen if we shook up a can before opening it. After we all took turns giving the can a big shake, none of us was brave enough to open the can. Jerry scouted around and found a rusty nail sticking through a 2x4 on the open wall. This would serve as a great beer opener, and it could be accomplished from a safe distance. All we had to do was throw the beer can onto the nail. The following four failed attempts allowed the beer cans to zip past the nail into the water below. We crept closer and closer to be certain the last beer would be a dead ringer on the rusty nail. Chris insisted he could throw the hardest and deserved the last shot. With all his might he hurled the hot can of beer onto the nail. There was a loud explosion, and a cloud of Schlitz foam made its mark on all of our clothes, covering us with the sudsy broth! About that time, Pop whistled the signal to come to the church service.

The three of us made a quick entrance and slid silently onto the back pew in a nonchalant manner. This was a particularly warm evening in July. The windows and the door of the church were fully opened, but nothing could hide the smell of beer on a muggy Saturday night. After several awkward stares from oglers, I was relieved when the meeting started and the attention was directed toward praising the Lord. However, I feared this was only a temporary reprieve, and the three of us would have hell to pay at the conclusion of the meeting. Much to my surprise something unexpected and quite wonderful happened. During the first song an old man who was obviously inebriated staggered into the building and sat down on the front seat. He was clad in dingy long johns, dirty overalls, and an old felt sweat-stained hat which he promptly removed, revealing his shaggy hair. He reached for a paper fan in the seat advertising the local funeral parlor and began vigorously fanning himself to seek relief from the heat. Very soon a biting aroma of body odor and alcohol began to permeate the building completely, masking the smell of stale beer that had soiled our clothes. I immediately knew I had been saved. This time it was not by Jesus Christ, but by the visitor who happened to bless us with his presence and his pungent odor at the most appropriate moment.

As automobiles approached the building from the road, they left behind a thick cloud of dust soon to make its way in through the open front door and the tall windows. The dust settled on the backs of the pews, making a perfect medium for roads on which I could drag my finger and drive imaginary road graders and automobiles. As usual, the time dragged by at a snail's pace.

I turned my attention to the loud hum of the katydids and crickets singing in the adjoining woods. Soon bugs and moths were dancing around the exposed light bulbs hanging from the ceiling. As the service progressed, experience had taught me that no one ever gets saved in the first twenty-five minutes of preaching. I braced myself for a laborious conclusion for the seventh straight night of drudgery. Much to my delight, a bat chased a moth through an open window into the church building. The bat scurried and fluttered around the light bulbs hanging from the ceiling for quite some time until it finally came to rest on the corner of the chalkboard behind the pulpit. As Pop would write a word on the board for emphasis throughout the sermon, the bat would rear up in a defensive position at Pop and chatter his teeth. Wow! What a show; the time zipped by so fast I thought I must have been at the swimming hole. This spectacular moment even caught me listening a little bit to the sermon. Pop concluded the sermon with one of his favorite illustrations: "Sitting in a church house no more makes one a Christian than sitting in a chicken house makes one a chicken."

On the way home after the service, we quizzed Pop about what he thought about the bat that rested on the chalkboard during the service. Pop said he never saw the bat, but he thought to himself that this must have been the best sermon he had ever preached because every eye in the audience seemed to be glued on his presentation. Knowing the truth was a little disappointing for him. He said he had also observed that no one had come from his home congregation at Summertown that night, and as a result he would present the same sermon to the Summertown flock the following morning.

Reminiscent of the story of Ezekiel's great vision, big wheels began to turn in Jerry's head about the following Sunday service. Later at home in the privacy of our bedroom, he double-dog dared me to crow like a rooster when Pop came to the conclusion of his famous chicken illustration. As a child growing up, there were certain unwritten rules defining bravery; a *double-dog dare* was something from which I could not walk away. I had no recourse but to accept the dare under the following conditions: all the boys at church would have to sit with me to provide camouflage, and no one could point a guilty finger toward me afterward. If I was ratted out, I would be facing a capital offense. The terms of the agreement were quickly ironed out and almost all of the boys of the church settled onto the back pew eagerly awaiting the crescendo of the chicken illustration. Unlike most Sundays that were spent drawing pictures and cracking jokes, this sermon captivated the entire congregation of boys as they waited for the grand moment. At the conclusion of Pop's illustration, and at the most appropriate moment to provide maximum attention, I crowed a very loud and impressive "Cock-A-Doodle-Doo"! Of course, I was too suave to look up for the immediate audience reaction, but as I continued to look down, I felt a congregation of eyes rubbernecking in my direction. Later I asked Jerry to describe the mood of the crowd immediately after my performance. He said "Sid, if looks could have killed we would all be dead."

Immediately upon our arrival at home, we began receiving one of the longest and most serious interrogations of my boyhood. Of course, we denied having any knowledge about the crowing incident and agreed the whole episode was appalling beyond words. To my great relief no one broke our agreed code of silence. Much to our surprise, prior to the beginning of the next church service, all of the boys were marched to the front seat and were instructed to remain there for all church meetings until further notice. That evening after church, Mom came into our bedroom and gave us a sermonette based on 1 Timothy 3:15 which states, "Thou mayest know how men ought to behave themselves in the house of God (KJV)…" Luckily for Jerry and me, we were just boys and dismissed the notion the scripture applied to us. We would have many future opportunities to learn otherwise.

When I started to school, it wasn't very long before my parents noticed that I was a very different kind of student compared to my two older brothers. Chris made relatively good grades in school, but Jerry made exceptionally excellent grades. As the report cards came home, Pop would dole out a dollar bill for each A on the card. Chris would make a little extra cash, but Jerry would really get into Pop's wallet. He almost always made straight As.

My school experience was much different. I couldn't sit still. I could not stay on task. I talked out loud to myself. I kept losing my books, my pencil, my coat, my lunch money. I was whipped almost every day my first year in school, and some days I received multiple whippings. Learning much later I suffered from attention deficit syndrome and dyslexia was no help at the time I started school. My school behavior was thought to be improved only if I was whacked sufficiently enough on the hind end. No thanks to my teachers, I learned how to overcome my learning problems, but it was a very painful experience for me. Overcoming my learning handicaps became an autodidactic exercise I learned through trial and error. I found that I could focus better on what I was reading if I used my finger to hold my place while whispering the words to myself. This technique helped me focus and kept me from skipping between lines. Some teachers frowned on what they called my bad habit and would whip me for it if they caught me using my hand to keep my place. I did eventually learn to read. In the beginning I was not one of the top readers in the class. I could read sufficiently enough to be on grade level, but I was never an exceptional student. My one great advantage that kept me moving forward was stamina. I worked hard and steady on my classes although I often received unsatisfactory grades in deportment. Being beaten so often at school by the teachers soon had a reverse effect on me. I found myself in a position of welcoming the punishment coming my way so I could entertain my peers and watch the teachers cringe. I began to act out in class just for the fun of it. Report card time was often a sad experience at home. Pop wanted me to be more like his other children. Mom cried and prayed often on my behalf, and I felt terrible about the whole ordeal. Much of my future success in school was due to the diligent effort of Mom, always closely monitoring my progress and rewarding me with positive reinforcement but quickly preaching a sermonette when all else failed. She reminded me often that I was given the name David because I was born when Pop was a student at David Lipscomb College, and it was her wish I would also graduate from David Lipscomb College. She further reminded me my name gave honor to King David from the mighty nation of Israel. David received his strength from his faith in God. Mom said this was a magic sword I would always carry with me to give me courage in the face of danger. I have used King David's magic sword many times in my life when I feared I was facing certain failure.

In first grade our class was preparing for open house (a time when parents were encouraged to visit their children's classrooms and view their work) by drawing and coloring a realistic picture of something that reminded us of our home. While most children drew pictures of their house, I chose to draw a picture of the barn and barnyard animals. My picture included a rendition of cows, goats, and chickens. I also added a barn, fencing, and a pond. For the finishing touch, I added a series of black dots scattered around the barnyard. When the teacher, Mrs. Alexander, came around to inspect our work, she curiously asked what the black dots represented. "Oh, those are cow piles," I replied. That night at open house I heard the teacher and my mom having a big chuckle over my artwork. I did not understand the humor, but I was very proud the adults were pleased and surprised with my work. (This was the only time I remember them being very pleased with me that first year in school.) During my era of public education there were no regularly scheduled parent-teacher conferences. The annual open house was the only time parents were invited to speak with the teachers. When Mom asked my teacher about my progress, Mrs. Alexander asked me to step out into the hall. This order had always preceded a spanking by the teacher, and I had no clue why she wanted to paddle me again in front of my mother. Out of view in the hallway, I closely listened to what my teacher was about to reveal. "I will have to say, your son is surely not setting the woods on fire." Shazam! I immediately wondered who had been my false accuser about setting the woods on fire. I was further puzzled at Mom's facial expression when she exited my classroom. I imagined Mom would have been delighted that I had been cleared of being the neighborhood arsonist.

Mrs. Anne Tate Crosthwaite (Burton's wife) was my second grade teacher. That year she developed cancer of the throat, and our class was taught by a substitute teacher almost the entire year. On the few days Mrs. Crosthwaite was present, she let me know she was the boss. Mrs. Crosthwaite would grab her paddle and make a sudden dash toward me, gritting her teeth while emitting a mad dog–type growling noise. This always frightened me more than the paddling that followed. Barry Roane sat next to me that year, and we became good friends. Barry taught me how to draw liquor bottles and rebel flags. His dad was an alcoholic and Barry had noticed the names and shapes of the liquor bottles, and he was most helpful in teaching me how to draw them in true scale. One day after school, Mom was going through my homework papers, and I accidently left one of the Barry Roane creations in the papers. Mom preached me a great sermon about wasting my time and studying such vices as alcohol. It never dawned on me that I was exhibiting inappropriate behavior at school. I cannot recall a single lesson learned in second grade from the substitute except "The Midnight Ride of Paul Revere," a poem the substitute teacher would recite to us every day. I sensed I was behind at the end of second grade, and I worried myself sick the last few days of the school term. On report card day, I was greatly relieved that I was passed to the third grade. However, my pal, Barry Roane, had been retained. How could this be? We were doing the same work, drawing the same pictures, and telling the same jokes. It remained a great mystery to me for many years.

Marie White was my third grade teacher. Marie was a fun loving and dedicated teacher who was bound and determined to teach me how to read. For the first time, I had a teacher who made me feel she was genuinely interested in me. I sensed she liked me. Early in the term, Mrs. White required me to stay in during recess and read to her. She began me in the pre-primer and moved me all the way into the third grade reading text. After about two weeks of missing recess, I was reading on grade level for the first time in my formal education career. I love her for her determination to this very day. She was not going to allow me to fail. By the end of the third grade, I had moved from the Jay Birds (the nonreaders) all the way up to the Eagles, her top reading group.

Marie White knew the secret of bringing out the best in her students. I also hated spelling class and dreaded those Friday tests until I came to her room. On Wednesday she would give the class a practice test on Friday's words. All the students who scored one hundred on the Wednesday test were excused from the Friday test and were allowed to play with her Rig-A-Jigs at the back of the room. Rig-A-Jigs was a first cousin to tinker toys but were smaller and made of plastic with about three times as many toy pieces. Since I was going to have to learn to spell the words anyway by Friday, I immediately saw the advantage of learning them earlier in the week. Last but not least, Marie loved teaching music and planning musical performances for the parents. I could always sing better than I could read, so quite often she would give me a leading role in the production. This was a huge confidence builder for me.

We participated in physical education for thirty minutes each school day. When the weather was pretty, we played outside games. The long school hall opened to an old gymnasium that was built by the WPA in the 1930s. The community raised $1000 for the building and all the labor was donated by the WPA program. When the school building burned in 1954, the gym was protected because it was not attached to the main school building. Unfortunately, the gym was in a poor state of repair and the roof leaked in numerous locations. On poor weather days, classes would assemble in the gym for PE class. Every Wednesday our class would have rhythms. Rhythms were particularly repulsive for me because I hated holding the girls' hands, and I had no natural rhythm in my body. Most rhythm activities were accompanied by music and skipping. I was thoroughly embarrassed because I could not skip. Mrs. White finally gave up on teaching me. No one ever broke skipping down for me in small steps. I eventually figured it out by myself that skipping was a series of steps and hops on alternating feet.

One side note about Marie White: She was the only teacher at Summertown Elementary School who did not have a formal teaching license. She only attained two years of college work during her entire teaching tenure which meant she taught on a temporary permit. I soon learned there were more important aspects to a successful teacher than professional credentials. Some of my worst teachers held the most impressive educational pedigree.

When I was ten years old, Pop hired a high school boy named Benjamin Luffman to help him put up rafters on a house. Benji arrived to work each morning pedaling an old bicycle. Much to my pleasure, he would allow me to ride his bicycle up and down the road while he was working. I soon discovered a bicycle opened the door to a new independence I had never experienced. I knew that my next objective in life would be to own a bicycle. One afternoon I asked Benji if he would consider selling his bicycle. After much persuasion Benji confided that he would sell his bicycle for $5. I rushed home to count the money in my piggy bank. Unfortunately, I only had $2.49. I tried to take out a loan with Chris and Jerry, but neither agreed to loan me any money. Next, I approached Mom. She said she would gladly loan me the money, if she had the money, but she didn't. She suggested I talk to Pop about borrowing the money. I had never asked a grown man for a loan, especially Pop. I already knew he was tight as Dick's hatband, and he had no time for foolishness.

At any rate the strong desire to own a bicycle dulled my sound reasoning, and I did the unthinkable. After practicing my speech for about an hour, I approached Pop and began looking for the perfect moment to spring my plan into action. Unfortunately, it was easier imagining the right moment than it was to find it. Finally, after about a half an hour of me squirming around like a worm in hot ashes, Pop asked, "Was there something you wanted to ask me?" There it was! The golden opportunity to make my request known was magically dumped into my lap! Forgetting the speech I had practiced, I cut straight to the chase and asked if I could borrow $2.50 to buy a bicycle. Pop never hesitated for a second. He reached for his wallet and forked over the money as if he were attending to business with an adult. As the money changed hands, Pop said, "This is a loan, and I expect to be repaid before summer's end." I purchased the bicycle that afternoon and began mulling over my employment options so that I could repay my large debt. The only kid that I knew that had a job was Bobby Bailey. He ran an afternoon paper route carrying the Nashville Banner six days a week. I approached Bobby to see if the possibility existed that I could assist him with the paper route in return for $2.50. To my dismay, Bobby wasn't interested. Then in about two weeks Bobby had an appendicitis attack and had an emergency operation. Bobby called and offered me the paper route.

The paper route was about twelve miles long, and on a good day it would take about three hours to deliver all the papers. I had been riding a bicycle for about six months, and my riding skills were really not up to par to make a twelve-mile trip six days a week. To complicate matters, I did not own a large paper basket to mount on front of the bicycle. The basket cost $5, a very expensive bicycle accessory for the fifties. Going deeper in debt was out of the question, so for the first two weeks I carried the papers out of a canvas bag that was balanced by a strap that went over my head. The bad thing about the bag was I could only carry about a fourth of the paper load at a time, requiring me to make three extra trips back home to pick up the rest of the papers. After about a month I had earned enough money to buy the paper basket and repay Pop the debt I owed. I soon discovered the paper route gave me new freedom I had never imagined. I had put myself in a position to earn enough money to buy most of my clothes and have all the spending money I needed, plus I was able to save about $5 each month.

Carrying the paper through all types of weather was a great experience. In the winter, a soaking rain exposed me to a new bone-chilling cold I never imagined existed. Before the paper route, I was a sickly child managing to come down with a good case of the croup a couple of times each winter. To everyone's surprise, the exposure to the winter weather elements made me stronger and gave me immunity from the croup. Also, learning to balance a bicycle with a heavy load of papers was no easy task for a ten-year-old kid. I always dreaded Thursdays because the paper was full of advertisements, adding to the bulk and weight. When I began my route, the paper cost twenty-five cents for six copies. However, I soon learned there was more money to be made by selling single copies at the stores for ten cents each. Sometimes I would lose count of the extra papers I had for sale and the customers on the end of my route would miss their afternoon paper. I dreaded getting a telephone call from a customer who complained of missing the paper. Mom would always preach to me that I had an obligation to my customers first. I also soon learned that some customers were not worth keeping. Deadbeat customers would not pay for the paper on Saturday, making me go around and continue collecting during the week. That process slowed production and ate into my delivery time. Believe it or not, some adults really thought they could take advantage of a ten-year-old kid by simply not paying. This taught me a valuable lesson about humanity and made me learn to stand up for myself. I realized I had leverage on everyone in the community who wanted an afternoon paper. My monopoly meant I could cut off dishonest customers at will.

When it came to hauling newspapers and having the only source in town, I recognized my status as a carrier put me on an equal status with my customers. When I first began my route, Miss O'Rear tried to intimidate me about how her newspaper must be delivered. Not only must her newspaper be neatly folded, she also wanted it placed behind the storm door of her back porch. In the summer when she was away on trip, the papers were to be placed in chronological order. This became a real headache for me. One summer she left instructions again concerning her newspapers while she was away. Instead, I decided to sell her papers at the local store so that I could double my profits during her absence. On the day of her arrival from the trip she was patiently waiting for me on her porch. Knowing that I was about to get a lecture, I began peppering her with questions about her vacation and killing her with kindness. I hastened to add that I had sold her papers while she was away and there would be no charge for my service during her vacation time. She was so flabbergasted that I stood up to her I was able to get out of her presence without rebuke.

During the summer of 1958, the Newspaper Printing Corporation of Nashville announced a contest for paper carriers. The carriers who added the most additional customers to subscribe for a thirteen-week period would be rewarded with a week's vacation to Chicago, Illinois. The very thought of me going to Chicago charged my batteries, making me work overtime combing the Summertown community for potential new customers. At summer's end I had doubled the number of paper customers from about forty to well over eighty. Much to my surprise and especially the surprise of my parents, I won the trip. At ten years of age, I had never been anywhere on my own. Two Trailway buses were chartered from Nashville where all fifty carriers and chaperones from the mid-state area assembled to begin the trip. The first day was spent riding the bus to Chicago. We arrived in downtown Chicago in front of the Conrad Hilton Hotel at about 1:00 a.m. My first new experience was to ride a chartered passenger bus. My second new experience was to be awake at one o'clock in the morning. When we exited the bus, I was totally unprepared for my third new experience. All of the suitcases were placed on the sidewalk in front of the hotel and I had great difficulty locating my suitcase. I soon discovered I was the last carrier on the walk with a suitcase. I quickly entered the hotel where I heard one of the chaperones calling out names and hotel room numbers. To my great dismay, I had arrived in the lobby after my name and room number were called. As the elevators started carrying the carriers and chaperones up to their rooms, my fourth new experience was to be all alone in the largest hotel lobby in Chicago. Out of desperation I asked an elevator operator if she knew what floor the Tennessee carriers had been carried. With a little luck I stumbled onto the party and into my room without any of the chaperones discovering that I had been missing. Unknown to the chaperones, all the other boys refused to be paired with the youngest carrier on the trip the next morning. This was totally fine with me because I preferred exploring on my own, and I had the whole morning to roam the downtown Chicago streets by myself. Finding the hotel in downtown Chicago was incredibly easy since the Conrad Hilton Hotel was the tallest building in the area. I had brought $10 with me from home to spend. Since it was an all-expenses paid trip, I needed money for souvenirs only. After a quick price check, I knew that I would have to be very selective in order to make my purchases meaningful. I especially wanted to buy souvenirs for Mom and Grandmother Emmons. By happenchance I wandered into a coin and jewelry store. Voila! I was having an experience of a lifetime. The glass cases were filled with expensive and rare gold and silver coins. I began pouring over the selections in the case when a clerk asked if I needed assistance. I explained that I was looking for two cheap souvenirs that could become valuable like the expensive coins in the showcase. He directed me toward a great selection of almost uncirculated Morgan silver dollars minted in the early 1900s that still contained their original mint luster. I purchased two Morgan silver dollars and two sterling silver bezels for $5. As he wrapped the gifts in beautiful foil paper, he congratulated me on making a wise purchase that would indeed increase in value with time.

Another great trip discovery occurred at lunch time. I

returned to the hotel restaurant for lunch and found I could order anything on the menu for free! I ordered ice cream with every meal. At breakfast the next morning I made another discovery called fresh-squeezed orange juice. This was absolutely the most wonderful taste my mouth had ever experienced. Since that first experience in Chicago, I have always been one to appreciate the taste of orange juice. This was something that rarely graced the James table at home. However, once I married, Carol and I decided orange juice would be a daily breakfast luxury regardless of the cost.

The second evening of the Chicago vacation was spent at Comiskey Park, the home of the Major League Chicago White Sox. The Sox were scheduled to play the New York Yankees, my favorite baseball team. The carriers were assigned excellent seats right behind the batter's box. All of my favorite Yankee stars were present for the game: Mickey Mantle and Yogi Berra were the most memorable. I especially enjoyed Yogi's trash talk to all of the White Sox hitters. The game was called after five innings for rain, but I also remember we were given $5 more to buy hot dogs and soft drinks. Thinking I had more money than I could ever spend, I soon discovered that $5 was just enough to buy one hot dog and soft drink. Since I had earlier filled up on ice cream at the Hilton, I opted to save my money for an occasion when I could get more bang for my buck. My favorite Chicago souvenir became the ticket stub from my attendance at a professional baseball game—my first and only experience.

The following morning my new ice cream diet had taken its toll and I had a splitting headache. The buses were off to transport the carriers to a natural history museum. As we exited the buses there was another tour bus of kids about the same age going to the aquarium across the street from the museum. I was bringing up the rear of the line and inadvertently transferred myself to the line of kids going to the aquarium. The aquarium was really great! I had never seen so many large fish before in my life. In about an hour after I had thoroughly toured the aquarium exhibit, I noticed that I didn't recognize anyone from my group in the aquarium. At that moment I knew I had been separated from the group. However, I still felt confident that I wasn't lost. When I walked back to the buses and discovered no one had returned, I decided I needed a plan. On the horizon I could see the shore of Lake Michigan. I decided to scout out the lake and check back to the buses every thirty minutes or so to see if my party had returned. On a rocky ledge of the lake, I discovered a group of crusty old men who were fishing and drinking beer. They were fishing with cut bait and I noticed that one man had tied bells to his rods to alert him when he was getting a bite. After entertaining my endless questions for about fifteen minutes, they told me to beat it. I continued my discovery of the shores of Lake Michigan and walked up on the beach with a boardwalk. The boardwalk extended itself about a quarter mile out into the lake. Toward the end of the walk, I found another group of fishermen that I enjoyed watching. After my third or fourth trip back to the buses, I arrived at precisely the same time as the rest of the carriers. I promptly took my place on the front seat of the bus. However, the buses did not leave after we boarded. We remained in the parking lot for at least another hour. Unbeknownst to me, the chaperones had discovered I was missing earlier in the morning and they were franticly searching for me. No one noticed that I had boarded with the group, and my buddies who were supposed to be watching out for me were not going to say anything for fear of reprisal. They finally discovered I was on the bus and I endured a barrage of questions concerning my solo ventures in Chicago.

The next morning, we traveled to Louisville, Kentucky. That evening we went to a large amusement park. One chaperone was stationed close to the carousel and handed out tickets for the rides. The great part about the amusement park was we could ride any ride we wanted as many times as we wanted. The first ride I approached was a giant roller coaster called "The Great American Scream Machine." No one under the age of twelve was supposed to ride this ride, but several of the carriers put me in their group so I could skirt questioning about my age. This was a really old ride constructed from huge wooden trusses. From the ground the ride looked like a blast. It was really fun climbing an eighty-foot incline, but when the coaster dropped off the hill, I thought I was going to die. I had never been so scared in all my life. The next two hills were smaller and easier to manage, but when the ride stopped, I knew I had all the roller coaster I wanted for the night. My next discovery was the bumper cars. I found the bumper cars to be incredibly satisfying, so I spent the rest of the night at the park riding the bumper cars over and over.

Upon my return trip home, I discovered the James family had moved into the new brick house on the corner of Monument Road. Pop had worked about three years on the house. Its greatest features were two baths (one with double lavatories), beautiful oak hardwood flooring throughout the house, the spacious kitchen/den combination room, five large bedrooms, and a long wide hallway. The hallway provided endless hours of fun for dodgeball and bowling.

Not long after I began delivering newspapers, I was introduced to my first lesson in politics. Frank Clement was a Democrat running for governor of Tennessee. One day while delivering the paper to Bucket Holloway, he offered me an opportunity to earn an extra dollar. My job was to insert a Frank Clement ad inside the remaining papers on my route. I quickly agreed, and everything was going according to plan until I stopped into Dwight Ivie's service station. Upon opening the paper, he bellowed, "What in the hell is this?" I quickly explained my arrangement with Bucket for the afternoon. Dwight countered, "I will give you another dollar if you will throw the remaining Clement ads in my trash can." I also agreed to Dwight's plan, thus earning $2 on my first lesson in politics.

Pop borrowed $10,000 from the First National Bank of Mount Pleasant to construct our new home on Monument Road. With the family's new indebtedness, money was tight, and all the unnecessary spending was cut to a minimum. Luckily, I had a steady income from my paper route allowing me spending money for candy and soda pop, and money to purchase most of my clothing for school, and I also managed to save a few hundred dollars that would go toward the purchase of my first automobile.

The year 1958 brought a radical change to television broadcasting. The latest technology allowed some of the shows to be broadcast live. This was a major accomplishment to spinning long reels of film on videotape. The first videotape reels were really huge, approximately two inches wide and a foot in diameter that spun the wide videotape through a very large reel machine about the size of a refrigerator. The live broadcast allowed studios to skip the taping process and broadcast the image live, producing a much higher resolution picture. One of the first live shows that aired in the weekday afternoons was the *Popeye* show. Guests were invited to fill the peanut gallery, watch the cartoons, and be interviewed by Captain Bob. Mom drove the boys from my Cub Scout den to Nashville to appear live on Captain Bob's show. This was an absolutely outstanding field trip for the den. Everyone piled into the family 1957 Chevy station wagon for the trip. Mom and Marie Barnett were the chaperones, so we had about a total of 12 cub scouts and two adults in the automobile. While in Nashville, we also visited the Ryman Auditorium, the L&C tower (which was a brand-new building in 1958), and ate a picnic lunch at Centennial Park. This was probably the most memorable scouting event of my childhood. Here is a side note about the live *Popeye* show: Sometime later we were tuned into the show at home and as Captain Bob was interviewing the kids in the live viewing gallery, one little boy said, "I want to say hello to my mom and dad, and this is for you, Herbie!" With that he quickly shot Herbie a birdie on live TV. Since this was before shows were delayed by videotape for editing purposes, the entire Tennessee viewing audience got flipped off by the *Popeye* Show. The live show was quickly canceled from the network as a result.

    Time moved at a snail's pace when I was a child. Chris and Jerry had been in the Boy Scouts for some time before I became old enough to join. Chris was given a uniform and was supported through his scouting efforts mainly by Mom. Pop considered the scouting experience foolishness and bluntly said he would not waste his time on such endeavors. Jerry received Chris's outgrown uniforms when he joined. By the time my eleventh birthday rolled around, there was no money to spend on my scouting activities, and Pop made it crystal clear my adventures in the scouts would be contingent upon my self-funding the activities. This was music to my ears. Funding the scout activities would be no problem because of my steady income from my paper route.

Mr. A.D. Prosser was the scoutmaster, and a very good one at that. He only had one son, Andy, and Mr. Prosser was determined to see Andy receive the rank of Eagle (Scouting's highest rank) before Andy graduated from high school. Mr. Prosser was a great motivator, and he worked very hard toward making his troop achieve their highest rank possible.

All Boy Scout candidates start with the basics. The first hurdle is the rank of Tenderfoot. The young Boy Scout candidates were jeered and harassed by the older boys in the troop which provided extra motivation to achieve rank as fast as possible. Residual lessons were also provided by the older boys on the fine arts of how to cuss, smoking grapevine and rabbit tobacco, and sex education. Since I had never received any formal sex education training at school or at home, I was happy to learn all I could from the older boys in the scout troop. At the ripe age of eleven years, girls were only good for teasing and chasing around the school grounds at recess. When sex was explained to me in detail the whole affair seemed appalling. I had no idea my pecker was useful for anything but a hose with which to piss. I learned the older boys often said, "I am going to drain my main vein to make my bladder flatter." That made more sense to me than poking it inside a girl. Another milestone for young boys was the ability to grow hair under their arms and around their privates. This hair growth also was accompanied with a growth spurt to the pecker. Boys spent lots of time bragging about who was endowed with the largest sex organ. It was many years later before I was convinced that girls could really enjoy the sex act. The closest sermon Mom ever preached on sex was for me to be good on a date. Pop said, "Be sure to keep your nose clean. You are a James. Do not tarnish the family name." Pop preached a lot about fornication at church in the pulpit, but never mentioned it to the boys on a personal basis. The mystery of fornication began to have a certain charm as the older boys described their sex acts in great detail and with enthusiasm. To add to my confusion about sex, I began to notice almost all of the Old Testament heroes also participated in fornication from time to time. I often wondered how could Abraham be a man after God's own heart when he had sex with Sarah's handmaiden, Hagar?

My first kiss occurred on a trip home from the boys' basketball tournament with Dale Marshall. I was 15, and Dale was 14. We had sat together at the ball game and it only seemed natural for us to sit together on the school bus on the way home. I was entertaining Dale with a joke a minute when, all of a sudden, I had an urge to kiss her. Dale gave me an encouraging smile as I went in for my first kiss. Boy was I ever surprised. I had never had a big sloppy kiss before, and I felt excited and confused simultaneously. A million thoughts raced through my mind as I began analyzing the moment. Did this mean that Dale and I would be going steady? I only wanted to experience a kiss. The next few days at school were terribly awkward and embarrassing. I had not given any thought on how I should proceed in the future.

My first large hurdle in scouting was to learn how to swim. I had never taken a formal swimming lesson, and at the age of twelve while I was working on the rank of First Class, I knew I would have to tread water for at least five minutes to earn the rank. In the summer, swimming lessons were offered at the week-long summer camp of the Boxwell Boy Scout Reservation on Old Hickory Lake north of Nashville in Lebanon. I saved my money that year and laid down the twenty-five bucks to cover the fee, and Jerry and I were off to camp.

Boxwell had recently undergone new construction and Jerry and I were among the first campers to experience the new campsites. The first night at Boxwell it began to rain. It rained all night and all the next two days. Paths were replaced with muddy mires more than ankle deep in places. The weather front also brought unusually cool weather. The normally warm lake water was an unseasonably cool forty degrees. The swim lessons went on without delay and I learned to swim in some of the coldest water I had ever experienced. Another great highlight of the Boxwell experience was the rifle range. Marksman Merit Badges were reserved for the best riflemen, and both Jerry and I qualified for the Marksman Merit Badge. We qualified shooting special NRA .22 rifles equipped with a peep sight at targets twenty-five feet away. (Some 50 years later I ran across one of the special NRA .22 Remington rifles that I learned to fire at Boxwell. Great memories rushed over me as I quickly made the purchase.)

I was a wee bit trepidatious upon my return home. I knew the next time we went swimming at the Pleasant Gardens swimming hole, I would be required to jump off the bridge. The old wooden bridge stood about twelve to fifteen feet above the water level, and the water under the bridge was about eight feet deep. Being a nonswimmer gave me a good excuse to refuse to jump, but since I passed the beginners' swim test at Boxwell, I had no excuse to stand behind. I still remember to this day the dreaded anticipation of the first jump. Of course, once I conquered my unfounded apprehension of drowning, the bridge jump offered great exhilaration!

One of the first lessons as a Boy Scout was to identify poison oak and poison ivy since they grew prolifically in Tennessee forests. As new boys joined the troop, the older scouts took turns teaching the recruits about the dangers of poison oak and poison ivy. One of the fun activities was to cut wild grapevines into four-inch lengths. The grapevine was pithy, making it a good substitute for a cigar. Poison ivy vines were sometimes mistaken for a grapevine by an untrained eye and smoking the ivy vine proved to be disastrous. Upon one occasion I was teaching a new recruit the first lesson about poison ivy when he told me the lesson didn't interest him since the plant had never bothered him. "Watch this!" he brayed, as he began rubbing the crumpled leaves on his arms and face. I warned him to go wash immediately, but he remained cocky and confident that he was not allergic. The next time I saw him a couple of days later at school, he was broken out in a terrible rash. Ouch! He was bound and determined to learn about poison ivy the hard way!

Other lessons in the Boy Scouts were knot tying, Morse code, lashing, knife sharpening, and many techniques used to cook over an open fire. I remained in the scouts for four years until I reached the rank of Life and lacked only three merit badges to become an Eagle Scout. Those three badges were swimming, personal fitness, and lifesaving. The gene pool had not been very generous to me. I had been a skinny kid my whole life with neither brawn nor brains. I had no chance of ever meeting the requirements fair and square. Of course, those scouts who had supporting parents paid for special summer classes that ensured their sons would meet the requirements sometimes by less than honest means.

When the local scout troop dissolved, I was Senior Patrol Leader, and had worked about a year on the God and Country award. I met all the requirements, but there was no adult support group to see that I was pinned with the award. Although I found this disappointing, my participation in the Scouts and my paper route were my two greatest childhood achievements.

I gained new independence when Jerry turned sixteen and received his driver's license. Pop had an old 1953 Chevy that became our wheels of independence. Pop made it clear that he would not fund any of our rat killing. If we wanted to joyride, we had to provide the gas and the oil for the trips. Oil was a larger expense for us since the car had needed a ring job for years, making the car smoke worse than a diesel truck. We used to joke about checking the gas and filling up with oil at the service station. Since oil was a large expense of the operation cost, Jerry came up with a novel plan for oil. In the back of the garage at Summertown, there was a fifty-five-gallon drum full of used oil that had been saved from the customer's oil changes. Since there was no market for used oil at the time, the attendant gladly gave us all we wanted. As a result, we would carry a five-gallon container of oil in the trunk. On the weekends we would drive to Lawrenceburg to the movies. We always tried to invite two or three of our friends so they could chip in the gas money pool. Gasoline was about a quarter a gallon at the time so if we could raise fifty cents to a dollar for the gas, we could ride around all weekend.

One particular winter trip to the drive-in comes to mind as atypical. That particular cold and stormy Friday night, Bob Washburn, Roy Martin, Jerry, and I decided to go to the drive-in movies. We were unusually short of cash for the trip, so Jerry hid Roy and me in the trunk of the car to save on the movie admission. About the time the movie began it started snowing. About every thirty seconds Jerry would have to start the car and run the defroster and windshield wipers so we could see. At the conclusion of the movie, we discovered we were the only patrons in the parking lot and it had snowed about five inches. As we eased out on the highway to go home it began snowing harder, making it difficult to see the road. We drove all the way to Summertown with sentries posted on both sides of the car to help steer Jerry down the middle of the road. Another peculiarity was we were the only automobile on the road from Lawrenceburg to Summertown. We were all very fortunate to arrive safely at home that evening, having carefully avoided the ditches.

Many of my childhood memories are associated with insects. My imagination was captured on many occasions by the insects that were in the yard.

As the early summer air warmed a large congregation of

fireflies would light up the evening skies. A fun evening only required a fruit jar and a little patience to catch the fireflies. The captive firefly audience delighted onlookers as the yellow intermittent glow filled the night sky. In the 1950s the night sky was especially dark, making the bumper crop of fireflies a beautiful sight to behold. There were no security lights in rural Summertown, and there was scarcely any night traffic on the highway. The late summer nocturnal sky gave way to a deafening cacophony of insect mating calls throughout the night. The crickets and katydids droned especially loud mating calls into the night air. The outside porch light would invite hundreds of insects to curiously inspect the artificial light with confused hyperactivity.

Around the first of July, the next exciting insect to appear was the June bug. These large jade green beetles were a joy to catch and fly around on a five-foot thread. The super strong beetle insects provided endless entertainment. At the bottom of the wood pile in half rotten wood, we would find supersized black wood borers equipped with giant pinchers. With just a little pestering they could be encouraged to latch onto anything we would put in front them. Reminiscent of cock fights, the black horned monsters would engage in deadly battle, making it especially entertaining when a nickel bet was riding on the victor. Other summer favorites were the news bees. They had a peculiar habit of just hovering motionless in the air, watching people do things. Those curious little creatures appeared especially interested in any activity that was going on, and after a few moments of studying the situation, they would make a quick exit to explore new horizons. The local yore was that it was good luck get one of those large yellow news bees to perch on one's finger, but woe to the one beholding the black news bee which warned of imminent death.

A variety of insects made good fish bait. Earthworms were plentiful out in the barnyard. An aged cow pile was a perfect place to dig worms. In the spring they were abundant and easy to dig. Later in the summer as the soil hardened, we looked for bait that was more readily available. Paper wasp nests provided excellent bait, but it was risky knocking down the nest without getting stung. In late May, the catalpa trees would be filled with larva of the sphinx moth. Those three-inch colorful worms provided an irresistible meal for black perch and catfish. In late summer, grasshoppers and crickets were favorite top water bait. The most unusual bait of the summer was larva found in horseweed galls that made a really ugly moth. These horseweed worms were exceptional bait because they were irresistible to the fish, and they were ugly and tough as nails. Horseweeds were actually giant ragweed plants, and Tennessee raises a bumper crop of these host plants each year.

I would have to say the most entertaining pastime was fishing for the world's meanest worm. He would lie motionless, attuned to the delicate vibrations made by his prey as they slithered along the ground. Crouched at the top of his burrow, he remained poised to pounce. As soon as the unsuspecting victim came close enough, the fight was on! Clutching his prey in vice-like pinchers, he would carry the new meal down into the safety of his burrow. This super-hideous hunchbacked creature was actually the larva of a tiger beetle. His ugly looks earned him the nickname chicken choker. Folklore taught the tough skin and hunched back of this fierce creature would stick in the unsuspecting chicken's throat, choking the poor chicken to death. Chicken chokers lived in a round, vertical burrow about the diameter of a pencil eraser. They were most easily spotted on a barren patch in the yard. Once located, a special lure was required to coach the monster out of its hole. A nice wild onion reed twelve to fourteen inches in length worked nicely, but if green onions were in short supply, a straw from a broom would also suffice. The lure was carefully inserted all the way to the bottom of the hole. With a little patience, the chicken choker would eventually grab "holt" of the foreign object with his pinchers and attempt to remove it from his den. When the lure wiggled, we would simply pull it out of the hole. Most of the time the angry chicken choker would not ease his pincher grip on the lure and voila, the predator became the prey.

Late summer gave way to the gigantic yellow spider called the golden orb-weaver. The yellow spiders faithfully spun their large webs on the back porch, taking advantage of the confused nocturnal fliers that paid homage to the back door light. As an insect would fall prey in the giant web made by the spider, the spider would quickly move to secure the prey by spinning a tight sticky web around its victims. For added entertainment we would catch insects and throw them into the web so that we could watch the ensuing battle for dominance. The big yellow garden spider would usually win the bout.

I would also like to honorably mention a few insects that were just fun to watch. Antlions live slightly below the surface of the ground at the bottom of a one-inch inverted pyramid in the dusty part of the yard. Unsuspecting ants would wander into the trap, and as they struggled to get free, the antlion would gently pull them out of sight. To add to the action, we would first catch a few ants in a jar so that we would have an immediate response from the antlion. In late summer, the beautiful yellow garden spider would build a large web near the back porch. They would come back year after year in almost the same location. I suppose the word got around in the garden spider community the James kids were most happy to throw grasshoppers into the web to see the immediate battle of the giants for domination. Occasionally the grasshopper would break free of the web, but all bets were on the spider who usually won the contest. Ladybug beetles would migrate to the back porch and end up in our utility room in enormous numbers when the autumn weather gave way to bitter cold. They would come by the hundreds looking for an escape from the cold. Toward the end of autumn, the praying mantis would drop large egg sacs in the flower garden. We once gathered one just for fun and placed it in the den window. In early spring, the egg sac hatched out with about a thousand babies crawling all around the window. One Thanksgiving weekend on a quail hunting trip, we located a large hornets' nest. Since it had been bitter cold outside for several weeks, we assumed the nest had been abandoned. After a few hours in the den, the heat of the Ashley woodstove proved us wrong. As the critters began flying about, we rushed the nest to a safer perch on the back porch.

As bats would begin to fill the Tennessee night sky, we would aggravate the bats by throwing small rocks into the air. The bats would home onto the rocks and follow them very closely as the rocks fell to the ground. The bats would give up the chase right before the rocks made it back to earth.

With two older brothers to serve as mentors, I had the opportunity of learning to drive an automobile very early. I remember I was eleven years old the first time Pop invited me to drive the '57 Chevy station wagon to a local store in Summertown to purchase all of the workers a Coke. That summer Pop was building a house just a few blocks down from Ross Dunn's store. As I carefully pulled away from the building site, I began to fear I would be pulled over by a patrolman. I noticed one of Pop's half smoked cigars in the ashtray. I quickly put the stogie in my mouth in an effort to appear more mature.

I had been saving my extra cash from my paper route, telling my mom that I was saving for college. As my sixteenth birthday began to approach, my priorities took a drastic change. My brother Chris had purchased a 1952 Chevy. About a year later Chris found himself strapped for cash and needed to sell the car. Since neither Chris nor I were twenty-one, the car was registered to Pop. Chris explained that for $225 I could have my own personal wheels and Pop would continue to be the legal owner. Chris added that the best part about the deal was Pop would not have to know about the arrangement. A few days after Chris returned to college, Pop quizzed me about the car. When I shared the details, Pop blew his stack! He tore into one of his longest lectures outside the Sunday pulpit. In conclusion and in no uncertain terms he promised he would not provide any gas, oil, or maintenance on the broken-down heap of a car. Since I never expected any help, this was actually a soft blow. I had worked independently outside the family since I was ten years old for five years delivering newspapers, followed by mowing yards in the summers, and as an extra farm hand during harvest seasons.

I confidently felt that maintaining an automobile would be a piece of cake. This proved to be another very important lesson in life. I wasn't nearly as smart as I thought I was. Nevertheless, the old Chevy brought me a new level of independence. Since I was driving without car insurance, a common occurrence during the 1960s, I managed to be super careful and avoided the wrecks commonly experienced by young drivers. My first maintenance problem was getting the cold collared auto running on a six-volt system to start in cold weather. By reading the latest *Auto Mechanics Illustrated* magazine, I discovered a new twelve-volt battery available that would start the motor on twelve volts, and then automatically return to six volts once the motor was running. The downside was the newfangled gadget sold for $35 and sales tax. This was about three times the amount one would spend on a standard six-volt battery. I saved my money and soon purchased the new battery that worked as good in reality as it did in my dreams.

Since the car was much more reliable, my next objective was to get a date and carry a female to the movies. I had met a young lady during cotton-picking vacation and we became good chums in the cotton field. I was never very good at picking cotton and this gal was a pro. Every time we weighed our sacks, she beat me. I took a good teasing about it, but I decided this gal would accompany me on my maiden voyage to the movies—and I would be driving my own automobile! When I asked her for a date, she gladly accepted and we agreed that I would pick her up the following Saturday evening around 6:00. That would give us a full hour to drive about ten miles to the theatre. When I arrived that evening, I met her father on the front porch and asked if my date was about ready. "She will be down soon," he replied. "Just make yourself at home in the porch swing." As I was waiting, little brother came outside and sat in a chair next to the swing. I noticed that his hair was combed and he was dressed to the nines. "Are you going somewhere?" I asked. "Oh, yes," he replied. "I am going to the movies. Not only me," he continued, "the whole family is going with y'all, and Pa is going to drive the family car." Kaboom! As the debris from the bomb began to settle, I suddenly realized this date was not going to be an instant replay of my first date dreams. The longer I sat in the swing, I began imagining how my date must also be feeling. She had to be as sick and embarrassed about the whole situation as me. I finally opted to take the teenage gentleman approach to solve this dilemma. Turning to little brother I quickly mumbled that I had taken a sudden stomachache, and regrettably I was not feeling up to the movies. I made a mad dash for the car feeling rejected, humiliated, and embarrassed. The very idea, I thought to myself! Her parents must have felt that I was a really immature sixteen-year-old kid!

One Saturday I was working alongside several of my high school buddies in the hay fields. Hauling hay was a miserably hot job, but it was also fun to hang out with my friends as we worked. We had hauled all day, and around seven o'clock we were bringing the last load to the barn. This last load was especially large since there were not enough bales for another load of hay, we just kept piling the hay higher on the truck. When we finished, the hay was stacked about fifteen feet above the bed of the truck. The four of us boys then climbed on top of the hay to ride the truck back to the barn. The barn was located about three miles from the hay field, and as we started down the road, we rapidly approached some low tree limbs. As we drove under the tree, I raised my leg to push the limbs out of the way. Unfortunately, on the other side of the limbs was a low hanging power line. When my foot hit the line, I was immediately jerked off the truck and up into the air by the wire. Thankfully, my buddies rescued me just in the nick of time toward the back of the hay load. Whew! I counted my lucky stars that day!

I had only one favorite teacher in high school. Mrs. Connie Hollman taught math. As a result, I took math every year in high school. When I was a senior, there were only four students in Mrs. Hollman's advanced math class, one of which was David Vincent, the high school principal's son. Our class was scheduled for the fourth period of the day that occurred immediately after our lunch break. David lived in a house that bordered the school campus. One day at lunch he was talking about a new pool table his dad had purchased and placed in their basement. As the discussion evolved, the four of us decided to sneak over to David's house and shoot a game of pool. Wow! This was really fun. We all were so engulfed in the pool table, we missed the entire fourth period class. Mrs. Hollman was a good sport and did not report us AWOL. The next day the four of us decided to hide in the math room before the bell. Mrs. Hollman came to the door and did not see any of her students. She made a quick exit out of the classroom, and we immediately sat down at our desks. About five minutes later Mrs. Hollman returned. She was not amused. We all were paddled for that.

A few weeks later on the way back from the cafeteria, I spotted a little green snake slithering across the lawn. I slipped the snake in my pocket and carried it to Mrs. Hollman's math class. All four of her students arrived early that afternoon to class, and while we were waiting for Mrs. Hollman, I opened her top desk drawer and inserted the little snake. When Mrs. Hollman attempted to remove her roll book from the drawer, the little snake slithered into her lap. Mrs. Hollman let out a bloodcurdling scream, and her four students doubled over with laughter. Mrs. Hollman failed to see the humor. I was paddled for that.

As the school year waned, Mrs. Hollman began to tire of my smart remarks. One day as she entered class she stated in a commanding voice, "Sid James, I am tired and have a headache. If you start with your funny business, I am going to paddle you." I couldn't resist the temptation. "Well, Mrs. Hollman, if that's the way you feel about it, let's go out in the hall and get it over." After she paddled me, I asked, "Do you feel better now?" "I most certainly do," she replied with a big smile on her face. I admired Mrs. Hollman's sense of humor. She was not afraid to laugh when something goofy happened in her class. One day after our class had taken the six-week examination, one boy innocently asked Mrs. Hollman, "Have you graded our testes yet?" Mrs. Hollman and most of the class broke into harmonious laughter.

On another occasion in Mrs. Hollman's class, a boy found a wallet in a desk at the back of the classroom. He brought it up to Mrs. Hollman's desk and said, "Look what I found at the back of the room." Opening the wallet, he continued, "I wonder who owns this wallet?" With all the class watching, two condoms fell out of the wallet and on to Mrs. Hollman's desk. Without breaking a smile Mrs. Hollman calmly said, "I know one thing for certain. It's not my wallet." The class exploded in laughter.

When I was a senior in high school, the only class that would fit into my schedule was general business, a freshman class. In advanced math we were working with algebraic logarithms and exponential equations. The general business teacher gave us a series of problems to determine interest using the archaic interest-date-time method. One problem would fill almost an entire page of cyphering using her method. I applied the algebraic method achieving the same answers with much less work, and the business teacher accused me of cheating. Being a smart aleck, I asked her how much she would like to wager on the accusation. Totally flabbergasted, she carried me to the principal's office. When the principal asked how I came by the correct answers, I simply replied, "Advanced math homework, sir." The principal laughed and asked the business teacher to check with Mrs. Hollman. When the befuddled business teacher carried me to Mrs. Hollman's room to check my work, Mrs. Hollman broke down in a hysterical laugh. The answers were correct.

I suppose I was the only student who had the dubious honor of being paddled every year in school. How I escaped the wrath of Miss O'Rear's paddle remains one of the great mysteries of my life. It must have been due to the euphony of charming compliments I graced upon her. Miss O'Rear would periodically patrol the halls. Any student who was sent out to the hall would abruptly receive a paddling from Miss O'Rear with no questions asked. Teachers sent me out to the hall on numerous occasions. Miss O'Rear was a very large woman and I grew accustomed to the massive clunking sound of her feet. When I heard her in the hall, I simply ducked behind the door. She never caught me.

Every summer vacation, Elmer came up with a project. Most

of my summers in high school were spent helping Elmer frame a new house. He built a house almost every year. Pop's plan was to get the house framed and all the exterior completed during the summer break, and he would complete the inside work in the afternoons after school. I remember one morning we showed up to one of his house projects before daylight and had to wait in the car for about thirty minutes before it was light enough to see to work. On another morning Jerry and I were busy digging the water line to the house. The last part of the job was to dig down at the roadside deep enough to place the water meter. I was down in the hole digging the packed roadway with a pick. "Be careful not to hit yourself with that sharp pick," Jerry cautioned. Sure enough, the next swing of the pick glanced off a rock and firmly landed in the side of my foot. Blood gushed from my leg, and I almost fainted. Six stitches and a great deal of pain and suffering were in store for me the rest of the summer.

Being friends with the high school principal's son gave us a unique advantage. On Saturday mornings a few boys would gather in the gymnasium to play basketball. Usually ten or more boys would congregate for the ball games. Most of the time we could play together unsupervised. If tempers flared, we knew the gymnasium would be promptly closed. Summertown High School offered no extracurricular activities other than basketball. Band, drama, chorus, and art classes were also not available. I did take agriculture one year and learned a great deal about woodworking and welding.

This is an indication of how times have abruptly changed since I was in high school. During dove season, David, the high school principal's son, and I decided we would hunt doves on the school campus one afternoon when school closed. That morning the two of us brought our shotguns and ammo to school and dropped it off in the principal's office. When school was out, we went back to the office and retrieved our guns and ammo to commence the dove hunt. This was such a natural occurrence; no one gave it a second thought. Almost all the boys carried a knife to school. Occasionally a teacher would ask to borrow a knife for a chore in the classroom. Practically all of the boys hunted and owned a shotgun. Squirrel hunting was so popular a squirrel dog was needed to help a hunter reach his bag limit. Bobwhite quail were very plentiful. A covey could be located in almost any honeysuckle fence row, sagebrush field, or adjoining a soybean field. The coveys were especially large, between 20 and 50 birds. When they became startled and began to fly, the thunderous commotion of flapping wings would make an unsuspecting person jump out of his wits.

I give both parents the grade of A+ for the excellent guidance they gave in raising me from an infant to adulthood. I never realized I was a privileged child until I was an adult. Elmer James was the hardest worker I have ever encountered. He always worked two jobs, and he was busy from dawn until dusk. Many evenings he would be completely exhausted and would go to bed with the chickens. Pop had little to say to me with the exception of report card days. He never understood why I was not as smart as the other kids, but rarely expressed his disgust for my behavior. Pop was an excellent provider, and he gladly shared with his neighbors—especially widows and older adults who were having financial difficulty. He taught his children by modeling an excellent example of hard work and honest Christian living. Pop did have much to say about the James name in the community. "The James name has been a venerable and well-respected name around here for 100 years. Everyone knows that the James family is honest, and we have offered hospitality to friends and strangers alike. Be certain you never do anything to tarnish the James name because Jameses always do their best at everything!" I suppose I heard Pop's James speech more than a hundred times as I grew up.

While Pop consumed his waking hours providing for the family, Alice Lou Emmons James nurtured the children. Mom taught us to say our prayers at bedtime starting when we were old enough to talk. This is the bedtime prayer she taught her children: "Dear God in Heaven, we thank you for our home and the ones we love. Help us to be kind when we play. Watch and guide us every day. When on earth our life is done, take us home with you to live. In Jesus's name we pray, amen." Mom was the one who checked our homework and helped us grasp the many educational concepts. Mom had a great sense of humor, and she enjoyed playing with the children. She was our confidant and our liaison when we needed to ask Pop for a favor. Mom did all the preaching at home. Mom always offered love and encouragement for us to do our best. Mom flogged us with the flyswatter when she thought we needed a dose of humility. She was a great cheerleader, and her goal in life was to make her children and grandchildren kind and respectful of others. Mom was also an excellent cook. In fact, with six children to nurture, there was always room at the table for our guests. The children knew their friends were always welcome to eat at the James table, and often the friends would appear unannounced to enjoy the bounty of the James harvest.

COLLEGE

In 1966, I was a senior at Summertown High School. I had taken all of the required college-prep courses, and the ACT college entrance examination. After Christmas vacation, I submitted my scores and transcript to David Lipscomb College. A few weeks later I received an acceptance letter from Lipscomb inviting me to the 1966 summer quarter. I had not made very good grades in high school, but I was determined to succeed in college.

In the spring of my senior year, Miss Vivian Shields, the high school guidance counselor, called me into her office. I began thinking to myself, "What have I done wrong now?" "Sid, I have reviewed your test scores and high school transcript," Miss Vivian began, "and I have determined the only possible school in Tennessee that might grant you conditional entrance is Austin Peay State." "Thank you for your interest in my education, Miss Vivian, but I will not be attending Austin Peay," I politely stated. I could tell this irritated Miss Vivian (which secretly entertained me). "Just where do you think you are going?" she asked in a huff. "I'm quite confident I will be entering David Lipscomb College the summer quarter after my graduation from high school," I stated with a smile on my face. Oooooh! There was that Sid James smirky smile that Miss Vivian found so irritating. To her chagrin, she continued the conversation. "You think you are so smart, Buster! With your pitiful grades and low test score, I am quite confident you will never be accepted to David Lipscomb College. Their standards exceed your academic ability!" Oooooh! This was fun! "This may come as a shock to you, ma'am, but I really don't need your help in gaining college acceptance. I have already received my acceptance letter from David Lipscomb." Being corrected by a smart aleck caused Miss Vivian to fly into a rage. As the veins began to bulge out of her head, she was determined to have the last word of this conversation. "Well, Mr. Smarty Pants, you may have been accepted to David Lipscomb, but you will never graduate. This I assure you!" "Sorry, Miss Vivian. I also plan to graduate from David Lipscomb College." Miss Vivian's goose was thoroughly cooked at this point. "Get out of my office," she sneered. As I walked out of her office, she was not quite through. "You may possibly graduate, but I promise you, it will not be in four years!"

Miss Vivian's anger was something I could never understand. Reminiscent of the *Leave It to Beaver* TV show, I killed Miss Vivian with my polite Eddie Haskell kindness. Miss Vivian had a reputation as a slapper. I was positive I would have to continue killing her with kindness the rest of my senior year to keep her slapping hands off my face. Soon afterward one of my friends heard Miss Vivian bragging that she was going to "slap Sid James down" before he graduated. Miss Vivian's gruff behavior stuck in my craw. She probably didn't realize it, but her confident assurance I would not graduate from David Lipscomb in four years was a challenge I could not allow her to win.

I made it my goal to graduate from David Lipscomb in three years. Miss Vivian was the resident temple goddess at Summertown High School because of the forty-five-plus years she had spent there. Unfortunately, she was also a bully and a misanthrope who ruled supreme through intimidation.

Okay, folks, I must admit I would have been an utter failure if Jerry had not taken on a role as college advisor for me. When I entered David Lipscomb in the summer of 1966, Chris and Jerry were seniors. Chris was having difficulty passing an organic chemistry class, and he was also studying getting married. Jerry never had any difficulty with his classes. He was the senior class president and was also working full time as a keypunch operator. My first day at school after I registered for my classes, I went to the bookstore and bought my books. Jerry came to my dorm room to check on me. "Why did you buy all of those books?" he asked. "They were on the list for my classes," I stated. "Don't ever do that again," he chided. Jerry showed me how to check the dorm bulletin board for used books and also to wait until the first class with the teachers to see if the books would be held in reserve in the library. Jerry explained used books were far superior to new books because they were cheaper, and many times the goodies had been highlighted by previous students. Before studying for an exam, he showed me how to search for old tests the teacher had given in the past, because many times the actual test would be a carbon copy of an old test. Jerry showed me tips on how to quickly write required papers. But his most valuable tip was to never listen to a college advisor. He said advisors liked to load students down with unnecessary classes making them take extra quarters to graduate. "The student academic catalog is your Bible," Jerry continued.

"The catalog will give you a list of every class that is required for college graduation. Work the classes into a long-range calendar to be certain you can graduate on time, because some classes are only offered on staggered quarters." (That was the best advice I ever received while I was a student at Lipscomb.)

Jerry also showed me how to sign up for the National Defense Education Act (NDEA) student loan. I kept the loan until I was a senior, and mysteriously, I was bumped off the list my final year in school. The second loan was from the First National Bank of Mt. Pleasant. It was called the Tennessee Education Loan. Interest on the loan did not begin until I finished my degree, and it would be delayed further if I entered military service after college. (When I entered the military, the First National president called Pop and asked what he was going to do about the loan. Pop just paid it off. That meant I had to pay Pop back while in the army making pennies an hour.)

On my second day at Lipscomb, the college dean of students met with all the incoming freshmen. Dean Craig began, "Ladies and Gentlemen, look to left. Now look to your right. In four years, two-thirds of you will not be here for graduation. This institution does not spoon-feed freshmen students. If you expect to be successful, you must study. Preparing for your classes is the only thing that is important. Good luck to you all." With those terse words, the meeting was over. The dean's remarks gave me a wake-up call. He made me realize my fun and games at school had come to an end.

On my third day at school Jerry introduced me to the college cafeteria manager. I was thankful she gave me a job. However, my day would begin at 5:00 a.m., and I would report to work no later than 5:30 a.m. The job paid $1.25 an hour with perks. The perks meant I could have unlimited food. This suited my voracious appetite very well. The first few days went smoothly until my lack of rest caught up with me. I would be sleeping so soundly in the morning I would not hear the alarm clock. I started setting five alarm clocks in the morning, and I would still fail to awaken. I found myself not being able to stay awake in class, and my grades began to slip. This really scared me. I could feel the dean's words of doom ringing in my ears.

One of the first Bible classes in which I enrolled was called Early Hebrew History. The course was accompanied by a five hundred question workbook which required all questions to be answered in detail. It took me a very long time to complete the assignment. Every student was required to take a daily Bible class, but the daily classes were only worth two quarter hours. In addition, daily chapel was also mandatory. Chapel chewed up a good hour each day as well. Despite the rigor of Christian education, I recall several amusing anecdotes.

During the first week of Bible class, the teacher said only two Bible translations could be used in preparing for the assignments: the American Revised Version, and the King James Version. One student promptly raised his hand and stated, "Well, if the King James Version was good enough for Jesus, it is also good enough for me!"

Daily Bible class began with a word of prayer led by student volunteers. The final exam was going to be administered on this particular day when one student rose up to pray. I just about lost it when he stated, "Dear God, please don't let anybody get caught cheating on this exam."

The Bible teacher invited a guest speaker one day to discuss the Jewish religion. After his brief lecture he called for questions from the class. One young lady innocently inquired, "How often do y'all take communion?"

Another Bible teacher who was also a professor of philosophy stated this in his course introductory remarks: "I do not allow freshman students to comment during class. Their comments lack substance. Imagine trying to fill one empty bucket with another empty bucket."

One ancient Bible professor had been a fixture at DLC for over forty years. He spoke with an unusual whistling lisp. He began his classes inviting everyone to pray a silent prayer. As the professor silently prayed, everyone could hear his lisp. Therefore, he had the dubious honor of being the only person on campus who could whistle a silent prayer.

Among all the serious discussions, the funny questions stand out in my memory. Which Biblical character is mentioned playing tennis? Moses served in Pharaoh's court. Who was the first person to smoke a cigarette? When Rebecca saw Isaac, she lit off a camel. What was Jesus's alias? It's mentioned in the song, *Tell it to Jesus, alone.* He is a friend, Maxwell Known. Breathing in the right places during a song was also important, or this could happen: "Are you sowing the seed of the King—Dumb Brother?" Automobiles were first mentioned in Acts. They were all in one Accord. Every floor of the men's dormitory contained four large community bathrooms. One day I noticed someone had named all of the fixtures: the two urinals were named First and Second Peter, the three commodes were named First, Second, and Third John, and the two showers were named Jude and

Revelation. On another occasion someone placed a sign behind one of the commodes that read, "Flush twice. It's a long way to the cafeteria."

Somehow, I survived the first quarter making all Bs and Cs. Then Elmer and I had a heart-to-heart talk. Elmer had funded about $500 of my first quarter's room and board. I had paid for the tuition and books. "Sid, I really thought you would be 'one and done' at Lipscomb. All the teachers at Summertown High were betting you would flunk out. I personally know your days are numbered, so don't expect me to fund any more of your nonsense at Lipscomb." First, it was Vivian Shields. Then Pop was also a naysayer. My mentor, Jerry, was also calling me an idiot. Doom and gloom were painted in my dreams.

The fall quarter at Lipscomb was the most miserable time of my life. I picked up extra hours in the cafeteria to make up the slack Elmer had provided the first summer quarter. I was working about 40 hours a week in the cafeteria and also doing my best as a full-time student. Jerry had no trouble doing both, but I was not Jerry. I was so sleep deprived I would fall asleep standing up. I had made a B+ in college algebra the first quarter, but I was failing trig. I dropped the class to keep an F off my record. Among the turmoil, I was assigned a new roommate. This guy was legally blind and recorded his classes. In the evenings when I was trying to study, he would listen to his recordings without earphones which just about drove me up the wall.

For just a little privacy, I carried my biology text with me to the dorm latrine to do my business. I took off my glasses after a while and placed them in my shirt pocket, and promptly fell asleep on the john. After about an hour nap I awakened confused. When my senses came back, I stood up and bent over to flush. I knew immediately I had made a terrible mistake as I felt my glasses slip out of my pocket and wash themselves down the drain. Reminiscent of *Hee Haw*'s, "If it weren't for bad luck, I'd have no luck at all," I called home and received permission to buy another pair of glasses. I rode my bike over to Aunt Era's for info to the closest optometrist. Her doctor was located in downtown Nashville on Fifth Avenue about five miles away. It was thirty minutes from closing time. I began my most treacherous bike ride of my life as I weaved around traffic to make the thirty-minute deadline. When I arrived five minutes before closing, the receptionist said I would have to return another day. I began talking fast and furiously pleading my exigency which was overheard by the doctor. He and Era attended church together and were close friends. He graciously consented to completing the eye exam so that I could receive my glasses ASAP.

One other distraction came into play. I would fall asleep around 10:00 p.m. Then between 11:00 p.m. and 12:00 a.m., the pay phone in the hall would ring. It was Aunt Era begging me to come over to her house to help get her sister, Lora, up off of the floor. Lora and her husband, Byrne, lived in the duplex apartment beside Era. Both Lora and Byrne had failing health. Lora and Byrne were in the habit of watching *Perry Mason* after the ten o'clock news before going to bed. Lora would take her sleeping aid while she watched *Perry Mason* so that she could drift off to sleep quickly. This worked well until her diabetes and heart disease had progressed, making it very difficult for her to get out of her chair and walk to bed. Byrne would try to help her up, but he wasn't strong enough to hold her up and walk to bed.

Inevitably, Lora would end up on the floor. They would call Era to help, but Lora's weight was more than Byrne and Era could manage together. When I would arrive, Aunt Era would fly into a tirade about how irresponsible Lora and Byrne had become to allow this to happen. When I would reach for Lora, Era would invariably say, "I don't know how you can pick her up. She's just dead weight." Lora would quickly counter, "I'm not dead weight just yet, Era! Just give me a little more time and your wish will be granted!"

I was introduced to the Grand Ole Opry by a few of my college buddies. At 8:00 p.m. on Friday nights, the Opry stars would take a brief intermission, the back doors leading to the stage would be opened, and many of the stars would step behind the Ryman Auditorium to take a smoke break. The college students would mingle into the crowd, and when the whistle was blown to return to the auditorium, we would walk right in with the crowd, free of charge. I saw several of the shows without paying.

Another free amusement was attending Metropolitan Nashville night court. It was entertaining to see the congregation of lowlife being arraigned. Most of the cases involved public drunkenness or assault. One evening two policemen brought in a drunk who had been in a fight. He had a large bump above his eye and dried blood was still on his shirt. The judge carefully looked the man over and said, "It looks like you must have received the worst end of the fight." "Oh no, your honor," the man countered. "You should have seen the other guy."

My bicycle was a lifesaver for making the nightly trips to Era and Lora's house. Their house was only about half a mile off campus, but I needed to return to the dorm and get back into the sack ASAP. I continued to make periodic nightly trips to their home until the last week of the fall quarter when Lora died. At the funeral, Era approached me and asked me to consider moving in with Byrne. In exchange for breakfast and a room at Byrne's, I would help Byrne by being his driver and being his companion during the week. Era would provide one meal in the evening for Byrne and me. I would also help Era with her flower garden, mow her grass, rake her leaves, and wash the dishes after our evening meal. We haggled over the weekends, but eventually they agreed to allow me to go home on the weekends. Going home most weekends was very important. Mom would take care of my laundry on weekends, and she would cook my favorite food. Since I didn't have an automobile, I would hitch a ride with someone from school headed to Lawrenceburg, or I would thumb a ride by traditional hitchhiking.

The used Schwinn 15 speed bicycle became my best friend in college. On the weekends I would ride the Granny White Pike south to the end of the street, and then I would pedal around in the ritzy neighborhoods in Brentwood. The traffic was very light on those streets back in the sixties. Another favorite destination was Radnor Lake. The street followed the secluded lake's banks making it a beautiful ride. Just for fun, I rode my bicycle home one beautiful Saturday during the summer quarter. I pedaled for a little over five hours to wheel into my Summertown home.

When I declared a major in elementary education, I was the only male student at Lipscomb in the field. Invariably I would be named committee chair for special projects. Over the years I had very few good teachers in elementary and high school. I intended to be the best teacher possible! While taking the course reading and language arts, I threw myself into my studies, learning every possible teaching strategy. I had been handicapped all through school because I was a poor reader. I had witnessed many students like myself struggling with reading, and I yearned to discover a better way to teach. My enthusiasm impressed several of my professors, and they offered encouragement on my quest to learn better teaching skills.

Byrne was a soft-spoken, easygoing guy. The room he provided was aptly named the little room due to its tiny seven × eight-feet size. The room had no closets. The furnishings included a cot and a small cedar wardrobe. A window air conditioner hung in a small window at the foot of the cot. I brought a card table, straight chair, and lamp pole from home, and purchased a cheap attaché case for transporting my books. Byrne and I had no problems getting along. He prefaced his gentle requests with, "If you have time, or if it is convenient, would you please…?"

Thank goodness for the good graces of my mother. She was just the opposite of Pop. She encouraged me and supported me in every way possible. When I came home on the weekend, Mom would give me $1.50 for my weekly lunches at Lipscomb. I could buy a small tossed salad at the Lipscomb student center for twenty-five cents. I would also purchase a pack of peppermint Life Savers for a nickel. The small salad with free student center crackers and the Life Savers would hold me until Era prepared the evening meal around 6:00 p.m. Era was flabbergasted at how much I ate. She always had a snide remark such as, "You are eating me out of house and home, Boy!" Byrne just smiled.

Washing the dishes for Era was always an ordeal. Era would begin emptying the dishes. If there were just a few bites in the dish Era would say, "I'm not going to let that go to waste. I'll just eat it. Era would generally eat her second meal as she cleaned out the dishes. The apartment kitchens were tiny with very little counter space. I would have to rotate the pots and pans on the floor as I prepared to wash them. Byrne would dry the utensils as I washed them. Frailty caused Byrne to lose his grip, and quite often he would drop a pot or pan as he was drying. This would cause Era to unleash one of her favorite tirades, "What are you trying to do; break up housekeeping?"

Working in Era's flowers was an impossible task. In the spring, Era raised poppies. After the poppies bloomed, they would reseed themselves. As I would attempt to remove weeds, Era would tell me to do so with unrelenting caution. If one of those thousands of baby poppy plants came up with a weed, Era would mourn, "Oh, my poor little poppies!" Mowing her grass was also a large challenge. The backyard was full of flowering bushes with little more than a path left between for mowing. In a day before the Weed Eater, I would use a hoe to remove the grass around her shrub collection. I would trim the shrubbery twice a year to keep them from growing into each other. Her forsythia bushes were notoriously vigorous. It was a Catch-22 to deal with those bushes. If I pruned too much, they would not bloom the following year, but if I did not keep them pruned, they would grow into the neighboring bushes. As a result, I planned most of the bush pruning when Era was gone away from home. I would beg forgiveness because I knew I would not be granted permission. In the fall I would rake the leaves and place them in large plastic bags. The city would only remove the leaves if they were placed in plastic bags on the curb.

Era's favorite bush grew in the middle of her flower bed at the end of her house. It was a pyracantha. Pyracantha literally meant fire thorn. The bush was covered in beautiful reddish orange berries, and the worst briars I had ever encountered. Her bush was a climbing variety, standing about eight feet tall and required being tied to a trellis. The prolific orange berries were heavy, and if the bush did not get regular pruning, it would fall off the trellis. Era quickly delegated the upkeep of the bush to me. Working without a good set of gloves meant I was subject to frequent battle scars from the bush. While caring for this beautiful bush, I vowed I would never have a pyracantha in my flower garden.

Era had an affinity for Russell Stover candy. She generally kept a box on the coffee table in her living room. The only time Byrne and I were offered a piece was after Sunday dinner. We knew better than to help ourselves without Era's permission. One Sunday afternoon the three of us retired to her living room to read the Sunday newspaper. Hearing a noise in the driveway, Era went to the window to peek out. "Oh, no! It can't be true," Era moaned. Her niece Juanita (Walter's daughter) and her two young preteen girls were out in the driveway, and on their way to the front door. Era continued her wailing. "Oh Lord, please make them go away. Maybe, they are just going to Byrne's apartment. Please Lord, let it be true!" All of Era's hopes were dashed when her doorbell rang. She quickly picked up her box of chocolates and hid them in her closet before opening the front door. As the front door opened, Era's mood made an about-face. Smiling from ear to ear, Era greeted her guests with all the southern charm she could muster, "Hello! Please come in! I am so delighted to see everyone."

Byrne was an excellent storyteller. He survived WWI and he clocked 45 years with the Tennessee Central Railway as a mail clerk. Byrne would ride the train to Harriman, Tennessee, spend the night and make the return trip to Nashville the following day. The 150-mile train ride encompassed an entire workday. The train made frequent stops to accompany mail parcels and passengers along the way. Sometimes the staggered shifts would give him a weekend layover in Harriman. Over the years Byrne developed some great fishing buddies on his Harriman layovers. When the weather was fitting, there was no question about his weekend activities. Byrne like to fish for bluegill in small lakes around Harriman and also in the Nashville area. He had been retired almost 20 years when I became his roommate. It wasn't long before he asked me to carry him fishing. It was quite an ordeal to take Byrne fishing. He walked with a cane but still needed to hold onto me for extra balance. On our first excursion, we traveled to a small lake near Franklin. We rented a boat, and miraculously, I was able to get Byrne seated in the boat without incident. We fished most of the day, and I sensed Byrne had a splendid time. It was immaterial that the fish were not biting. Byrne just wanted to get away from his boring routine at home. While we fished, Byrne told endless stories about his life.

Byrne grew up on the Caney Fork River near Cookeville, Tennessee. When he was a teenager, he and a friend became partners on a twelve-foot jon boat. He recalled a terrible flood on the river that closed off all transportation over the river since the water was flooding over the bridges. After a week, the flood waters began to subside. He and his friend decided to maneuver their small boat to the other side of the river. They picked out what appeared to be a good place for the venture. However, once they entered the full current of the flooded river, they realized they had made a grave tactical error. Byrne said he had never paddled so hard in his life. Eventually they made it to the other bank about two miles downstream from their intended destination, and the little jon boat was half filled with water. After coming to their senses Byrne and his friend examined their hands to find the desperate paddling had blistered their hands. He mused, "That was my first and last experience of paddling a small boat in a flooded river."

While fishing at the small lake in Franklin, Byrne told me about the proprietor who was in charge of the lake. When Byrne and his buddy would check in, they would inquire if anyone had caught any fish. The proprietor would always tell the same story. "Yeah, a feller caught a nice bass that weighed three and a half pounds yesterday." It was always the same story, and the weight of the fish never changed.

Occasionally Byrne would have to work a double shift and would ride the train from Harriman to Nashville at night. One night the train came to a screeching halt. Byrne opened the mail room door and walked down to the engine of the train to see what brought on the commotion. The train had run over a man and the wheels had cut off his head. Everyone was searching for the man's head. Byrne used his flashlight to help search and noticed what appeared to be a fresh path leading off the railway. He followed the path for about fifty feet and found the man's head looking up at him. Byrne picked up the head by the hair and carried it back to the authorities. Byrne said the vision of the man's head looking up at him was something he would never forget.

Byrne had a good fishing buddy who lived in Harriman. One morning the two of them caught a hundred-plus nice-sized bluegill. By early afternoon they had dressed the fish and ended up with two, five-gallon buckets full of cleaned fish. They approached a friend who ran a café in Harriman about having a free fish fry that evening. For a ten-dollar bill, the friend agreed to cook the fish and provide free coffee and hush puppies, if they would agree to help wait on the customers. After the agreement, Byrne and his fishing friend roamed the streets of Harriman spreading the word about the free fish fry that evening at the café. Byrne said the people poured into the restaurant, and they served for several hours. Byrne said it was one of the most exhausting days of his life. He said that was the last time they decided to keep all the fish they caught.

Byrne was a live bait fisherman. He rarely fished for anything but bluegill. One particular day he and a friend decided to tie up to an overhanging tree near a large fish hide of debris in the lake. As they eased into position, a largemouth bass weighing about five pounds jumped into the boat with them. His buddy quickly lay down on the fish to keep it from jumping out. As they were checking out the proprietor asked Byrne and his friend what they were fishing with at the time they caught that big bass. Crickets.

On one occasion Byrne and his buddy were fishing under an overhanging tree and a large water moccasin fell into the boat with them. They were both terrified of snakes, and quickly grabbed the oars from the boat, and commenced beating the snake. Byrne said the snake would go from the front to the back of the boat over and over again. Finally, the snake flopped out of the boat and back into the water. This scared the dickens out of Byrne, and he was determined to be better prepared in the future. He bought a little snub-nosed .32 pistol from a friend and placed it in his tackle box. He said they never had a snake get into the boat with them again. Years later his buddy asked Byrne to retrieve the pistol from the tackle box and shoot at the great blue heron on the bank. Byrne said he had never fired the pistol but just that one time, and he hit the heron with one shot.

Byrne was nineteen years old when he began working for the Tennessee Central Railway. He had been on the job for just a little over a year when he was drafted into military service during WWI. During basic training, he was assigned to mentor a big, awkward fellow because Byrne said he couldn't do anything right. Byrne had helped him for a couple of weeks, and one day he noticed the guy had packed up all of his gear. He told Byrne he was going home. "How did you get out of the army?" Byrne asked. In his usual country drawl he replied, "They told me to go home because I was too tall for my height." *(I have frequently used the quip to jokingly describe myself.)*

While in basic training, the great influenza pandemic of 1918 hit his company. The flu hit his company particularly hard with over half the company being sickened by the disease. Unfortunately, Byrne was also struck with a mean case of the flu. He said he remembers lying in his bunk for two straight weeks suffering from incredible pain and he became delirious from the high fever. After the fever broke, he was too weak to walk or stand alone. As a result, he was sent to a convalescent hospital and was eventually medically discharged from military service. Byrne said that most of the soldiers who managed to escape the flu from his company were later killed in France. Byrne said the flu was the worst and also the best thing that ever happened to him. After Byrne recovered from the flu, he returned to his job with the Tennessee Central Railway. He retired at age sixty-five with forty-five years in service. His friends took up a collection upon his retirement and bought him a nice railroad watch which became Byrne's prized possession. Byrne said in the forty-five years with the Tennessee Central Railway, he only changed jobs one time.

In the afternoons when I returned to Byrne's apartment from school, I would inquire how Byrne was fairing. "Tolerably well" was always his answer. About twice a month Byrne asked me to drive him to the funeral home. I was very amused the first time I accompanied him to a wake. As if Byrne had downed a whole bottle of Geritol, he entered the wake with unusual pep to his step. Byrne was surrounded with old friends, and everyone was laughing and having a jolly good time. This boisterous behavior at a funeral home was new for me. I inquired why everyone was behaving in such a jovial manner. Slightly grinning, Byrne replied, "The only time I see my friends now is at the funeral home. This is a celebration of all the good times. This is exactly what the deceased would expect!" I was too young to recognize that a wake could be an invigorating experience.

One Saturday Byrne carried me to a new lake about forty miles outside of Nashville. The small lake was about three acres in size. No boats were available, so I backed the car close to a shade tree on the bank of the lake and we sat on the ground. We caught several bluegill which Byrne wanted to bring home for a fish fry. I noticed movement close to the stringer. When I retrieved the stringer, only fish heads were left. Turtles had eaten our fish right off the stringer. I decided to fish with one of the remaining fish heads and caught a turtle about the size of a wash tub. That tickled us both. From that day forward when Byrne talked up a fishing trip, he would say, "How about us going turtle hunting?" Occasionally Byrne would ask me to take him fishing and I would tell him I had to go home to take care of my laundry. "Maybe next week," I replied. "Don't count on it," Byrne would often retort, "I might not be kicking next week."

Chris had recently married and he often needed a little extra cash to get by. Although I did not have much extra money, I traded with Chris for three items: a baritone ukulele, a tenor guitar, and a double-barrel shotgun. The ukulele was a constant companion while I was in college. I spent many nights in college strumming the uke and serenading Uncle Byrne. This amused Byrne very much!

One week between quarters, Era decided she wanted her kitchen cabinets repainted. Jerry and I agreed to paint for her. When we began, we noticed she had only bought two small pint-sized cans of paint. "Where's the rest of the paint?" Jerry inquired. "I discussed this with the man at the paint store, and he said a professional painter could easily paint the cabinets with two pints of paint." Jerry replied, "I hate to break it you Aunt Era, we aren't professionals." Under protest, she allowed us to return to the store and buy enough paint for the job. When we finished, she decided we also needed to paint Byrne's cabinets as well.

Aunt Era had a black lady who came one day each week to clean house for her and Byrne. Era scolded the lady as if she were a dog. "You are about the most worthless no accounting individual I have ever seen! I would be ashamed of myself if I were the culprit of such pitifully sloppy work." I can't understand why you (people) don't have any pride!" It reminded me of Mr. Dithers chastising Dagwood Bumstead in the funny papers. The lady just smiled and kept right on working. She had worked for Era for more than twenty years and had learned Era's bark was much worse than her bite.

One afternoon while she was cleaning for Byrne, I asked the lady about her family. As she was telling me about her children, she incidentally added, "You probably didn't know this about me, but I am three thirds Cherokee Indian." After she left that afternoon Byrne said with a smile, "She might be part Cherokee Indian, but I'm positive she flunked her math class." Deep down, Era was a sweet and caring person. She paid the 14 percent (both parts) into Social Security for her help for more than 25 years so that her helper could draw Social Security at age 65. One regular topic of conversation between Era and Byrne was about how the black population had begun to move out of the inner city of Nashville and into the suburban neighborhoods, and they might someday have black neighbors.

One evening Byrne and I were washing the dishes when Byrne accidently dropped a plate on the floor. It shattered into pieces. Era went into one of her usual laments about breaking up housekeeping, and how Byrne was totally useless around the house. When we returned to Byrne's apartment, I asked, "How do you just sit there and take it?" "Take what?" Byrne looked surprised. Byrne continued breaking a smile, "I haven't paid any attention to Era in years."

One evening during dinner it began snowing. As the snow began to accumulate, Era became edgy. "Every time it snows like this I am reminded of Lora and Byrne. One afternoon they were eating at a café when it began to snow. Instead of hurrying home, they just sat there, drinking coffee and talking to their friends. When they attempted to leave, they couldn't get their car started so they called me. I hate driving in snow. Here I was safely at home, off the streets, when these silly children call and ask for a ride home. I had to ride out there on slick streets and bring them home. *The very idea!*" Byrne just smiled.

After a couple of years, Era's discontent with my unsatisfactory help began to escalate. One day she accused me of coming into her apartment and stealing her money. "You can't deny it," Era continued. "I know it's you." That evening, I told Byrne I was thinking about moving out. Era's criticism had reached a new height. Now she was accusing me of being a thief. "We have no one else to help us," Byrne pleaded. "Please ignore Era and stay with me." A few years later, Jerry and I were helping clear out Era's apartment so that she could move into an assisted living facility. As we began emptying out her bedroom furniture drawers, we found over $2000 stuffed into numerous bank envelopes. Poor Era had forgotten where she had stashed her money. When we presented Era with her money, she apologized for accusing me of stealing.

Era's hobby was stamp collecting. She had been collecting

stamps for over 50 years and had amassed a very large collection of stamps that included first day of issue and plate block stamps in mint condition. Era asked me to carry her stamps to a nearby dealer and sell them. When I approached a dealer with the large collection, I noticed the man studying the stamps with great concentration. "These stamps aren't worth much. $250 would be all I could offer you for them."

"The face value of the stamps is far greater than $250," I countered. "Those old stamps cannot be used by the Post Office anymore. That's my final offer; take it or leave it." I was really in a negotiating bind. I had no other source to sell the stamps, so I was stuck with the one offer.

"Okay. I will accept the offer, but I am going to keep this old stamp book."

"Nooo," the man moaned. "That is the most valuable part!"

"How can they be valuable if they can't be used in postal currency?" I asked. I agreed to accept $225 and keep the old stamp book. When I returned with the money, Era said, "You keep the money, honey!" I refused but did accept the old stamp book. I consider the book one of my prized possessions. Had I known Era was going to offer me the money for collection I would have asked her to give it to me instead.

Jerry had a large truck that we used in cleaning out Era's apartment. We moved what furniture she needed into her new apartment. The rest was divided among Mom and her siblings. Era had nice mementos throughout her apartment, and she insisted on carrying as much as possible with her to her new home. Years later when Era required a sitter, the sitters stole all of her treasures. The last part of our job was to clear the attic of her apartment. Jerry and I removed five truckloads of cardboard boxes. After surviving the depression, Era never threw away a good box. In the attic of my garage, I also have a small cubby used to hold cardboard boxes. The door of the cubby holds a glossy black and white photo of Aunt Era that is entitled "The Era Emmons Room."

Pop once asked Era why she never married. She began explaining she had dated when she was younger, but never could find a man with the exceptional qualities necessary to be her husband. Era was the epitome of an Amazon woman. She tirelessly worked fifty years as executive secretary to the president of the Life and Casualty Insurance Company. The president took special interest in Era and advised her on her investments. When Era passed away in 1974, she left six shares worth approximately $15,000 to each of her nieces and nephews.

There was a lengthy Christmas break between fall and winter quarters at Lipscomb. I found a temporary job working at the Cain-Sloan department store at the Green Hills mall. The mall was in walking distance from Byrne's apartment. I worked three straight Christmas breaks making $1.50 per hour. I was a flunky working in the packaging department. The money came in handy to help with my college expenses. During my first job there, Chris, Jerry, and I decided to buy Pop a Browning automatic shotgun for Christmas because I received a 15 percent employee's discount on their merchandise. For $150, we bought him a Belgian-made Browning automatic 16-gauge shotgun called the Sweet Sixteen. The three of us had seen Pop admire the Browning shotguns at Richardson's Hardware in Lawrenceburg on several occasions. After holding one a few moments, he would always place it back on the shelf. Pop always put the financial exigency of providing for his family ahead of his personal desires. Pop was really surprised with the gift. For years, the three of us would go on a quail hunt every Thanksgiving and Christmas vacation. Before Pop's surprise, no one had a very good shotgun. Pop would usually carry the 28-gauge shotgun he inherited from his father. All three of us boys were broken into the hunt with that old 28-gauge shotgun. Bucket Holloway was the owner and operator of a general hardware store in Summertown. Since most boys were short on cash, Bucket would break up boxes of ammo to accommodate smaller budgets. He sold .22 rifle shells for a penny each and shotgun shells for ten cents each. He also dealt in used and new guns. I bought my first shotgun from Bucket when I was in high school—a used Sears & Roebuck J.C. Higgins bolt-action 12-gauge for $40. I learned to shoot quail and dove with that old shotgun. Mom would slow bake the game birds we brought in from the hunt. She would wrap two or three bird breasts together and add salt and butter and slowly bake the meat so that it would be tender to eat. It was always tricky eating the game meat because occasionally one would chomp down on a lead pellet hiding in the meat. Over the course of the thirty years I hunted, I have wondered how many of those lead pellets escaped undetected and ended in my digestive system. Lead pellets were not outlawed in all shotgun shells until the 1990s. I suppose I could blame my addled brain on lead poisoning. The first items Jerry and I purchased after the army were Browning automatic shotguns. My Browning Automatic Light 12 remains one of my most valuable possessions.

While working at the department store, I also treated myself to a silk tie. The following Sunday while I was sporting the tie, I asked Byrne if he had ever owned a silk tie.

"Not that I recollect. How much did it cost?" he asked.

"$7.50 and sales tax, less with my 15% employee discount," I reported. Byrne was flabbergasted!

"I would wear a seagrass string around my neck before I would pay that much for a tie!"

I had managed to pass all of my classes with Cs the second quarter at Lipscomb. After I moved in with Byrne, my grades began to slightly improve. The third quarter at school I was introduced to English literature. The text was an oversized book that resembled an unabridged dictionary. Daily assignments were over one hundred pages. I bought a pillow for my cot called the bachelor's friend. The newfangled pillow would allow me to lie in bed in the supine position and read. I detested the class, but I am confident reading the large literature book helped me hone my poor reading skills. I managed to eke out a C in the class. By my junior year, my grades made a dramatic improvement. I managed to make the college honor roll several times and actually made the dean's list one quarter. Along my college path of elementary education, I met one professor who truly believed in me. I am confident this rare encouragement propelled me to success.

When I was a senior, I met with my assigned college advisor. I told my advisor I was scheduled to graduate at the end of the spring quarter in 1969. "Really?" my advisor answered. "I don't think you have enough credits or have met all the requirements for graduation." As the advisor reviewed my transcript, he was surprised I had successfully completed all the required courses for graduation and I had completed 198 quarter hours—the exact number necessary for graduation. "How did you manage to cram all of this in just three years?" he asked. I had followed the college academic directory perfectly. I had also completed a correspondence class on manuscript and cursive handwriting and successfully passed the National Teacher Examination, allowing me to qualify for the INCATE seal on my college transcript. This certification made me eligible to teach at any school in the United States. Jerry's advice about planning my work and working my plan proved to be most helpful. I managed to graduate from Lipscomb with a 2.88 grade point average—just a little shy of a B average in 12 straight quarters. Elmer James, Miss Vivian Shields, and Dean Craig were right about me. My naysayers all agreed I would never graduate from Lipscomb in four years. By the grace of God and the encouragement I received from my mother and one college professor, I managed to graduate in three years at the age of 20.

In March of 1967 I was enjoying a week break from classes at home in Summertown. Jerry and Chris just happened to be home during the same time. One sunny afternoon, the three of us walked down to the pond in the corner of the pasture to fish. The fish were not biting on this particular afternoon when Jerry had an idea. With one hand stuck in his pocket he said, "Hey, Sid. I'll bet you won't take your clothes off and swim across the pond for all the money I'm holding in my hand." Intrigued by his proposal I sought more information. I had been tricked too many times in the past. I needed assurance this was a bona fide offer. "Sorry, Jerry, I have to know how much money you are holding in your hand." Jerry eagerly responded by pulling the money out of his pocket to reveal a quarter, dime, and two pennies. Seeing the money, I took the dare. After removing my clothes Jerry handed over the money, and I swam across the pond. Wow! The water was icy cold. It took my breath away as I made a fast dash across the pond. Chris yelled, "Sid is an idiot!"

Standing on the opposite side of the pond I yelled to Jerry, "Hey, Jerry, I'll bet you won't swim across the pond for all the money I have in my hand."

"How much money do you have?" Jerry yelled.

Playing the buffoon, I opened my hand and counted the money. "How about thirty-seven cents? I'll bet you won't swim over here for thirty-seven cents." Following my lead, Jerry took off his clothes and swam across the pond to join me. I applauded as Jerry whooped and hollered the whole way. I quickly gave Jerry his thirty-seven cents prize with my congratulations.

Thoroughly flabbergasted, Chris yelled, "You two idiots just swam across the pond for nothing!"

"Not true," we retorted. "We did it for thirty-seven cents." Exchanging a wink and a nod, Jerry and I proceeded to swim back across the pond and retrieved our clothes.

While we were dressing, Jerry turned to Chris and said, "Hey, Chris, I'll bet…"

Chris quickly interrupted, "Don't even go there. I'm not as stupid as you two fruitcakes!"

My best friend in college was Jim Miller. Jim took an interest in me when I began college and encouraged me to stay on the required path for graduation. Jim was brilliant but could not manage to heed his own advice. One quarter his roommate ordered an amplifier kit. Jim became so possessed with building the amplifier, he quit going to class, working night and day on the amp. At the end of the quarter the amp had been assembled and was working perfectly. Jim made straight Fs because he did not complete the required coursework.

Occasionally on weekends, Jim and I would walk to Green Hills or Hillsboro Village to take in a movie. Jim funded the outing since I had no extra money for frills of any sort. When I was a senior, Jim dropped out of school and began working for Commerce Union Bank. The bank was in the beginning stages of offering a special credit card called the Super Card. Jim encouraged me to sign up for one, but I told him a person with no income had no business owning a credit card. I became Jim's junketeer as he began to treat me to some of the finer restaurants in Nashville on weekends. One evening he carried me to hear the Nashville Symphony. I told Jim I was concerned about the amount of money he was charging on his new credit card. "Don't worry," was Jim's standard reply. Two years later, Jim realized his staggering credit balance was financially ruining him. Jim cut the Super Card into little pieces and temporarily swore off credit card debt. Jim's example taught me a valuable lesson about living within one's means. After college graduation Jim and I lost touch with each other. Thirty-five years later the phone rang in the middle of the night. It was Jim. We talked for hours on the phone, and eventually Jim twice visited me from Alaska on extended vacations.

Jim's father and mother were living in Alaska at the time I graduated from college. I applied for a teaching position at four locations: Alaska, Metropolitan Nashville, and Coffee and Lawrence counties in Tennessee. On the day of my graduation from college, Pop brought in the day's mail. My draft notice was included in the mail. I had managed to secure my diploma and draft notice on the same day. Considering the military a good learning experience, I did not attempt to apply for a teaching deferment with the local draft board. Eventually, and while in the army, I received acceptance letters from all four of the locations I had applied, and I was accepted into graduate school at George Peabody College for Teachers. Elmer was gagged once again with my decision to enter the army.

My college experience taught me how to play the game of life. I had single-handedly honed my reading and study skills, and I had actually impressed a few of my college professors with my work ethic. Mom was right when she drilled the idea home that I would attend and graduate from David Lipscomb College. She never gave up on me. I never considered attending any institution but Lipscomb!

When Jerry and Chris were seniors in high school, Mom and Pop bought them class rings. When I was a senior, Pop offered a new set of class ring rules. "I consider class rings nonsense. However, I will buy you a class ring when you graduate from college." I was the only senior in my high school class not to order a class ring. I knew what Pop was thinking. He considered me too stupid to graduate from college, and he thought he would never have to buy me a class ring. Of my senior high school class of sixty-eight, only five elected to attend college. During my senior year in college, I mentioned to Pop it was time for me to order my senior class ring from David Lipscomb. Pop made a quick exit to his bedroom and returned with his 1948 class ring from Lipscomb. "Here," he said. "You can have this one." Much to Pop's chagrin the ring would not fit over my knuckle. Pop flew into a hissy fit about how he was wasting too much money on my foolishness. "You just taught me a valuable lesson, Pop. I thought you were a man of your word." Wreathing with anger, Pop handed me a blank check and said, "Go buy the stupid ring!" Wearing my classic Sid James smirk, I said, "Thank you. I intend to." I wore the ring for twenty years until the ring would no longer fit over my knuckle.

I owe a great debt of gratitude to Era and Byrne for allowing me to live with them while I completed my education. I also have to thank my weird friend, Jim Miller, for taking me under his wing and showing me a good time. Even Pop offered a few words of wisdom along the way. Although he never directly said he was proud of me for my college accomplishments, I sensed he was. I learned stamina and dogged determination were more important attributes than intelligence. I was extremely fortunate to have great models who taught me that hard work and perseverance will always win in the end.

ARMY EXPERIENCES

In 1968, I was a senior in college, and frequently made weekend trips home, going down to the Dipper to hang out with my friends. What made this year unusual was most of my friends had been drafted into military service to feed the Vietnam War machine. The Vietnam War had really heated up after the 1968 Tet Offensive by the North Vietnamese, and the horror stories of Hamburger Hill had been on the evening news. As the war dragged on, it was becoming more unpopular with Americans every day. When my friends came home on leave, they would chide me because I had received a college deferment from the draft. I sensed some of my drafted friends held somewhat of a hostile attitude toward me because I had been deferred from the draft. I didn't like being called a "draft dodger," "privileged," "chicken liver," and "unpatriotic," and decided to do something about it. I had heard that being a college graduate made the road to becoming an army officer less complicated, so I began exploring my options with an army recruiter. After I took a competency examination and was given a thorough physical examination, the recruiter said I was a perfect match for Infantry Officer Candidate School.

During my last quarter at school the local draft board notified me that my draft notification would change from college deferred to 1A (immediate eligibility for the draft) upon my graduation from college. This cheery letter came at about the same time I began weighing my post-graduation options. Finding myself between a rock and a hard place, I took the army recruiter's advice and decided to join for a three-year commitment of active duty. In order to sweeten my deal, the recruiter agreed to allow me to spend six months in the Army Reserve before I would be called to active duty. On June 27, 1969, I graduated from David Lipscomb College with a BS degree in elementary education. After packing my bags and saying my goodbyes to Aunt Era and Uncle Byrne in Nashville, Mom and Pop drove me home to Summertown. Upon arrival I discovered a letter for me from the local draft board. I had been inducted in the U.S. Army and was to report to the Fort Campbell, Kentucky, Induction Station the following day. I simply picked up the telephone and reported that I was already in the U.S. Army Reserve, and I was promised six months of inactive duty before I would be called to active duty. Soon thereafter I learned of the army's first lie: instead of six months of downtime, I actually had only one month. I was unaware they had started the clock on the day I signed the papers five months earlier. On July 27, 1969, exactly one month after graduating from college, I reported to Fort Dix, New Jersey, to begin basic training in the U.S. Army. That memorable day introduced me to a series of new experiences. I had never flown in an aircraft of any sort prior to the army. My first flight was from Nashville to Pittsburgh to Newark, New Jersey. I had never been in a commercial airport terminal before that date. While Nashville's terminal was quite small and easy to maneuver, the terminal at Pittsburgh was a monster. I had forty-five minutes to meet my connecting flight and found myself in a hard run trying to make the connection (that happened to be on the other end of the airport). When the plane landed in Newark, I hastily found myself boarded on a military bus for transport to Fort Dix. I was one of about sixty new starry-eyed inductees, and soon learned the majority were there after they had volunteered for the draft. They said the judge back home had given them an offer they couldn't refuse—either volunteer for the draft or go to prison. That was only the beginning of new surprises that awaited me in the army.

When the bus arrived at the induction station, an army corporal (two-striped NCO), boarded the bus and started cursing at the top of his lungs. (Every other word was the *F* word. I soon learned the *F* word was the army's favorite adjective that was used in a variety of creative and humorous situations. I also heard the *F* word being used as a noun, verb, adverb, and gerund. In fact, the army's idiosyncratic style of the *F* word could be used as both subject and verb in the same sentence. It amused me wondering how my father, Elmer, would have diagrammed the sentences. (I'm sure he would find a way, since he was the diagramming king at Summertown High School.) As the corporal made his way to the back of the bus, his instructions were that every swinging dick had to be off the bus in ten seconds. All he wanted to see was assholes and elbows. (Please pardon the language. I really can't tell the story about the army unless I use a smattering of their language.) There was a mad scramble to exit the bus, and unfortunately during the confusion, one guy fell on the steps of the bus, and the rest of the men just stampeded over the top of him. This poor guy had just arrived, and he had successfully dislocated his shoulder in the first thirty seconds of army life.

The next two weeks were spent taking aptitude exams, receiving official army uniforms and gear, and hearing a variety of orientation lectures on the army way of doing things, like how to avoid syphilis and stay out of the stockade. After they shaved our heads with a neat GI haircut, we learned the wrong way and the army way of doing things. One lecture I found quite humorous was learning the difference in right and left. This seemed so juvenile to me, until a few days later when I discovered some of the men really didn't know their left from their right.

The day finally arrived when we would be introduced to our drill instructors (called DIs). As the bus arrived, we had already been introduced to the army way of debarking a bus. So as soon as the bus arrived, everyone gathered their duffle bags full of gear and stood up in preparation of making a swift exit. Having learned from the earlier experience, I found my way to the back of the bus figuring I had a better chance of survival. Just as soon as the bus door opened, the first guy started to exit when he was met by one of the biggest and meanest black DIs I had ever seen. The DI hit the unsuspecting guy right in the jaw and laid him out. He then said, "Who told you pussies to get off this bus? From this moment forward you never do anything without requesting and being granted permission. We are paid to do the thinking for all of you dumbasses! Furthermore, every sentence out of your mouth will end in 'drill sergeant.'" After our first official lecture we fell into our first official formation. After about thirty minutes of yelling, cussing, and ass kicking, we stood at attention in four perfectly congruent rows. The time soon arrived for our first roll call, and after we heard our name called, we were to yell, "Here, drill sergeant," at the top of our lungs. No deviant response would be tolerated. As the roll call began, each recruit seemed to be doing a marvelous job at following the simple instructions until one poor soul answered with a whiney, "Here." At that moment all four of the company DIs, the field first sergeant, four platoon lieutenants, and the company commander all wore a terribly disparaging face. In an almost shocking reply, the DI said, "What did you just say?" Again, the whiney reply of "Here." The DI countered, "I'm going to give you one more chance to answer by the correct response of 'Here, drill sergeant.' If you fail this time, God have mercy on your soul." Once again, the muddled cry of "Here." All of the DIs present converged on the poor recruit at the rear of our formation and proceeded to beat the crap out of this guy. He was on the ground screaming and begging to go home, but no one else could actually see what was happening because our orders were to remain at attention with eyes front! After about fifteen minutes of the alleged beating, an army ambulance came and hauled the guy away. The indoctrination of our new life in the army had begun. Here's an interesting side note to this story. Toward the end of the nine-week basic training exercises, the truth slipped out about our introduction to the DIs. The guy on the front of the bus who got knocked out by the DI and the guy who failed to say, "Here, drill sergeant," were merely actors. They were part of the skit performed for the benefit of the new recruits to be sure the DIs had our undivided attention.

Basic training was designed to introduce civilians to the army and convert them to mean, lean fighting machines. The main components were following orders in a concise and particular manner, orientation to warfare, and physical conditioning. Each day began with reveille at 6:00 a.m. regardless of the time we went to bed. Some nights we would be up till the crack of dawn on night training maneuvers. Before we could get in the sack, our weapons had to be cleaned and turned into the supply sergeant for inspection. Also, a member of each platoon had to remain awake for guard duty of the barracks bay (the area where we all slept). The rotation of this guard duty was a particular bone of contention. The rotation shifts were supposed to be one hour each governed by a clock on the bay wall. However, the unlucky ones who drew the shift prior to reveille would sometimes face a longer shift since some of the buddies tampered with the clock to shorten their shifts. Another thorny issue arrived when some of the buddies on guard duty would steal the keys to footlockers that would be around the necks of those who slept. One morning our platoon awoke to discover we had been hit by thieves. Soon thereafter, I changed to a combination lock that went with me throughout my military career. I became so accustomed to the feel of the combination I could open the lock in complete darkness.

I soon discovered the DIs liked me. I could run and I could shoot a rifle. Like my father before me, I was only one of four in the platoon who scored expert at the rifle range. I was amazed at how dumb some of the recruits were. Everyone had to qualify on the final day at the rifle range before the platoon could leave the field. When it became almost sundown, there were still about three recruits who had not qualified. The only one I remember was named Marzetta. Marzetta had been drafted while he was writing his PhD dissertation in nuclear physics.

Although he was a brilliant man, he had no common sense whatsoever. Among his faults as a soldier: he hardly did anything right. He couldn't march; he didn't know his left from his right; and every time he tried to fire his rifle, it would bounce back and hit him in the chin. Out of exasperation the DIs came to the rifle line where Marzetta was trying to qualify and asked him why he couldn't follow instructions. By this time Marzetta's cheekbone was bloody from the numerous kicks by the rifle butt to his face, and his sighting eye had almost swelled shut. One of the DIs took Marzetta's rifle away from him and quickly qualified for him. Everyone was called to a hasty formation to have a quick check to be certain all weapons were empty before boarding the bus. While in formation, Marzetta's rifle discharged right in front of the DI. All of hell's fury was about to descend upon Marzetta. The DI asked, "Marzetta, you are undoubtedly the dumbest recruit ever to enter the army. I was just wondering. Do you know your ass from a hole in the ground?" Marzetta just stood there stone-faced fearing to make a sound. With that the DI said in a commanding voice, "Demonstrators, post!" One DI came before Marzetta and the platoon formation, pulled down his pants and mooned Marzetta. Another DI took the heel of his boot and dug a hole in the sand. The DI in command said very sarcastically, "Marzetta, please observe very carefully.

On your right is a hole in the ground. On your left is an ass. Do you understand, or will it be necessary for you to kiss the ass?" Marzetta mumbled that he understood, thus ending one of the funniest lessons I had ever witnessed. The next morning Marzetta reported to formation and had failed to shave. The DI said that was quite alright. Marzetta could shave while he was in formation. An old safety razor with an extremely dull blade had been saved for such an occasion. After Marzetta had attempted to dry shave in formation his face was a bloody mess. This was just too much for the guy. He fell down and started crying like a baby, requesting to be excused from the army. All he wanted was to go home. Of course, this just brought on more harassment. The DIs offered to carry Marzetta to the shower so he could slit his wrists and easily wash the blood down the drain so he wouldn't make a large mess. The following day something unexpected happened. While we stood at attention at the morning inspection, Marzetta was called out of the formation because new orders had come for him the night before. He was given a direct commission of second lieutenant and was ordered to report to Langley, Virginia (CIA headquarters).

Exercise became everyone's middle name. Before entering the mess hall, recruits had to complete an exercise routine that included walking on the monkey bars, pushups, and a twenty-five-meter low crawl. The low crawl was a new experience for me. The object was to crawl while keeping one's body completely on the ground. Forward movement was achieved by moving one's arms and feet in a systematic method similar to a crab while keeping one's stomach on the ground. While under watchful eyes, if someone's head, heels, or butt became elevated, the high body part was met with a swift kick. The correction was also combined with a string of expletives and a reminder if a soldier wanted to live, he would learn how to stay close to the ground. Of all the exercises introduced to me, the hardest for me to conquer was the low crawl. As a result, the DIs loved to pull me out of line and gave me the opportunity to perfect my low crawl skill. They kept saying the low crawl would save my life someday when I found myself looking down the wrong end of a rifle barrel. All of the extra practice I received paid off. I eventually mastered the art of the low crawl.

In the entrance of the mess hall was a soda machine. Of course, this was reserved for the cadre. Our diet was regulated to army chow only. Care packages containing homemade goodies from the family were also taboo. These were opened by the DIs and distributed among the cadre. They would usually eat the contents in the presence of the recipient. On one occasion I asked Mom to send me some banana bread. I told her to write "Civvies/Undies" on the outside of the box. Sure enough, the deception worked. As soon as the coast was clear, the box was opened and passed around to my buddies with such haste, the contents were devoured in less than thirty seconds. After a few weeks, we learned that by working together we could treat ourselves to a soda on the way into the mess hall. This is the way the deception worked. Four guys worked together. The first put in the money, the second pushed the button, and the third and fourth chugged the drink when the coast was clear.

The army had a special way of doing everything. All the GI bunks had to be made in a certain army method, and each footlocker was organized according to a special army code down to the finest detail; even the lid of the shoeshine can had to be attached the army way. The DIs held regular surprise inspections, but the big inspection of our basic training occurred in the final week of training. This was the so-called inspector general (IG) inspection conducted by the battalion commander (an officer in charge of five companies). The IG inspection was very important to the DIs because their evaluation and rank was dependent upon a favorable IG inspection. As the big inspection commenced, all the men in the barracks were ordered to stand at attention by their bunks and footlockers. Upon command, all the footlockers were opened, and the inspection commenced by the battalion commander and the command sergeant major who was taking notes from the commander. Everything was moving like clockwork until the commander happened upon a recruit who had stuffed a bag of cookies in the bottom of his footlocker. The commander called the DI forward, locked his heels to attention, and proceeded to curse the DI up one side and down the other. When the inspection was complete, the DI focused his attention on the cookie hoarder. In a sweet, sarcastic voice he asked the recruit, "Sooo, you like cookies. Is that true?"

The recruit, standing at attention in front of the DI, responded in a weak, timid voice, "Yes, drill sergeant."

"Fine," answered the DI, opening the bag of cookies, "Have a cookie." The recruit reached in the bag and took a cookie and began eating it. Being coached by the DI at his every move, the DI commanded him to eat faster, faster, faster. One by one the recruit continued eating the cookies as fast as he could. After he had eaten about half the bag, he said he couldn't possibly eat any more. With that the DI ordered the recruit to sit on the floor, Indian style. The DI stomped on the remaining cookies in the bag and then poured the contents over the recruit's head. Next the DI neatly draped the recruit's poncho over his body, forming a nice plastic tent over the recruit. Then he ordered the recruit to stay under the poncho until all the cookie crumbs had been eaten. This was a very hot July day, and of course, there was no air conditioning in the barracks. It was at least ninety degrees in the building, and probably about one hundred degrees plus under the poncho. After about thirty minutes under the poncho, the recruit passed out and keeled over. After that episode, I learned that nonconformity required extreme sneakiness.

It didn't take long for me to realize that the army loved doing stuff in total darkness. Most of our training, bivouac, and maneuvers were nocturnal activities. Trying to keep up with my gear and my buddy in total darkness took practice. We were taught to gauge the distance from the enemy; this required fine tuning my ears to subtle noises and the report of their weapons. I also learned that my second most important piece of equipment (next to my rifle) was a shovel about two feet long called an entrenching tool. Uncle Byrne Puckett told me years ago that he thought I was too tall for my height. While engineering foxholes, I gleaned a deeper appreciation for his expression. I also learned that most of the foxholes I dug were in the middle of the night. Digging was quite a challenge, but one hasn't really had any fun until he tries to spend the night sleeping in a hole knee-deep in mud and in the pouring rain.

My basic training occurred in the hot summertime. On one particular adventure, we were sleeping in pup tents. Pup tents were made by snapping two shelter halves together to create a two-man tent. Almost everywhere we went we carried a poncho and a shelter half. There was a malaria outbreak at Fort Dix that summer due to the increased number of mosquitos brought on by the surrounding swampland on the base. Our company commander was alarmed by the malaria outbreak, and being a proactive gung ho soldier, he ordered someone to spray inside the tents every hour on the hour for mosquito protection. In about two days about a third of the men developed a reaction to the mosquito poison, and they required medical attention.

During the last week of basic training, the outstanding recruits were promoted to E-2, and given a three-day pass. I had managed to save about $50 from my first two month's pay of $65 per month. I decided to board a bus to New York City, and spend the weekend seeing the NYC attractions. The round-trip bus ride to NYC cost me about $20. The first thing I did was buy a guided bus tour of the city for $24. This left me $20 for a two-night stay in a hotel. Much to my dismay, everything in NYC was two to three times as expensive as the usual costs in Tennessee. I finally walked into the biggest hotel I could find in NYC and explained my financial problem. The clerk took care of me by giving me a small tucked-away room that was saved for the overnight custodial staff for $10. Yay! This left me $10 for food. I asked directions to the USO club for servicemen and ate almost all of my meals there consisting of coffee and stale cake. Of all my personal excursions, this had to be my favorite one. By being frugal, I managed to see the attractions and also bring home a few cheap souvenirs.

After my graduation from basic training at Fort Dix, I was transferred to Fort Lewis, Washington, for nine weeks of advanced infantry training. Fort Lewis was just south of Tacoma and sprawled over more than a hundred square miles. The first thing we were issued upon reaching Fort Lewis was rain gear. During my nine weeks of training there, it rained about 80 percent of the time and snowed about 10 percent of the time. I stayed cold and wet for about the entire time. Our only regular sleep came riding the bus to the rifle training ranges and on the weekends when passes were issued. The trainees at Fort Lewis were an extremely low caliber of humanity. The officers were arrogant, and the NCOs majored in giving the trainees an exceptionally hard time.

I particularly remember Thanksgiving Day. Of course, we were in the field in the pouring rain when our fancy Thanksgiving dinner arrived on the meal trucks. A meal line was hastily constructed, and each man went through the line holding his canteen cup (the only cutlery provided to infantry soldiers in the field). Turkey and dressing, cranberry sauce, and pumpkin pie were quickly poured into the cups. The conglomeration was mixed very quickly with the rain downpour. That was the first and last time I ever drank a thanksgiving meal.

One E-5 sergeant, a recent graduate of Shake and Bake school, was especially big on trying to steal the guys' rifles when they laid them down by their side during breaks. After about seven weeks of this torment, the guys in the platoon decided that enough was enough, and we began laying plans to teach him a lesson. One day while we were taking a break during a forced march, the sarge laid his rifle against a tree. The temptation was too much for me. I picked up the rifle and quickly passed it off to a buddy who hid it behind a tree about fifty meters away.

In about three minutes when the sarge reached for his rifle he found that it was gone. Reporting the loss of his weapon to the lieutenant would make him appear incompetent, so in a panic, and ever so quietly, he began to scurry around until he finally found his weapon. He never tried to steal a rifle again after the incident.

After the evening maneuvers, our rifles had to be cleaned before they could be turned into the weapon vault. There was a corporal in charge of the weapon vault, and he had the authority to decide when the weapon was clean enough to be turned in for the night. He really enjoyed pulling rank over all the privates, regularly sending us back to do more cleaning—sometimes two or three times. After several weeks of this fun and games of cleaning our rifles and his refusal to check them in, we decided enough was enough. Most everyone in the platoon carried their rifles to their bunks and strapped them securely to their arms so they could not be removed without waking us. After the corporal waited for the rifles to be returned until the wee hours of the morning, he came to the barracks and pleaded for everyone to turn in the rifles so that he wouldn't get into trouble. After that incident he didn't try to jerk anybody around about a clean rifle.

About a week before we had finished advanced infantry training, we were issued our dog tags. Immediately I noticed that my new dogs contained an error that made me very uncomfortable. The tags listed my blood type as O positive instead of O negative. I had given blood several times while I was a student in college and I certainly knew that this was an error so unacceptable for me that I would not wear the dog tags into combat in Vietnam. The next morning, I reported to the company commander and requested that I be issued new dog tags with the correct blood type. I really expected this to be a minor request, and that the company commander would immediately help me rectify the error. Instead, the commander flew into a cursing rage and threatened to carry me straight to the stockade if I refused a direct order to wear the erroneous dog tags. "Well sir," I calmly said, "You had better call the MPs right away because I refuse to wear these dog tags." The CO was flabbergasted that I had called his bluff, and quickly restated that I would be issued sick leave to have my blood type retested, but he hastened to add, "If you are wrong about this, you will go to the stockade."

"That is fair," I replied, "because I am certain that I am not wrong." The next day I was issued new dog tags with the correct O negative blood type, and without apology. (In the wee morning hours of August 5, 1970, I was administered four pints of O negative blood. I am confident I would not be here writing this memoir had I not insisted the dog tags be corrected.)

The particularly low caliber of the assembly of thieves, pickpockets, and downright ignorance of my buddies soon made me realize I had probably made a monumental mistake to volunteer to lead this raggedy congregation into combat. Realizing my orders for Infantry Officer School would not be rescinded, I decided to bide my time and try to make the best of a bad situation. At least I knew I was about to receive the best infantry training the army had to offer, and I was more than willing to learn all I could that I hoped would keep me alive during my tour in Vietnam.

The best part about my stay at Fort Lewis was the beautiful view of Mount Rainier. Rainier is located about forty-eight miles southeast of Tacoma. Rising more than 14,000 feet above sea level, it makes a beautiful silhouette on the horizon at Fort Lewis. Formed by a volcano eons ago, Rainier's last eruption was over a thousand years ago, making it a likely candidate for another eruption in the near future. The glaciated, snowcapped peak forms five major rivers in the area.

The second best part about my stay at Fort Lewis was viewing the beautiful fern- and moss-covered temperate rain forest. The supersized base at Fort Lewis sprawled through the forest, and many of our maneuvers placed us in some really spectacular landscapes. In many places the ferns were as high as my head and green moss covered almost all the ground vegetation.

At the conclusion of our training at Fort Lewis, most of the guys were really uptight about the possibility of being sent to Vietnam. We were called to an assembly by the company commander, and while in formation he announced that our orders had been cut, and every swinging dick was assigned to Germany. This was every soldier's dream—to somehow luck out and not be sent to Vietnam. Furthermore, the commanding officer of the company (CO) gave everyone the rest of the day off and encouraged the company to move themselves to the beer hall so they could celebrate in style. Knowing this could not be true since my orders for Officer Candidate School (OCS) had already been cut, I was somewhat suspicious of the announcement. However, everyone was so elated and in such a jolly mood, I decided to stay mum.

Around two in the morning, everyone was back in their bunks sound asleep. Then suddenly, the DIs appeared, cussing and shoving and ordering everyone to get up for an emergency formation. We staggered outside to our second company formation of the day with the CO. Formations with the CO present were rare. Normally, the formations were held by platoon with the drill sergeant in charge of the formation. After everyone was brought to attention, the CO stated in a sarcastic voice, "Do you idiots remember earlier in the day when I announced that the whole company had new orders to report to Germany? Guess what? I was lying. Everybody is going to sunny Vietnam. I just wanted you guys to have a good time for a few hours before you learned the miserable truth!" A horrid groan fell over the audience of disappointed soldiers, soon to be replaced with a rage of anger. Most everyone had already phoned home to tell parents, wives, and girlfriends the wonderful news. Now they were forced to make another expensive phone call home to report their betrayal. I had only been in the army for four months. After that, nothing surprised me.

My next assignment was Officer Candidate School at the Infantry School in Fort Benning, Georgia. This was a six-month intensive training course in the best the infantry afforded. It was in the dead of winter and the winter of 1969 was especially cold. We ran everywhere we went—never marched. The good part about the running? It kept me from freezing to death. I liked running, and I had good stamina, so this was not a problem for me. That all changed one winter night when one of the new second lieutenants decided to take us out for nice run. It was pitch dark outside, and difficult to see anyone except the person directly in front. In the new lieutenant's wisdom, he ran the platoon right into a big metal pipe that had been driven in the ground. My knee smacked that pipe and I thought I had broken my leg. My leg was so sore I could hardly walk the next few days. Since I couldn't run, I was not allowed to train with the troops. This happened at the three-month interval of training. The CO called me into his office and asked what I was going to do about my situation. After I told him I was quitting, he said, "Fine, I'm sending your ass to Vietnam!" I said, "Thank you, sir!" I was looking forward to a thirty-day leave at home before my departure.

I was grateful for the opportunity to be a student at the Infantry School at Fort Benning. While I was there, I was able to hone my infantry skills that I knew I would soon be using. I had received demolition training, combat assault techniques, and important lessons of how to call air strikes from mortar positions and Cobra helicopters. I also spent a great deal of time at the rifle range with the M16 and M79 grenade launcher. One other tidbit I picked up was an infantry marching song. Here are the lyrics:

"Your left, your right, your left. Your left, your right, your left. Oh what a way to fight a war! Vietnam, Vietnam! Late at night while you're sleeping, Charlie Cong comes a creeping all around, all around Vietnam.

The Saigon girls are pretty. Their hair is long and black. And if you don't watch it, they'll stab you in your back. Vietnam, Vietnam! Late at night while you're sleeping, Charlie Cong comes a creeping all around, all around Vietnam.

A bayonet sticks right through you, you hear your buddies say. You're in another ambush, God let me live today. Vietnam, Vietnam! Late at night while you're sleeping, Charlie Cong cones a creeping all around, all around Vietnam."

While on my thirty-day leave at home, I had an opportunity to say goodbye to my friends and tell my girlfriend to wait for me because I would soon be back home. On the day before I was to fly to Oakland, California, my departure point for Vietnam, my Mom told me she had something very serious to discuss with me. I braced myself for a talk about the possibility of not coming home since I was entering a war zone as a combat infantryman. That greatly increased the likelihood a negative experience was awaiting me. Instead, she said she had dreamed that while I was away in Vietnam, I would fall in love with a native woman and bring her home with me as my wife. She said she could not bear the thought of having someone like her in the family. That was a relief. I was afraid my Mom was going to get emotional and tear up. She had no idea that I was about to enter hell. I decided at that moment all of my letters home would be only the cheeriest of news.

Upon arriving at my departure station in Oakland, I was ordered to wear my dress uniform to the departure station. California locals did not warm up to the army uniform. After leaving the airport, I was insulted, jeered, and chanted with "baby killer" and "we won't go, GI Joe." I received lots of birdies and feared that I may not make it to the departure station without being rolled. I was actually relieved when I finally made it to a very large, outdated indoor sports arena. I was greeted at the door by MPs who checked my orders and pointed me through the doors to the open arena. I noticed the MPs were armed with M16 rifles, and there were signs posted everywhere that those attempting to escape would be shot. I never expected a reception like this in a million years. Obviously, escaping the departure area had been a big problem for the army, and this was their solution to the problem. Now I understood that my prison sentence had begun.

The first order of business was to swap U.S. Army dress greens for Vietnam jungle fatigues. Next, we were ordered to turn in all of our U.S. currency in exchange for military pay certificates (MPC). This was necessary because U.S. currency could be sold for about 100 percent profit on the Vietnam black market. MPCs were used to eradicate this problem. MPCs looked very similar to Monopoly money. All of it was paper, but the coin money was a smaller version of the dollar money. They were printed in bright colors, illustrating American propaganda about the war. The lifers who were going back for multiple tours called the MPC funny money. I was already given a heads up about this by a lifer who was about to go on his third tour to Vietnam. He advised me to hide about twenty bucks in my shoe so that I would have some spending money at the first layover in Hawaii.

My boarding manifest was on a commercial DC10 jetliner that held about one hundred passengers. We were instructed to ride this same bird all the way to Vietnam, about a twenty-four-hour flight of a little more than ten thousand miles plus layovers. After several hours in the air, our first stop was Honolulu. With about a two-hour layover, I had time to get off the plane and explore the terminal. I found a flower shop in the lobby and ordered Mom an arrangement of exotic native Hawaiian flowers and paid postage to have it shipped back home to Tennessee. I remember the flowers and the postage cost just a little over $20, almost exactly what I had squirrelled away in my shoe. I also found a tourist with a Polaroid camera who agreed to take my picture to send home as a souvenir and evidence that I had enjoyed a two-hour vacation in Hawaii. Several hours later we landed on Wake Island for refueling. This was about halfway into our trip. By this time, flying on a jet plane had lost its charm, and there was a steady line at the latrines. It seemed that everyone had to go—not so much to take a leak, but more to break the monotony of the long trip by finding a different seat. Our third stop was the U.S. Air Force Base in Manila, Philippines. By this point everyone's tongues were hanging out. The last stop was Bien Hoa Air Base, Vietnam. I was so happy to get off the plane. It was a horrible trip, and adding insult to injury, I realized I had wasted an entire day of my life on that jet plane. Much to my chagrin, many more horrible episodes were just around the corner.

As we traveled through the terminal of this massive air base, the enormous American commitment to the war began to sink in. There were planes, helicopters, tanks, and soldiers everywhere. It only took a moment to discover that Vietnam carried a peculiar rank smell. The smell was a combination of filth, jet fuel, DEET, and incredibly strong body odor. All of a sudden, I sensed the body odor was magnifying as a company of U.S. infantrymen moved their way through the terminal toward me. The soldiers' faces were filled with a combination of fatigue, anger, and blank stares. Returning from a forty-day combat assault in the jungle, they had not had the opportunity to bathe, shave, or change clothes. Their utter filth took me somewhat by surprise, since in training I never went more than a week in the field.

After a quick roll call, we were marched outside the airport for our first Vietnam briefing. About ten minutes into the presenter's message, a Viet Cong B40 rocket exploded about twenty-five feet from our assembly area, throwing rocket explosion debris over the crowd. As everyone scrambled for cover, the presenter remarked, "Welcome to Vietnam!"

The next few hours were filled with more processing, and finally after about forty hours of no sleep, we were assigned bunks in large tents to get some rest. The f'ing new guys (FNGs), also known as cherries and the short timers (those going home after their tour) were assigned the same bunking areas. Making small talk, the short timers asked about my military occupational specialty (MOS). Following each inquiry about my MOS, they would pause and say, "Good luck. You are going to need it." It was a fact. Infantry soldiers made up the lion's share of casualties in Vietnam. Of their three hundred and sixty-five-day tour, they would see combat an average of two hundred and forty days. I was definitely going to need a double portion of good luck to survive. As the sun set on my first evening in Vietnam, I observed the commencement of boozing and smoking by the soldiers. Both cigarettes and beer were free, and marijuana was dirt cheap. I never cared for smoke, so I felt no attraction to the cigarettes or marijuana, and generally I adhered to a two-beer limit, because I also did not like the drunken feeling of excessive booze. As the evening progressed, the party atmosphere gave way to loudness, arguing, staggering, and puking. Having my fill, a new acquaintance, also uncomfortable in the surroundings, suggested that we take our bedrolls and find another place to park for the night. We headed toward the short timers' tent to seek solace. As we entered the tent, a short timer was playing with a .45 pistol. He aimed it at my new friend and pulled the trigger, shooting him right between the eyes. My friend fell dead in the tent. "My God, what have I done? I didn't know it was loaded!" cried the short timer.

Panic-stricken, I ran for my life and found an old French bunker that became my new home. I had been in Vietnam for less than twenty-four hours, and had already been shot at twice, and witnessed the death of an unnamed friend. Contemplating my situation, I again resolved to sugarcoat my letters home to shield my family from the horrors I was about to witness.

The next morning the FNGs were ordered to load up in duce-and-a-half (two-and-a-half ton) trucks and take a short ride into Saigon. This was my first experience to see the Vietnamese landscape. Since we were near the delta, I saw many rice paddies, water buffalo–drawn plows, and coconut palm trees. The weather was steamy hot, nearing the one-hundred-degree mark. Ominous clouds hung heavy with a coming monsoon. The road we traveled was filled with potholes and large mud puddles. As the trucks sloshed their way through the puddles, the spray would come over the top canopy and into the area where we were seated. The road was very crowded with carts drawn by donkeys and water buffalo, small mopeds, and medium-sized Cushman-type scooters manufactured to seat six to ten people. However, all of the scooters were overcrowded with several extra passengers riding on the top and the sides. This mass sea of the native humanity riding bicycles or simply walking with their livestock eased its way along this tiny road that had become a filthy canal of mud and water. Housing along the highway was made from adobe, and shacks made from tin, bamboo, and thatch dotted the countryside. I was witnessing a new concept of poor. Never in my wildest dreams did I imagine life being so destitute for the indigenous people of Vietnam.

Just a few clicks (kilometers) outside of Saigon, our truck convey came under attack. A lone VC machine gunner had hidden himself in a berm that rose about four hundred meters from the highway. As the machine gun rounds came piercing through the canvas sides of the trucks, everyone aboard jumped out of the backs of the trucks and took cover wherever it was available. The only weapons aboard our convoy belonged to the drivers, and after a brief firefight, we were ordered back into the trucks. Thankfully no one was injured during this attack.

Upon our arrival in Saigon, we boarded helicopters for a short ride to Nha Trang. Nha Trang was a beautiful coastal city north of Saigon nestled among mountains that came right up to the South China Sea. The mountains formed an inlet and a crystal white sandy beach. This would be my home for the next few weeks while awaiting orders for a regular infantry battalion. Nha Trang was absolutely beautiful. The accommodations were safe, and the food was the best I had eaten since leaving the states. We were assigned light duty from 7:00 a.m. till 3:00 p.m. The rest of the time was off time, and we were free to swim or do whatever in the compound. I saw my first USO show while in Nha Trang. Although it was only natives attempting to sing American rock and roll music, I found it amusing and mildly entertaining. That evening when I returned to my quarters, a guy came in and asked if anyone wanted any nooky. He said he had bought a prostitute for the whole night for twenty bucks, and he didn't think he could do any more "bam-bam" with her. "She's out there in the bunker if you want a free piece of tail." Guys began to line up. I was rather appalled at the situation and did not partake which surprised several of the guys in our tent. A few days later all the partakers began paying for their sins, lining up a second time for a big dose of penicillin in the hind end.

While the beach at Nha Trang was absolutely beautiful, lying on the beach playing homage to the sun god was a bit tricky. The direct rays of the sun magnified by the crystal white sand would burn a feller's butt in a matter of minutes. FNGs were warned not to stay out in the sun for longer than fifteen minutes per session until our bodies became accustomed to the sun's ferocity. Any FNG becoming sunburned so badly they could not report to work the following day would be fined $50 for each consecutive day missed. I personally thought it was good advice to watch the sun. However, some FNGs did not listen and became baked to a crisp in a New York minute. One poor guy was forced to miss two straight weeks with his severe sunburn. We were only making about $150 monthly. His $1000 fine represented about half of his pay for a one-year tour. Double ouch!

One day in Nha Trang I wandered into a used college bookstore. Realizing I was going to have plenty of downtime, I browsed around until I eyed two psychology books by B. F. Skinner and Sigmund Freud. I had always been fascinated with my college psychology classes, and I felt sure these books would prove to be interesting. I carried one of the two books with me almost everywhere I went in Vietnam. The grunts thought I was a book nerd since I chose to read these books. Unlike most of my college courses, I actually read these two books, and I believe this experience paved my path toward special education, becoming a reading specialist, and later becoming a teacher of teachers as principal.

After being in Vietnam for about a month, I received orders to fly to LZ Betty outside of Phan Thiet. I was assigned to Company B, First Battalion, of the 50th Mechanized Infantry Division. Its nickname was First Field. LZ Betty housed the rear echelon barracks; battalion headquarters; a mechanics' bay for the APCs, trucks, and Huey and Cobra helicopters; an ammo dump; a metal landing zone for small planes such as C-130s; the 192nd Assault Helicopter Company; a PX (GI general store); mess hall; bunk tents; officers' and enlisted men's clubs; a green line of fortified bunkers along the perimeter of the landing zone; a first aid station; and latrines. Everything was lined with sandbags for protection against a mortar or rocket attack. I arrived with three other FNGs. The first sergeant met us for our first briefing. The first sergeant was a salty old infantry soldier who earned the Combat Infantryman Badge (CIB) in WWII, Korea, and Vietnam. He was a strictly by-the-book lifer who considered himself an authority on about every subject. As we stood in a formation of four soldiers, he locked our heels and commenced giving each of us a thorough once over. He then went into a lengthy tirade of how everyone in Vietnam hated FNGs because an FNG could get a seasoned soldier killed in a heartbeat. Until we proved our worth in combat, we would be considered pariahs. He kept saying, "Remember your training, and with some luck, you just might make it back home." His next question was surprising: "Now I want to know what you FNGs prefer. Are you juicers or heads?" When he asked me I was a little bumfuzzled, so I correctly answered, "Neither, sergeant."

"Okay, let me break it down for you," yelled the sergeant in a snarling voice. "If you prefer alcohol, you are a juicer. If you prefer marijuana, you are a head, and that 'neither' shix will be out of your head very quickly because you are on your way to hell, sonny boy, and you will be driven to one of the two very quickly if you are lucky to survive!" Next he asked each of us where we received our training. When I responded with Fort Dix, New Jersey, and Fort Lewis, Washington, he looked me right in the eye and said, "You need to write a letter home immediately, because you will never see home again. Yep, they will bury you right here in Vietnam! Now, get out of my f'ing sight. I can't stand to look at FNGs!" Wow! That was sobering. I started to tell him that I had also gone to the Infantry School in Fort Benning, Georgia, considered the premiere infantry school in America, but I knew it would probably be better to leave well enough alone.

That evening, having a little time on my own, I ventured into the enlisted men's club. The club was a ramshackle metal building with a makeshift bar and a few tables and chairs. There was a small window air conditioner that struggled to keep up with the outside heat. Although the temperature was not really comfortable, it felt much better than anything I had experienced since landing in Vietnam. Beverages at the bar included beer, cokes, and nothing else. The beer was served lukewarm since the refrigerators also struggled to keep up with the heat. Beer sold for twenty-five cents a can, and cokes were a dollar. There was a reel-to-reel tape deck, an amp, and two large speakers on a shelf above the bar and *Playboy* playmate foldouts decorated the walls. And, did I mention it was crowded? Very crowded—too many bodies to sit in too few seats. Therefore, most of the patrons stood or mingled around the crowd. While I was there, I met several of the guys from our company. One of the first people I met was a cook in the mess hall. When I asked him about his MOS, he said, "I fix the shix you eat." Later after eating at the mess hall I found his explanation to be amazingly accurate.

The next morning the first sergeant assigned each of the FNGs to our platoons; he took me by the hand and gave me to one of the seasoned infantry guys. For the next week, this guy showed me every little thing he had learned while in Vietnam. He was gruff, but very thorough, and I appreciated all the time he spent cueing me in on things that training back home did not cover. As we prepared for our first combat assault, I learned the First Field Battalion was unique since it rotated regularly between going in the mountain jungle via Huey helicopters and traveling the flat lands via mechanized armored personnel carriers. My first mission with the company would be the Central Highlands of Vietnam.

As we prepared for the mission, I was issued an M16 and was allowed to pop off a few rounds to be certain that it was well sighted-in and just to get used to the feel of the rifle. Next, the platoon prepared their rucksacks together by squads. Each squad was a group of five to six soldiers, one of whom would carry the M60 machine gun that weighed twenty-six pounds. The man with the M60 also carried about 500 rounds of ammo. Furthermore, every soldier carried an additional two hundred rounds of machine gun ammo; a towel and poncho; DEET bug repellent; a can of foot powder; a small mirror, comb and toothbrush; an entrenching tool; a pound of C-4 plastic explosives; a minimum of four canteens of water with one canteen fitted with a metal cup; a small bottle of iodine tablets for water purification; malaria pills; rifle lubricant; two hand grenades; ten magazines of M16 ammo that fit into a cloth bandanna; one Claymore mine; enough C-rations for three to four days; and a two-pound steel pot helmet, liner equipped with a camo cover.

The soldiers' helmets were uniquely decorated with catchy slogans. The seasoned grunts usually had a calendar with the last month's days to mark off until the tour was over. Those who had scored their first combat kill often carried the ace of spades on their helmet with the phrase "Death comes in spades." "Born to Kill" and "Natural Born Killer" were also popular. One helmet said, "God have mercy on the enemy because I am one bad MF." There were many euphemisms referring to combat, killing, and hatred for the enemy and for the war like "Kill 'em All!" and "F Peace, F Love, F Vietnam, Bomb it all!" Those that had found love back in the world often decorated their cover with their darling's name. And lamenting real life in the world, I saw many peace signs, "Wake Me When It's Over," and "I know I'll Go to Heaven, Cause I've Spent My Time In Hell." After several weeks in the field, I decorated my helmet with, "Nixon's Hired Gun," because I wanted something original.

Short timers, those with just a few days left in the field, were extremely superstitious, and for good reason. They were near the end of their tour and they didn't want anything to go wrong with their last days. The middle of the march was reserved for the short timers and the FNGs. However, short timers refused to communicate with the FNGs for fear it would bring them bad luck. On their last day in the field, the platoon would throw a celebration by filling up their helmet steel pot with beer and the short timers were to chugalug the beer from the pot. The joyous celebration also brought wisecracks and jokes such as, "That's the last time I will ever drink from a pot!"

To conserve space and weight, the C-rations were broken up so that a soldier did not take any more than he could carry. As we were divvying up the rations, I noticed that each meal had its own unique calling card and special army nomenclature. For example, they called ham and lima beans ham and MFs. The round chocolate bar was called the John Wayne bar. The ham and eggs meal was called the sick stomach casserole. Then there were all the mystery meats. The best parts of each meal were the crackers, hot cocoa mix, coffee, toilet paper rolls, and assorted fruits. Bartering and swapping broke out immediately as the rations were doled out. Out of the blue one guy said, "Does anybody want my pears?" I responded with a quick "I do!" The whole squad broke into laughter. The pears were by far the absolute best can of fruit in the whole case of meals. A case of rations rarely had more than four or five cans of pears. This was a routine joke to play on the FNGs. Yep, if I were going to get respect from the rest of the squad, I had better heed their instructions and learn fast.

After my ruck was packed, my mentor said, "Now pick up your ruck and put it on your back." As I struggled with my ruck the squad members laughed at me again. My mentor asked, "Do you know your mistake?" I had packed too much food and did a poor job of placing everything in the ruck. The towel was placed around my neck first to help shield the weight from my shoulders, the poncho was placed on top since it rained almost every day in the jungle during the rainy season. Hand grenades were attached to the front of the shoulder straps of the ruck to offer a counterbalance to the weight of the load. Everything had a special place for safety, convenience, and efficiency. My second attempt of getting my rucksack on my back went much more smoothly as the squad broke out into applause. Wow! This sack was much heavier (between seventy and eighty pounds fully loaded) than what we carried during training. Most FNGs washed out the first day, unable to tote their weight or were killed in their first firefight. I was determined that would not happen to me.

That first Huey helicopter ride was also much different from training. The doors had been removed, making it easier to load and unload. Also, each Huey had a crew of three to four: a pilot, copilot, and machine gunners on each side. All of the crew members were strapped into their seats. Seats or straps were not available for the squad members. When the helicopters banked, we had to find something to hold onto to keep from sliding right out the cargo hold. Most of the time as we arrived at our destination, the helicopter would go in hot, assuming that an enemy greeting committee was awaiting our arrival at the landing zone. That meant as the helicopter prepared to land, both machine gunners would fire off a burst of about a thousand rounds each. At six hundred rounds a minute, that took less than two minutes. The moment we landed, everybody scrambled as they moved to cover as fast as possible. Loading and unloading was always the most dangerous part of the trip. I struggled keeping the loaded ruck balanced while attempting to successfully make my first run for cover.

If we landed in an area that was confirmed to be enemy occupied, we would begin our assault with a mad minute. A mad minute meant everyone was firing automatic weapons on the rock and roll setting, and we would throw everything we had at the new perimeter for a full minute. This gave us a psychological edge that many times would encourage the enemy to hightail it. After the mad minute, vegetation would be mowed down to the ground.

I thanked my lucky stars that I had survived my first jungle landing. Soon we were in a thick jungle canopy between eighty- and one hundred twenty-feet high. The vegetation was dense, making it difficult to see very far into the perimeter. We humped in single file about ten to twelve feet apart. The point man had an exceptionally hard job picking the right course of travel and keeping a keen eye peeled for the enemy. Traveling in the mountains was exhausting. Going uphill meant overcoming the force of negative gravity. Going downhill meant overcoming the force of positive gravity. Finding the right foothold in either direction was a treacherous task. All of the combined factors gave me a terrible backache. After several hours of hard humping and as the sun began to sink below the horizon, we made camp.

When we stopped, one or two members of each platoon were sent out about fifty meters from the camp perimeter on a listening post (LP). This precaution was taken to keep the enemy from catching us in a sneak attack. The mood of the men was very different in the bush. No talking, only whispering, and then no sound after dark. My mentor kept warning me to quit thrashing around on the ground. The first and most difficult assignment was to learn to sleep in a foxhole or flat on my back with weapon always in hand. We all slept close enough together so we could wake each other for guard duty or in case we heard the enemy approaching our perimeter. After a little practice I learned to sleep on my back with my steel pot helmet as a pillow. I also used the rucksack to help shield my body from the perimeter. We slept in a circle with everyone's feet pointing inward and our heads outward with the rucksacks offering a shield.

At dusk we would all unwind the wires to our Claymore mines, placing them about ten to fifteen meters in front of our position. The Claymore mines weighed about two pounds each. They were packed with about two hundred buckshot-sized balls that were propelled by about a pound of C-4 explosive. They were ignited by a handheld clacker that provided an electrical surge to the fuse for detonation.

The extra pound of C-4 explosive was always packed at the bottom of the ruck so that it would hug the ground at night. A lucky shot from a machine gun tracer round would ignite the explosive. The purpose of this explosive was to blow up Viet Cong bunkers and to blow a large enough perimeter to land helicopters. Generally, the squad leaders carried the detonation (det) cords and blasting caps for this operation. Det cords were a plastic cord about one-quarter inch in diameter that contained C-4. Multiple charges could be detonated at one time by hooking the plastic explosives mounted on designated trees simultaneously.

The jungle was filled with all sorts of eerie sounds. The monkeys became rambunctious right at dusk, but the two most regular sounds of the jungle were tokay gecko and the re-up bird. The re-up bird would tweet in a very loud burst of three re-ups, answered by the gecko that was better known to us as the F you lizard in an erratic burst of several F yous. Most nights in the rainy season the jungle was pitch black, making it impossible to even see a hand directly in front of one's face. Over the course of the next few weeks in the field, our platoon opened fire and killed several monkeys, a Bengal tiger, a mule deer, and more VC than I cared to count. The nice thing about killing the enemy was the next day we would be served hot chow in the field. (It was the army's way of rewarding Pavlov's dogs.) Although the chow wasn't very good, it was hot and much better than the C-rations.

I also learned the only time I could remove my boots and socks were during my guard duty shift. Each shift lasted one-and-a-half to two hours, depending on how many soldiers were in a squad. In the most expedient manner, I would remove my boots and socks, drench my feet and socks in foot powder, perform a very quick foot rub, and be back in the boots in less than a minute. Not knowing what was around the corner meant that I always had to be ready for combat when we were in the field.

We also had to wear garters around our britches' legs (trouser blousers) to keep the scorpions from crawling up our legs at night. Scorpions were plentiful and very pesky in the bush. They rated a close second to mosquitos that were everywhere. We had to treat all exposed skin at night to keep from being carried off by the mosquitos.

Early in the morning on the second day, the monsoons hit us with all their fury. This meant even poorer visibility than before. Since it was raining so hard, we had to stop and go into a night formation much earlier. We all dug a hole and got in. I dug my hole backed up against a very large tree and placed my back against the tree and hunkered down in the hole. My hole was about waist deep. Very soon the hole was full of water. It poured down rain that whole night, and I thought I was going to freeze to death although it was at least 85 degrees for the low that night. I still recall the adventure very vividly. It became my new worst night in Vietnam. The monsoon rains also made me realize that I was an ineffective marksman with the M16 because my glasses would get so messy I could not see out of them. Therefore, I jumped at the chance to trade the M16 in for more firepower, accepting a rotation between the M60 machine gun and the M79 grenade launcher. My logic was if I could get more lead in the air, I would have a greater chance of surviving.

The next morning it continued to rain. We built makeshift hooches over our foxholes by snapping two ponchos together. This offered some relief from the relentless rain. We stayed up in the mountains for two weeks that first outing. I recalled the grunts that I had seen in the Bien Hoa Airport on the day of my arrival. Now I really knew how miserable a human being could feel. Grunt was an excellent name to describe my condition.

We were in a state of constant danger when we were humping in the jungle. Of course, we never knew when the enemy might attack, but when the enemy was not in the area, we had to be wary of the surprises they left behind. They would prepare booby traps using trip cords attached to mines or grenades that would automatically explode if the cord was tripped during a hump. Also, they were really sneaky, leaving punji pits along the trails. The pits contained bamboo stakes one to two feet long that had been sharpened and hardened by fire. For an added bonus, the tips of the stakes were coated with poison or human excrement. Stakes in the bottom of the pit were pointing vertically, and lateral downward positioned stakes were located on the sides of the hole to injure one on the way out of the hole. Most of the punji pits were prepared by the Viet Cong using a rice hook to sharpen the stakes. Bamboo was very plentiful everywhere in Vietnam, and there were no shortages of punji pits. As a result, we rarely walked down a beaten trail in the jungle but instead chose to cut our own path to avoid Charlie's surprises.

On the final day of the assault, we began our preparations to leave the mountains. The C-4 explosives were used to blow down enough vegetation to land the helicopters. Secondly, we hooked all the machine gun ammo together and shot it all so that we would not have to clean it upon our return to LZ Betty. A platoon carried about six thousand rounds of machine gun ammo. At six hundred rounds a minute, it only took about ten minutes to deplete our supply. After the pop-off, the trees were leveled for about fifty meters. The barrel of the machine gun turned white-hot. The M60 was definitely the workhorse of the infantry.

We returned to LZ Betty for what was supposed to be five days of rest. Of course, being an FNG meant that my name was at the top of the duty roster. Almost immediately on our return the first sergeant grabbed me and said there was no use for me to get spruced up, I was on the shix burning detail. So that I would learn the ropes, he also added a seasoned hand who knew all about the detail. His name was Benjamin Franklin Whittington. Ben was extremely agitated about the assignment and kept shouting that he was no f'ing FNG. He told the first sergeant he would not help with the detail. The first sergeant said he would give him an article 15 if he disobeyed his order. (An article 15 was a $50 fine.) That infuriated Ben even more. He dug the Claymore mine out of his rucksack, positioned it under the latrine, and clacked the clacker. Kaboom! The latrine was knocked off its foundation and the tin shell of the latrine went flying everywhere. Ben got busted to an E-2 private and he was known as Frag from that moment forward. Shix burning was a smelly but necessary job at the base camp. Since there was no traditional sanitary plumbing, excrement was collected in fifty-five-gallon drums that had been cut off to about eighteen inches in length. All of the drums were gathered and placed close to an open dump at the edge of the green line (perimeter). Next, diesel fuel was added to each drum and set on fire. Oh wow! A feller ain't truly lived until he has had the opportunity to inhale the wonderful aroma of burning diesel and shix. It's a never forgotten maggot-gagging odor earning the shix drum the clever name of honey pot. The last step was cleaning and depositing the remaining contents of the drums in the open landfill. Sickening is literally too nice of a word to describe the shix burning ordeal.

After my first combat assault, my clothes were so filthy I began my bath wearing my clothes. Since the latrine was demolished, I had to take my first bath under a hose pipe standing buck naked in ankle deep sand. As bad as this may have sounded, I smelled much better afterward.

One thing that stood out in my mind about this incident and many more similar situations later on was a feller had better be careful when he messed with a grunt; particularly one who had just spent the better part of the past two weeks in the jungle. The agitation factor was multiplied by a series of combat situations, and especially aggravation was the norm if he had lost some of his buddies in combat. Although I didn't see much disrespect in the field, back at the base camp was a totally different matter. Tempers were short, and when someone said, "Back off or I will kill you," most of the time they meant it. Another fascinating observation was the great number of soldiers at the base camp awaiting court-martial. I observed the majority of the soldiers awaiting court-martial were black. One night I was just settling into a real bunk at the base camp when two black soldiers started arguing. As the argument escalated, they pulled out their M16s and pointed them at each other. I rolled out of the bunk and low crawled out of the tent as fast as I could before shots were fired.

There were about twenty large bunkers that encircled the perimeter at LZ Betty. Each bunker was equipped with an M60 machine gun, an M79 grenade launcher, a large box of hand grenades, and a green starlight scope. In addition to the regular high explosive M79 grenade ammo, there were also special star-cluster rounds that would provide illumination at night. They were equipped with a parachute that would allow them to slowly drift back to earth after being fired in the air. Encircling the green line was about a twenty-foot-wide area of concertina razor wire and barbed wire. The wire was rigged with booby traps and rattlers to wake up any unsuspecting guard, to alert of the enemy approaching. The guard duty roster always began with the FNGs. About four guards were placed on each bunker, alternating guard shifts so that one guard was awake at all times. As the night progressed, M79 grenades were lobbed out past the green line so that Charlie would know the guards were awake.

After about six combat assaults over a two-month period, our company switched to riding the armored personnel carriers (APCs) in the delta area. Everyone was ready for a break from the humping and ready to ride. An entire squad would ride on one APC. No one rode on the inside. The back hatch remained open to provide cover in case of an attack. Each APC was equipped with one 50-caliber machine gun that covered the front direction and two M60 machine guns on the back right and left flanks that covered the sides and the rear. There was one commander who sat directly to the rear of the 50-caliber and a driver. Everyone else rode on the top carrying M16 rifles. Each APC had a graffiti-decorated hatch representing the sentiment of the soldiers riding. The one I was riding said, "Killing is our business and business is good!" This slogan was not unique to our APC. I saw it scrawled on everything from helmets, C-ration boxes, the door of the latrine, and on the front of many Huey helicopters and Jeeps. Since we were not humping, we wore flak jackets. A flak jacket was a low-tech, sixteen-pound vest designed to provide a shield against light shrapnel. It was heavy and hot, unlike the Kevlar armor modern infantry soldiers wear. We also wore our steel pot helmets that weighed over two pounds. After a long day in the field, it was a pleasure to take off the helmet and the flak jacket. When it was too hot to wear, the jackets made a nice cushion for the bumpy APC ride. A company of men would head out in a convoy of sixteen to seventeen APCs. The lieutenants boarded alongside the enlisted men, and the company commander (usually a captain) boarded a separate APC toward the rear of the formation with protection and his radio telephone operator (RTO). Each lieutenant also had an RTO to provide communication between the platoons and the company commander.

As we prepared to leave LZ Betty, we gathered up all the C-rations we refused to eat, placing them in large boxes on the top of the APCs. Immediately outside the green line less than a click away was the city of Phan Thiet. Highway 1 ran directly through the center of the city and provided our exit to the delta countryside. As the APCs made their trek through town, the city streets would be lined with the locals (especially children) who would be awaiting our arrival. Reminiscent of the Christmas parades back home, soldiers would throw out the cans of discarded C-rations to the children. This always provided plenty of excitement for our trips out. We were not greeted with the same fanfare on the way back because we didn't have an opportunity to prepare the discarded food.

I was amazed at how fast the APCs could travel on the street. Of course, we rarely saw that speed in the field unless we came under attack. The APCs tried to follow the same tracks as the lead APC. In case there were mine fields planted for the APCs, this decreased the possibility of exploding the mines. The Russian-supplied tank mines were about fifteen inches by three inches. They were detonated by a spring-loaded mechanism on the top of the mine and would be buried under two to three inches of soil to provide camouflage. They were packed with plastic explosive very similar to the army's C-4 explosive. The mines packed a mean wallop that almost always provided a body count for the enemy.

As we moved farther into the bush and out of view of civilization, the missions almost always became more dangerous.

One of the hazards provided by Mother Nature was flying termites. Termite colonies were massive. The mounds were generally between ten to twenty feet high. The vibration of the APCs would disturb the colony, and soldiers would be greeted by a swarm of flying, stinging soldier termites. There were also stinging hornets, flies, scorpions, poison snakes, and disgusting sand fleas. The termites were the most aggravating when the APCs were moving, and the scorpions rated a close second when we were on the ground.

The APCs were very loud as they trekked through the terrain. Since the roar of the engines left little doubt we were approaching, all of the APCs had a large radio mounted on top that blared rock and roll music from the one American-Vietnamese radio station. Occasionally we would tire of this broadcast and tune in to Radio Hanoi that produced a thirty-minute propaganda program that would air three times daily. The radio voice belonged to a lady we called Hanoi Hannah. She began each of her broadcasts with the same greeting. "How are you, GI Joe? It seems to me that most of you are poorly informed about the war. Nothing is more confusing than to be ordered in a war to die or be maimed for life without the faintest idea of what is really going on. The war protests in America are increasing every day. The American citizens hate what you are doing to the poor people of Vietnam." Occasionally she would surprise us, giving detailed accounts of our location in the Central Highland jungle. She would also play music from Bob Dylan and Joan Baez. However, the most upsetting part of her broadcast was when she would read a list of the latest U.S. casualties, followed by, "Your government has abandoned you. They have ordered you to die."

The Vietnamese landscape was also littered with propaganda fliers produced by both the Americans and the Vietnamese. Both sides pledged fair treatment and a great cash settlement for deserters. In fact, the Vietnamese government was offering more money to deserters ($20,000) than the Americans were giving to families of deceased soldiers ($15,000). Ouch!

Remembering my first conversation with the first sergeant, I also noticed that most of the guys were smoking marijuana. Marijuana, they explained, was a copacetic necessity making a very agitated grunt mellow. I was invited to try, but not liking smoke I declined. However, I observed that the mosquitos did not care for the smoke. The guys not smoking weed were smoking cigarettes or cigars. I chose the lesser of two evils and was surprised how much more comfortable I became without dozens of mosquitos circling my head. Cigar smoke worked the best for me because it had the grossest smell that sent the mosquitos on their merry way. I learned how to hold one in my mouth and by taking random puffs, I learned how to keep one lit for a very long time.

Our kill and casualty rate was about the same whether we were humping in the mountains of if we were riding aboard the APCs. Dehumanizing the enemy made it easier for us to do our jobs. We called the VC "gooks" and had no compunction for taking their lives. Hesitation in the moment of battle yielded disastrous results, making a killer's instinct the only possible option for survival.

The VC would try to anticipate our path across the terrain and lay mine fields. It was always a sad day for the troops when the APCs exploded a mine. Most of the time a mine would blow an APC to oblivion. Occasionally we would get lucky when a mine would become partially uncovered by the APC tracks, giving us an opportunity to detonate the mine so the VC couldn't use it against us again.

If this strategy wasn't working for the VC, they would dig holes equipped with debris tops matching the terrain and jump out of the holes for a quick ambush against us. The 50-caliber machine gun was a great psychological weapon because one round could tear a man in half. Just hearing the slow hum of the 50 generally sent the VC running. I remember one day that was exceptional. We were engaged in an extended firefight with the VC and the barrel of the 50 glowed white hot. The temperature magnified to a point that the rounds would pop off before reaching the chamber of the gun. The brass casings of the ammo would send shrapnel in all directions, putting the gunner at highest risk of injury. Any other time, the gunner sat in a relatively safe position shielded with half inch plate steel. The monsoons also created challenges for the APCs. Attempting to ford ditches filled with water from flash floods was always tricky. I remember one occasion when our APC became waterlogged and had to be pulled out with another. Of course, when the dry season hit, the APCs sent up large clouds of dust that infiltrated our eyes, nose, mouth, and all of the equipment. This feature of the APC earned it the nickname Duster. I preferred the monsoons to the thick dust of the dry season.

After three months of fighting, I graduated from the M16

rifle and the M60 machine gun to carrying the PRC-25 radio and the M79 grenade launcher. No longer shunned by the rest of the squad, I had proven my worth in combat and was able to carry my weight as a grunt. The added weight of the M79 and/or machine gun held an additional perk. These gun bearers were allowed to hump in the middle of the squad file since the larger firepower needed protection from the commencement of the firefight. I especially liked the M79 in the Central Highlands of Vietnam. By April, the dry season had begun, and water was scarce even in the mountains. I filled up my canteens in some of the scummiest water imaginable, added an iodine tablet, and gave the canteen a good shaking to dissolve the tablet. The water tasted awful but had a wet quality about it. Humping in the mountain jungle was exhausting because of the stifling heat and humidity and the steep terrain. Six quart canteens of water would not last long. Once we were dying for water and a Huey supply helicopter flew over and dropped two large duffle bags full of hot beer above the jungle canopy at about 125 feet. Our latest mail from home was also in the bags. When the hot beer hit the rocks below, most of the cans exploded on impact, ripping our mail into a zillion pieces. Mail call and USO shows were the only two morale boosters for the grunts in the field. We were mad as hornets about the mail, but happy we had something to quench our thirst. I had to sleep with my canteens secured in my cargo pants pockets at night to keep my buddies from stealing my water. On one occasion, the supply helicopter confused our drop shipment and dropped mortar ammo on our position. The mortar platoon was located on top of the mountain and we were about a click down in the valley. We had to hump the mortar cases back up the mountain to the mortar platoon. The mountain was very steep, and the mortar cases weighed about forty pounds, making our hump up the mountain extremely treacherous. After about an hour of hard humping, we reached the mortar platoon location, but it was almost dark. As a result, we had to spend the night on the side of the mountain. I dug a hole as fast as I could for my head and shoulders and threw the dirt downhill to level my sleeping spot. That night I had to brace my feet against a large rock and lock my knees to keep from slipping down the mountain. This became my newest worst night in Vietnam.

I fondly remember one combat assault that was hyped as especially dangerous. Intelligence had spotted a large concentration of VC in a particular area, and our company was ordered to combat the enemy who was considered extremely hostile. We flew in on the Hueys hot and fast and quickly began forming a perimeter adjacent to a secondary road that cut between rice paddies. Expecting to confront the enemy, we began digging our foxholes. Sure enough, along the horizon we spotted about a dozen individuals coming directly toward us. As they came closer, we also noticed they were riding bicycles and were not carrying weapons. Among the troop of natives were a pimp and six prostitutes, a concessionaire selling cokes and snacks, an artist selling glow-in-the-dark prints, and a barber. All the locals anticipated a profitable business with the grunts. I bought two glow-in-the dark paintings on black velvet so that I would remember this event. How did the locals know our exact landing zone (LZ) and ETA? Instead of engaging the enemy, we were met by a welcoming committee of locals.

We generally traveled with a Kit Carson Montagnard (French for mountain man) Scout. The Montagnards were the natives of the Central Highlands and among the poorest tribes in Vietnam who lived in huts made of grass and cane. We also traveled with about a dozen soldiers of the Army of the Republic of Vietnam (ARVNs). The ARVNs hated the Degar Moi (Montagnard Savages), but the Kit Carson Scout was an excellent asset for maneuvering in the mountains. The troops began to complain about being out of water, and the scout carried us to a small stream. After filling our canteens and drinking all we could, we noticed there were some small fish swimming in a pool that was about waist deep. The lieutenant exploded a small charge of C-4 in the water. Instantly the little fish began swimming on top and the ARVNs jumped and caught the fish. Being such a delightful spot in the mountains, we camped there that night. The ARVNs cooked the fish and we dined on a rice and fish feast that night. The next morning the scout began searching for holes along the stream's edge. When he found what he was looking for, he would lie down on the ground and stick his arm in the hole as far as he possibly could. Most of the time when retrieving his arm from the hole he would be gripping a Chinese Water Dragon, a large green lizard about thirty inches long. He promptly broke the dragon's back so that it could not crawl off. The locals humped with the dragons until it was time to make camp. That evening we ate rice and water dragon. This made an extremely tasty meal in the bush. After that, relations between the ARVNs and the Montagnard Scout were much better.

And then there was the elephant grass. Usually about halfway down the mountain we would encounter large expanses that would be eight to ten feet high and thick as a shag rug. The blades of the grass were sharp enough to cut right through the skin. It took two soldiers up front hacking a path with machetes. We would rotate every five to ten minutes because it was a gruesome task. Visibility was limited to the path, making our descent down the mountain more treacherous and putting everyone's nerves on edge. About the only thing we did not have to worry about with the new paths was booby traps. The enemy hated the elephant grass as much as we did.

Upon our return to LZ Betty, the first sergeant called a formation. He loved pulling his rank on everyone and jacking everyone around. Some of the guys were smoking dope and were pretty high when the formation was announced. Jim Falooga was lying naked in his bunk when the order to fall out was given. To everyone's surprise, Jim attended the formation in his birthday suit. This was one of the funniest moments I witnessed during my tour. When the first sergeant caught sight of Jim, he was totally flabbergasted! For the first time first sergeant was speechless. The rest of the company was cracking up at the sight as well. A few moments later the first sergeant appeared with two MPs and they whisked Jim off. No one heard a word about what finally happened to Jim until one of his buddies received a letter from Jim. Jim said everyone thought he was crazy for attending the formation in his birthday suit, but he was sick and tired of killing! "Anyway," he replied, "I'm in Japan and you guys are still in Vietnam! Who is really crazy?"

Carrying the radio gave me firsthand information about what the brass was thinking. Hearing the company commander's lack of concern for his men wounded and killed in battle made me angry. I vowed that I would volunteer for anything to get away from him. Our next field trip put us back on the APCs and I was placed on the right flank of the track with an M60 machine gun. The APC in front of us hit a mine and two men were killed. The company commander was extremely angry about losing an APC but showed no concern for his men.

That evening I developed a bad case of dysentery. Since I was puking and crapping everywhere, I requested a medevac to carry me to the first aid station, but my request was denied. I thought I was going to die that night, making it my new worst day in Vietnam. The next day the company commander called a rare assembly in the field. He said he was looking for someone to volunteer for a suicide mission. "The good news," he said, "is you will have a chance to get away from me. The bad news," he said, "is you will probably die on the suicide mission." I immediately stepped forward and volunteered for the mission. That evening a Huey landed, delivering an FNG to take my place on the APC and picked me up for my new assignment. I had no idea what awaited me but figured if I stayed in the bush one more day with dysentery, I would die anyway. That decision proved to be the right decision for me. The very next day my formerly assigned APC hit a mine and the FNG who took my place broke his back as a result of the explosion.

My assumption that I would initially be granted first aid was wrong. I was carried directly to a Military Assistance Command Vietnam (MACV) compound right outside of Phan Thiet located in a small hamlet called Ham Thuan. The fortified area at the MACV compound was much smaller than LZ Betty. It was home to a group of Ruff Puffs as well. Ruff Puffs were the local Vietnamese militia assigned to guard their hamlets across the Vietnamese countryside. The Ruff Puffs had little formal military training and I found that my new job was to help train the locals so that they could defend their homes from the Viet Cong. The Viet Cong would go into the hamlets at night and terrorize the citizens. Many times, they would pick out the teenage females in the hamlet and demand that locals pay them a ransom to keep from raping them. The VC would also attempt to steal rice, chickens, and eggs from the locals. I became part of one of the first six-man advisory teams of infantry soldiers in Vietnam. Very soon two more teams were assembled. Our team had one seasoned squad leader, two riflemen, an M60 machine gunner, and an RTO. I was assigned the position as RTO and I carried an M79 grenade launcher. We reported directly to an MACV major at the MACV base camp who was the best commander I had ever had the pleasure of knowing in the army.

Our first assignment was to change our appearance from regular infantry soldiers. We were to wear jungle camo fatigues, berets or boonie hats, and no rank on our uniforms. I chose the boonie hat that would help shade my eyes and keep the rain off my glasses. Since we were working directly with the militia from the local villages, we decided to wear ARVN rank on our uniforms. Our mission had four important components: teach the locals how to properly use their newly issued American weapons; teach them how to sweep the main roads into their village at daylight for Viet Cong; provide instruction about ambush sites for the VC at dusk; and provide the locals with Cobra helicopter gun support in the event of a firefight.

WARMING BY THE FIRE

The only thing novel about this mission was the small number of American soldiers carrying out missions. Instead of being a member of a five-hundred-man battalion team, we were six-man teams accompanying the locals with heavy weapon fire support. Soon after I volunteered, I learned that this used to be the mission of special force units, but regular special force units were spread too thinly to complete all missions required. The Ruff Puffs were impressed at how fast we could get Cobra helicopters to come help us in a firefight, and this made us a valuable ally. As a result, we traveled in the middle of the patrols—the safest position.

Rifle firing was a rather straightforward concept that the Ruff Puffs learned rather quickly. A more difficult lesson was to teach them to hug the ground during a firefight. They wanted to sit up to view the fight. The machine gun was something they could not master. Machine guns are designed to run best with an initial thirty- to fifty-round rock and roll burst with no hesitation on the trigger finger, followed with seven- to ten-round bursts. The Ruff Puffs wanted to shoot the M60 with two- to three-round bursts, causing it to jam the magazine and making the weapon ineffective. Our first decision was to take the M60 out of their hands. They were too small to carry the weapon, and they were afraid to fire it properly once the fight began.

Our first extended orders were to provide extra security for a Ruff Puff compound just outside the hamlet of Phan Rang. The perimeter of the Ruff Puff compound was not much larger than a football field, equipped with a WWI-style trench and one antiquated French bunker. Our home for the next three weeks would be in that old French bunker. It was a ten-foot concrete reinforced cube with a small door and three small portholes large enough for the barrel of a weapon. Although the most secure location in the compound, it was also the hottest location. I continued to suffer from stomach problems after three trips to the medic. The smell of food made me sick to my stomach. Reflecting on my symptoms now, I am quite sure I had a *Clostridium difficile* (C. diff)-type infection. I continued a surge of weight loss for a month, losing about forty pounds. One night we staged an ambush and I began passing some terribly disgusting gas, offending the whole team. The squad leader ordered me to catch a ride into LZ Betty the next day and not come back until I was over my illness. The fourth trip was my saving grace. The paregoric I requested had arrived from home at the same time, and I was given new medicine with three days of rest at the base. Thank God I was ending the latest worst ordeal of my life in Vietnam.

My most memorable day at the Phan Rang Ruff Puff compound began early one morning when the Ruff Puff commanding officer called at formation and asked the Americans to also attend. Two AWOL Ruff Puffs were returned to the base by the MPs. As they came into the formation, one of the Ruff Puffs kicked the commander. The commander grabbed a bamboo cane about five feet long and an inch in diameter and began giving the unruly Ruff Puff the beating of his life. I counted forty lashes across his back. Next, they placed the AWOLs into separate razor wire cages about forty inches long by twenty-four inches wide and high, making the fetal position very uncomfortable if they decided to move. The cages were placed in the middle of the compound under the direct sun, and the AWOLs stayed in the cages about six hours that day. Ouch! I thought to myself, "Two new Viet Cong have just been recruited."

I also remember the first day we carried the Ruff Puffs out to Highway 1 to show them how to clear the road at sunrise. This was necessary to keep the Viet Cong from ambushing the civilians as they went about their daily duties. About thirty minutes into the sweep, two of the Ruff Puffs opened fire. All of the Americans hit the dirt with lightning speed just to discover the Ruff Puffs breaking formation and running toward the field of fire. We later discovered the excitement was over a rabbit that had crossed the road in front of them. I knew right away that training the locals would be more difficult than I had first imagined. Instead of taking cover and hugging the ground at the first sound of gun fire, the Ruff Puffs wanted to look around, making them an easy target for the enemy. They also wanted to stand up to fire their weapons. Unfortunately, these bad habits could cost them their lives on the battlefield. As soon as Highway 1 was officially cleared, it immediately filled up with an assortment of traffic. I saw carts loaded with bamboo pulled by donkeys, water buffalo, and small trucks. I also saw lots of mopeds and bicycles. However, the most unusual conveyance was the Cushman buses. The buses were about four feet wide and ten feet long. Three seats fit snugly behind the driver's seat inside the cab. The cab was generally packed with passengers sitting inside, on the roof, and standing on the back bumpers. I wished a hundred times I had taken a photo of the spectacle.

On a brighter note, I really enjoyed the freedom of roaming the Vietnamese countryside. Many mornings we would stop at the local markets and have breakfast. The mama-sans cooked an egg dish resembling an omelet over an open fire that was quite tasty. In the evenings we would buy strawberry wine, fresh-baked bread, and canned sardines to supplement our bowls of rice. I really wasn't that fond of strawberry wine—it just happened to be the only kind they sold. Another great perk was after our initial stay with the Ruff Puffs, our commanding officer moved us back to the MACV compound where we had a latrine with a shower, bunks, and maid service. The six of us paid a mama-san five piasters each per month, giving her a thirty-piaster monthly salary (about $15, MPC), plus all the cigarettes she cared to smoke. Free cigarettes were available to the troops. My cigarette allotment was two cartons every week. Since I didn't smoke, we gave them to the mama-san. In addition to making our bunks, washing our clothes, and keeping the bunkhouse and latrine clean, she also shined our shoes. Beer was cheaper than sodas and more plentiful, and we could buy ice from the natives to keep our beverages cold.

 We were on duty for about three hours in the morning and carried out ambushes about three nights a week. The rest of the time we could do whatever we wanted. We played lots of spades and horseshoes, wrote letters home, and would get into a big poker game after payday. There was a kitchen at the compound, and we took turns cooking up wild dishes with the C-rations and long-range reconnaissance patrol supplement (LRRPS). LRRPS was an instant dehydrated meal in a bag. When hot water was added to the mixture, it became chicken stew, chili, or a flavored noodle dish. I preferred the chicken stew to all the other flavors.

 Another pastime was dreaming about the world. The world

was what we called home in the United States. Our days were filled with utter boredom that would ignite into intense hair-raising excitement at the report of a discharged weapon. Our routine of killing and surviving left us bewildered and angry because we knew the folks at home were insulated from our daily nightmare and were beginning to protest the war. I suppose that was why the army was so tolerant of soldiers drowning their fatigue and sorrow in alcohol and marijuana. I truly believe that reading letters from home was the only thing that kept me from going over the deep end.

My army pay was a whopping $150 monthly. Seventy-five dollars of that amount was called combat pay which came to about an extra $2.50 a day. I placed $50 monthly in savings bonds. I had promised Pop that I would repay my college loan of $1000 at $50 monthly increments. However, Vietnam service was paid in MPC—a currency having no value except in the war zone. Pop had to wait for his payment until I finished my tour in Vietnam. The rest of my pay went to the housekeeper and food I purchased from the natives. I managed to save an additional $50 a month. After five months in Vietnam, I had saved $250. There was a safe at the MACV compound that would hold my savings. I had toyed with the idea of buying a stereo from the Pacific Exchange (PACEX) system; it was about half the price of the same unit stateside.

While I was stationed at the MACV compound, I began receiving Lawrenceburg's local newspaper, the *Democrat Union*. Everyone at the compound who read the newspaper received a big charge out of the local stories that showed photos of big tomatoes, rattlesnakes, and especially the weekly columns about country gossip. Reading about Uncle Leroy driving to Nashville, or Grandma coming over for Sunday dinner and such was a novel and humorous experience for everyone. The all-time favorite story featured the county sheriff and his deputies raiding a whiskey still and confiscating several hundred gallons of wildcat whiskey. Intrigued by the whiskey story, several of my buddies promised to visit me back in the world when we quit playing war games with Charlie Cong.

Since we were the first STAG teams formed in Vietnam and after stunning success combating the Viet Cong as Ruff Puff advisors, our reputation caught the attention of the Secretary of the Army. Around the fourth of July, the three STAG teams stationed at the MACV compound were visited by Secretary of the Army, Stanley R. Resor, and General Arthur S. Collins, Commander of Task Force South, Vietnam. During their brief visit, several Cobra helicopters hovered overhead to provide the brass cover. They shook everyone's hand and congratulated us on our fine soldiering and encouraged us to continue giving Charlie hell. About a week later we were featured in *Stars and Stripes*, the army's official weekly publication.

I remember once not long after the visit from the honchos, I had shot up all of my M79 ammo in numerous firefights. The ammo supply truck was not scheduled to be back for another week, and our team was chosen for an ambush that night. When I explained to the CO that I had no ammo, he said, "What are you waiting for, James? Hitch a ride back to LZ Betty and get your ammo." This was really a very different way of requisitioning ammo. Generally, an order would come down through battalion headquarters and would flow through the officers. I had never been on a one-man, twenty-click operation. I borrowed an M16 and a Colt .45 pistol and headed back to LZ Betty. Luckily, I flagged down a ride on Highway 1 rather quickly and made it to the ammo dump with little difficulty. When I asked the supply sergeant for the M79 ammo, he refused because I didn't have any authorization from headquarters. While I was making my request, I noticed that my friend, Frenchy, from Bravo Company was working there. I waited for the supply sergeant to disappear and sneaked into the ammo dump from the rear. Frenchy agreed to fix me up with the M79 ammo in exchange for a favor. I had to accept a footlocker filled with assorted dirty ammo, rescuing Frenchy from a cleaning detail if the dirty ammo remained at the dump. We placed M79 ammo and the footlocker on the first jeep heading back toward the MACV compound. I hopped up on the back of the jeep and sat on top of the footlocker for a very bumpy ride back to the MACV camp. Upon arrival I was curious about what kind of ammo Frenchy had unloaded on me. I opened the lid and found that it was chock-full of hand grenades and one additional surprise. A small box of fifty blasting caps had jarred open and spilled into the loose grenades. It was a million wonders I wasn't blasted to kingdom come on that return trip to the MACV compound. I carefully removed all the grenades and returned the blasting caps to their insulated package. Reflecting upon my newest worst day in Vietnam, I never would have dreamed I would have to steal ammo to shoot at Charlie Cong.

It was always interesting to have the opportunity to socialize with the natives. Like Forrest Gump's box of chocolates, a feller never knew what he was going to get. One day while we were patrolling through a cornfield, we came upon the farmer's small hooch. The hooch was made of cornstalks and bamboo. The roof consisted of laced cornstalks. There were two small rooms about six feet square with a dirt floor. He constructed a clay firepit in the front room, and a raised bed made from bamboo cane in the rear room. The front room had open sides, and the rear room was protected with lashed bamboo cane. When we encountered the farmer, he was cooking his dinner. He asked us to be his guests for dinner. Happily obliging, we pooled our rations to add to his meal. We generally carried the LRRPS rice packs because this was a favorite of the natives. We also supplemented the meal with fruit, crackers, and John Wayne bars from the C-rations. The farmer had cooked up a tasty meat that was added to the rice dishes. After we had eaten, he said he was depressed about his pet dog recently dying. I am quite certain that was the first time I had ever eaten dog meat. I added it to the list of exotic cuisines that included rice paper, nuoc mam sauce, lemon grass, lime leaf, water buffalo, Chinese water dragons, and a variety of fish and rice dishes.

My personal experiences with the natives gave me an opportunity to respect the Vietnamese culture. Given their deplorable living conditions compounded by the ravages of war, I was amazed that most of the natives were happy and upbeat. The children were especially friendly, and many knew enough English so that they could beg for food. The adults had a very strong work ethic and worked from dawn until dusk. I remember one night we had established an ambush site on the edge of a hamlet near a cane break. About three in the morning, I heard something approaching our position. Everyone was awakened and ready to blow away the uninvited guests when it occurred to us they were a family of locals who were working late into the early morning. They were merely navigating a large cart loaded with bamboo pulled by two water buffalo. Realizing they posed no threat, we allowed them to pass our position unharmed. Ignoring the evening curfew, they passed our ambush site oblivious of the danger that awaited them that evening. I have thought many times about their perilous situation and am happy we figured out they were no threat just in the nick of time.

4 Aug 70: I still remember almost every detail of that evening as if it just occurred yesterday. Perhaps since this day was my personal nightmare for forty-something years, the events of that evening never faded into forgotten moments of time. As we prepared to leave the MACV camp, we were briefed by Major Wells in the usual manner. We had been training the Ruff Puffs for about three months, and we wanted them to take an active lead in preparing an ambush for the Viet Cong that evening. They were sent forward to the site about an hour before us and they were instructed to prepare the ambush site and anticipate our arrival. We normally began preparations about one to two hours before sundown, but this evening we started on a five-click hike to the site right at dusk. The moment we arrived at the site, I immediately noticed the Ruff Puffs had made no preparation as instructed. Almost immediately upon our arrival, we came under attack. This attack was different than any I had ever experienced. We immediately recognized we were being attacked with American weapons. The first reports of the attack came from an M60 machine gun in two-round bursts. Thankfully, the untrained hand on the M60 caused a weapon jam, rendering the

big firepower useless. Following the M60 was a field of fire from M16s and M79s.

At the opening of the firefight, the Ruff Puffs fled. I don't remember them returning a single shot during the battle. That put the battle greatly in favor of the Viet Cong that easily outnumbered our six Americans and one interpreter. Under heavy fire, we began to withdraw in pairs. One soldier would return fire while one soldier ran for his life, making quick ten-meter trips in reverse.

The ambush was occurring inside a Vietnamese cemetery. The graves were mounded up in two-feet berms. This factor allowed our withdrawal to coincide with the grave berms providing much-needed cover. We were all busier than one-legged men in an ass-kicking contest, but I also had an additional duty. I was on the radio sending info about our perilous situation back to headquarters. Upon our third withdrawal attempt, my buddy caught some M79 grenade shrapnel in the hind end. Unfortunately, it softened his appetite for the firefight. My next withdrawal attempt was noticeably absent of return fire. As I was diving for the grave berm, I felt a large explosion of an M79 grenade under my feet. I am certain that if I had been running upright when the explosion occurred, I would have been immediately killed.

The first sensation I felt was being engulfed in a ball of fire. My body reeled from the hot shrapnel as it laid into my skin. I immediately sensed a horrific pain in both legs, rendering them useless for my withdrawal. Sensing the enemy approaching, I began to low-crawl. Remembering the words of the DI from basic training, that "low-crawling can be a matter of life or death," I commenced on the fastest, lowest, and longest low-crawl of my life. Since I was now at the perimeter of the cemetery, there were no more grave berms to shield my position. About three hundred meters out I spotted a giant prickly pear cactus. This particular cactus was about six feet high and wide, making it much smaller than the largest I had seen in Vietnam, but sufficient to provide cover for me. Meeting the pain from the multiple barbs of the cactus was one of my smallest concerns at the time because the cover of the cactus was a welcome site. As I crouched down in complete exhaustion in the cactus, I realized I had also been hit it the right arm because my right hand had gone numb. The pain in my legs and buttocks was excruciating, masking the pain of the cactus barbs.

Within minutes of my arrival to my new cover, I saw five VC approaching. One man stopped about two meters from my cover. Upon his arrival, I discovered our Vietnamese interpreter was only ten meters away from my position. Strangely, the interpreter and the VC engaged in conversation. I could tell the VC was also wearing the Ruff Puff uniform we had furnished. This rebuttal continued for about thirty seconds when the VC and interpreter exchanged rifle fire, immediately hitting each other. The other four VC came rushing to the firefight, claimed the interpreter's rifle and carried their injured soldier away about thirty meters under the canopy of a dead tree.

Almost immediately I saw the four VC returning toward the cactus plant where I was hiding. The four of them stayed there about fifteen minutes smoking and talking. They were close enough that I could have touched them with the end of my outstretched weapon. During all of this commotion, the dusk daylight had dissipated, leaving me in a good cover of darkness.

I could see the silhouettes of the VCs setting up their night perimeter under the dead tree, and I could also hear their jabbering. They were not observing the night silence we had learned in our training. Seeing that the enemy was a safe distance from my position, I called the MACV compound to send mortar fire. I was beginning to fade in and out of consciousness because of blood loss, and I never saw the first mortar explosion sent to mark a position.

While lying in the cactus for about two hours, I really thought this was going to be my last hurrah. I could hear the interpreter moaning for help and I realized I was in no position to come to his aid. After about three hours, Major Wells and a reactionary force appeared. I was quickly administered two shots of morphine and given a small drink of water. The Cobra gunships were now in the air, and I directed their fire upon the enemy night position, making it my last official act of combat while in Vietnam. This was becoming my newest worst night ever.

After about three-and-a-half hours after the beginning of the firefight, the wounded interpreter and I were placed on a medevac helicopter and carried to the first aid station at LZ Betty. As the two of us lay on prep tables, I was greeted by the battalion commander, Lt. Col. Hooker. He wanted to hear every detail of the attack. While I was giving him a quick recap of the evening's excitement, the Vietnamese interpreter died on the table next to me. The first aid team cut off my uniform and hosed me down with antiseptic and did the best they could to stop the bleeding. I was rushed back to the medevac helicopter for about a thirty-minute ride to the 6th Convalescent Center in Cam Ranh Bay.

That thirty-minute ride was the second coldest experience I had in Vietnam. I knew I had lost a tremendous amount of blood because I was so cold and thirsty. As I entered the hospital emergency room, I spent the next thirty minutes in the x-ray room. I'll bet they made a hundred x-rays and all the maneuvering on the cold table exhausted me so that I could no longer turn myself at their command. Around midnight they sent me to the operating room. I was placed under anesthesia for six-and-a-half hours. Around seven in the morning, I woke up in the recovery room. I was covered in bandages on both legs up to my knees and around my right arm. The incredible pain from the night before had subsided to a tolerable level so that I noticed all the barbs from the prickly pear cactus sticking in my hands and arms. Both arms and legs were also hooked up to blood packs, and I was equipped with a catheter. For the next few hours, I slept the most peaceful sleep in my life. Around one in the afternoon the two doctors who performed the surgery came by to check on me. Also, two nurses appeared, and they were pushing a cart loaded with new bandages and antiseptic. I thought, how nice. They are going to change my bandages. I was not prepared for what followed next. They raised my legs and slipped under a rubber mat and gave me two shots of morphine. Next, they soaked the bandages in saline solution. I had no idea what fun was just ahead. As they began removing the bandages, I thought I was going to die. It literally felt like they were skinning me alive because the dried blood had caused the gauze to stick to my wounds. I relived the agony of being wounded just like the night before. After about ten minutes, the wounds were prepped and I saw for the first time the extent of my injury. The doctors had sewed me up with over one hundred regular suture stitches and eight metal stitches in my upper right arm. I had several open wounds on my left leg that were too large to sew up and they reported my left leg was fractured just below the left ankle bone. I then learned the disturbing news that my arm injury was probably the worst since one frag had partially severed my ulnar nerve in my right arm. This explained why I had no feeling in most of my hand, and the condition would probably be permanent. This was my newest worst day in Vietnam.

For the next six days, my routine was the same. When I wasn't sleeping, I ate three hot meals a day, and I was getting my bandages changed. Each day the bandaging pain was less severe. Then almost exactly one week later, the hospital came under a Viet Cong rocket attack. The hospital was being bombarded by B40 Chinese rockets. Since I could not get out of the hospital bed, the nurses placed a mattress on top of me and all patients who could not get out of their beds. Then everyone else scrambled for the bomb shelters. The next thirty minutes became my new worst day in Vietnam. My horrific nightmares were jump-started by the rocket attack as I lay helpless in a bed covered by a mattress. After that event, every time I would fall asleep, I would wake up in a cold sweat thinking I was dead reliving that moment over and over again. This was my newest worst day in Vietnam.

While in the hospital at Cam Ranh Bay, I was visited

by three of my buddies from the MACV STAG team. They informed me that Battalion Commander Hooker had put in a request to headquarters for me to be awarded the Silver Star for my 4 Aug 70 action on the battlefield. They informed me the air strike I directed killed 38 Viet Cong. Of course, most Silver Star requests were batted down by the upper echelon. I knew this because twice before requests had been made in my behalf for the bronze star; both of these were either watered down or thrown away. One friend offered to write a letter home for me, and I was very happy to finally tell my family that I had some pretty good knocks, but I was planning on surviving. I sincerely appreciated the surgery work by the doctors and the great care I received from the nurses. The staff was very professional and exceptionally kind. They had definitely saved my life.

After my fifteen-day stay in the Cam Ranh Bay Hospital, I was placed on a C-141 Medevac Jet with about thirty other guys on stretchers and flown to the 249th General Hospital in Tokyo, Japan. My new home became Ward 884 D. This ward was narrow, but about 120 feet long containing approximately forty beds. The smell of dead flesh almost made me sick to my stomach as they wheeled me to a bed. I saw guys with horrific injuries. Many of them were amputees and several were multiple amputees. A couple of the guys had half their face shot off. That night the ward was filled with shrieks of pain and chagrin. All of us had seen the horrors of war, and we continued to live the nightmare. I was thankful to be out of Vietnam, but this night became my new worst day in the army. The doctors and nurses in Japan were about the most hateful group I had ever witnessed in the army. I still have a keen memory of my first operation in Japan. They wheeled me into the operating room and began ripping off my bandages before the anesthetic had taken effect. One nurse stood out as being the most hateful woman I had ever met. She would regularly walk down the row of beds and pull at the patients' bandages and scream, "Wake up! I can't sleep and you are not going to sleep either on my shift!" She threatened to give Article 15s to those she found sleeping on her shift. It didn't take long before the guys would shout out "Sadist Alert!" when she entered the ward. She was the meanest bitch that ever graced our planet. She excelled at making each day my worst day in the army.

My third and fourth operations after the ambush yielded eleven large metal staples in my left leg and a straight-leg cast that went all the way from my foot to my hip. When I was in recovery, the nurses took my wheelchair away from me and made me walk back to the ward on the cast. This was a very large challenge to balance my weight on the heel that was built into the cast. It also hurt like hell as I went back to the ward. The next morning, I noticed the cast was a bloody red color around the area of the larger wounds that could not be sewn back together. I soon discovered a storage room filled with older wicker chairs that must have been left over from WWII and Korea. I dusted one off the best I could, and I hid it in a cloak room outside the ward so that I could ride the chair to the Mess Hall.

It had been almost three weeks since I washed my head and what hair remaining was driving me crazy. My right arm and hand were not strong enough to wash my hair, so I found the hospital barbershop and a kind barber who agreed to wash my hair for a dollar. When the guy lathered my hair, big clumps of hair fell out and covered the barber's hands. The anesthetic given to me during the surgery had taken its toll on my head, causing my hair to fall out. I repeated trips to the barbershop every two days for the rest of the time I was in Japan. The only good part about my stay in Japan was the excellent food served in the mess hall, and I could eat as often as I wished. I felt stronger every day, but realized my injuries were more severe than I first suspected. While in Japan, I left the hospital one time in a wheelchair to go outside and take a photo of the corner of the hospital closest to my ward. Six weeks after my injury, I was finally going to the States. I boarded a C-141 Medevac on a stretcher and was flown first to Alaska, then Chicago, and finally to Washington, D.C. There I was loaded onto a medevac bus and carried to Walter Reed Army Medical Center in Bethesda, Maryland, just outside of Washington, D.C.

Walter Reed was a sprawling hospital and research complex of buildings sitting on a 113-acre campus with fifty-five hundred beds for patients. There were thirty-six orthopedic wards dedicated to treating Vietnam War injuries. I was placed on Ward 35 that was situated over in a far corner of the campus. It was almost a quarter-mile trip from my ward to the mess hall. I was very happy to find the doctors and nurses at Walter Reed to be kindhearted people, and the hospital served the best cafeteria food I had ever eaten. This made my time spent in Walter Reed a much more pleasant experience.

When I arrived at Walter Reed, I was allowed one free telephone call home. Everyone passed the phone around at home and I had my first conversation with my family in over seven months. Mom surprised me when she told me her bags were packed and was coming to see me. I really appreciated her gesture, but I did not want Mom to see the horrible site of so many wounded men lying in the large wards of the hospital. I immediately talked her out of the idea since I knew I was scheduled to come home for thirty days on a convalescent pass in a couple of weeks. As the day approached for my first trip home, I was sent on a series of chores that required me navigating outside the hospital with my straight-leg cast and a cane for balance. I first went to the quartermaster to be fitted for a dress green army uniform. Then I had to make about half a dozen checkpoints to get various departments to sign off on my release. By the time I was finished with the assignment, I suffered from writhing pain and exhaustion, but I dared not complain in fear of jeopardizing my trip home. I had been prescribed a large bottle of darvon (a schedule II narcotic) and was encouraged to medicate for the pain. That night I took a double dose, my first step in a five-year progression of becoming addicted to pain medication.

The next morning, I took a bus to Washington National Airport to board a flight to Nashville. Mom and Pop were going to meet me at the airport and give me a ride home to Summertown. I had great difficulty getting to the concourse to catch my flight. The cool reception at the airport reminded me of my trip to Oakland, California, when I departed for Vietnam. Once again, I was shocked at how many people were angry at me while wearing the army uniform. Disgusting remarks were once again directed toward me because many did not like what I represented to them. I was given the finger by many whom I passed in the airport terminal. I was ecstatic to finally board the plane but immediately faced another problem. My straight-leg cast made it impossible to sit in the seating available on the plane. The head stewardess informed me I could not be accommodated on the flight home. At that point I commenced to offer the most sugarcoated appeal of my entire life. I offered to stay in the cargo hold, lie in the aisle, stand up or do anything in order to get to remain on the flight. My appeal caught the sympathy of one of the stewardesses who offered her seat to me up front by the pilots' quarters. This was a single seat at the very front of the aisle. "Thank God," I said to myself, "I'm free at last!"

The reunion with my family marked one of the happiest moments of my life. Becky, Deena, and Joe met me as I exited off the plane. We hugged and kissed and moved down to the baggage area with all possible speed because Mom was waiting in the temporary parking outside with the car. I had to sit in the back seat of the car, placing my long cast along the seat with Joe sitting in front of the cast. Hugging Mom felt especially good after such a long time. The trip home was filled with laughter and stories as everyone began catching me up on the news at the home front. When we arrived home, I noticed that everyone had been busy making welcome home banners and signs. They were posted on the back door and throughout the den. I had never received so much affection from my mother and siblings at one time in my life. Mom had been busy cooking all of my very favorite foods for my reception. She had cooked fried chicken with all the trimmings and also had made my signature chocolate birthday cake with chocolate candy icing. Mom's cooking was always the best! This was my best day in the army.

Approximately six months after my return to the States, a large box holding my Vietnam personal items arrived in

Summertown. I quickly rifled through the box to discover that most of my war souvenirs and many of my photographs had not been returned. Also, the $250 I had tucked in the safe was not returned. About half of my uniforms were returned and that was the whole kit and caboodle. I was familiar with the routine of divvying up the stuff of the dead but was surprised it also applied to the injured. I added this up as another sad Vietnam experience, marking it among a long list of bad days of being in the army.

The first night home was a mixed blessing. My bed in my room was a full bed which meant I had to sleep diagonally. My recurring nightmares came back to haunt me, and as I thrashed around in my sleep, Mom and Pop could hear my cast banging against the bedroom wall. After about a week of the nighttime drama, Mom had had enough. The next day she shopped for a new queen-size bed. I told her it was unnecessary but her will prevailed, and I had a new bed to sleep in after that. The new bed kept the cast from banging against the wall, but nights of peaceful sleep were over forever.

Just a few days after I came home from the hospital, Jerry received a leave from the air force, and we were home together for a few days. He insisted on carrying me dove hunting. He was very attentive to my every need on the hunting trip. He drove the car to a nice spot under the shade of a small tree, set up a folding chair for me to sit in, and left our bird dog, Beau, to retrieve any birds I had killed. My stamina was not up to the trip, so he brought me home and said we were going to hunt sparrows instead. There was a large willow oak close to the barn that was teeming with sparrows. I sat under the tree and killed several. We joked about it later when I told him the sparrows were my first kills since leaving Vietnam.

After about a week at home, Terry Pierce came by and offered to drive me around. He drove me down to the Dipper to see some of my friends. As we approached a group of guys standing around the service station next door, one of the guys aimed a pistol at me and opened fire. My battlefield instincts were still sharp, and I immediately hit the ground. Then everyone laughed—but me. The pistol only held blanks, but the report of the gun brought back painful battlefield memories. After that I was ready to go back home. Over the next few weeks, I found that many of my friendships I had made were lost forever. Terry remained loyal and helped me get around while I was stuck with the leg cast.

Pop had built a house across the street from our house and he was working on installing the drywall. I came over one afternoon to help him. Holding the hammer was a huge challenge since I had lost most of the use of my dominant right hand. As I attempted to nail the drywall, I noticed a blood trail that was following my hammering. Since I had lost feeling in most of my hand, I was not aware that while nailing, my little finger was banging the wall. My finger was a bloody mess where it had repeatedly hit the wall. The episode made me realize my recovery was going to be much slower than I had initially assessed.

I established a routine over the next five months, returning to Walter Reed for ten days or so, and then I would return home for thirty more days of convalescent leave. The doctors had changed my leg cast four times during that time, and they were waiting for the larger open wounds to heal before they planned to release me from the army with a medical discharge. They were also testing my right hand to determine how permanent my arm injury was going to be. During that time, a small amount of sensation returned to my hand, but two of my fingers were badly drawn into a claw. They said they wanted to give the injury more time before taking surgical action.

My days at Walter Reed were filled with utter boredom. I spent a great deal of time at the recreational center playing pool and volunteered to help out at the hospital medical record center located in the basement. The record center was gigantic. Since this was a time before computers, patient records became very large and cumbersome. After a few months, the records staff knew my name and relied on my clerical skills in helping to find lost records. I also became familiar with many of the patients at Ward 35. One day I saw some of the patients talking to an officer. Being curious, I asked what was up. They were giddy about being discharged from the army in just a couple of weeks. All they had to do was sign a waiver releasing the army from any responsibility toward their disability. I pleaded with them not to sign, but they signed anyway. This made me absolutely furious! I began trying to call my congressman to report the outrageous behavior of the hospital. The word must have gotten out that I was causing trouble. The next week the doctors who were treating me said I would have to go back to duty because they could not find any record of my Vietnam injuries.

Unbeknownst to the brass, I could navigate my way around the medical record center. The next day I found my file stuffed into an old locker where I had found lost records in the past. I made a personal carbon copy of every document in the record for my safekeeping and returned my original medical record back to its proper place. I noticed a cool change in the atmosphere by the doctors after that. I immediately knew someone up the chain of command had learned of my complaint.

About a week later, the doctors removed the cast from my leg. I had three open wounds, but they were slowly healing. The largest was about the size of a half dollar. It now became my responsibility to change the dressing and apply new 4×4s to the wounds. The next day the doctor came in with a box full of 4×4s, topical antibiotics, two extra-large bottles of darvon, and a hospital discharge. They had decided to put me back on active-duty status. "Doing what?" I questioned. They said someone had read my file and saw that I was a good typist, and they needed a good typist. "That was before my injury making my dominant hand useless as a typist," I countered. "What about the medical discharge?" I asked. That too was no longer on the table. "What about the open wounds?" I wondered. I was told to manage the best I could because it was now out of their hands. This became the angriest moment of my entire life!

The Silver Star Award: After I left Vietnam, I had no communication concerning the award. While I had lots of downtime at Walter Reed, I began to regularly read the *Stars and Stripes*, the army's official weekly publication. I noticed that every week they listed the new Silver Star recipients. I decided to make it my weekly task to check if, by any chance, my name was on the list. I knew it was a long-shot gamble, but sure enough I found my name on the list just a couple of weeks before I was discharged from the hospital. Then I began to wait to be notified of the award. After two months of waiting, I realized the communication trail between my Vietnam unit and Walter Reed was too far removed to ever hear official word. I resolved to go to the post exchange (PX) and buy the Silver Star ribbon. I thought this may draw speculation, but most likely suspicion, on someone's part to get the situation officially investigated.

My new assignment was clerk typist with the United States Army Topographic Command in Washington, D.C. This base was about a fifty-acre campus that housed the army's mapping service. There were several large buildings and I worked at headquarters of a fancy air-conditioned office building. The large bay was filled with approximately thirty typists. My assignment landed me with some very nice people. Only the warrant officer in charge was a stick-in-the-mud. I was given a cubicle and a new IBM typewriter. I explained to my superiors I had not typed since college and did not expect to be able to type with my crippled hand. The warrant officer heard my comments and told me my record said I could type sixty words a minute. I explained that was before my injury. I was going to be "a typist at any rate so get used to it," he countered. I was still angry about being back to duty after months of promises of a medical discharge.

The next few weeks were difficult. I didn't complete a single error-free assignment, making the work useless. However, I learned to type again using four fingers on my right hand. Once I learned to accommodate my handicap, I made improvement and began to contribute my share of the office load. (I am quite certain my typing skill would have been lost forever if I had not been forced to sit at a desk and reteach myself how to hone a modified typing skill.)

The Topographic Command did not have any housing

facilities for its staff. As a result, my housing was located about twenty miles across town at Fort McNair, one of the oldest army bases in the United States. Built in 1791 on a twenty-eight-acre campus of Greenleaf Point on the Potomac River, Major L'Enfant included this in his plans for Washington, D.C. Fort McNair was famous for the 1865 tribunal of the conspirators of the assassination of Abraham Lincoln, and for hanging the first woman, Mary Surratt, under federal orders. Later the fort became a general hospital for the army, preceding Walter Reed. While I was stationed there, it was known for the National War College. The housing was old, but nicer than anything I had lived in while in the army. I had a personal cubicle about ten feet square with a bunk and a chest of drawers. The mess hall food was adequate but could not compare with the excellent chow I ate at Walter Reed.

I commuted in a military sedan with four others to work and back to Fort McNair. We worked a five-day, forty-hour week with an hour lunch break, and all the free coffee we cared to drink at our workstation. Weekends were free time with no extra duty. Fort McNair was in walking distance of all the historic sites of Washington, D.C. I spent almost every Saturday for six months exploring the Smithsonian museums, monuments, and tourist destinations.

The only downer about my new job was I had to wear my dress green uniforms every day at work. I was given extra clothing, but none of the dress shirts fit. I was able to wear a civilian dress shirt and no one seemed to notice. One day after about three months on the job, one of the sergeants eyed the Silver Star ribbon I was wearing. He called me into his office and showed me that my military record was not indicative of the award. I pulled out the notice I had found in the *Stars and Stripes* where my name was listed as a recipient. This intrigued the sergeant very much and he promised to investigate the incident on my behalf if I would remove the ribbon in the meantime. This was exactly what I hoped would happen. About a week later, he called me back into his office and reported the award was in fact legitimate. "James," he said, "I thought you were the biggest liar I had ever met when I dug into this situation. Now I just want to shake your hand!"

The office began to buzz with gossip about my coming award ceremony. One day I received an invitation from the Command Sergeant Major of the U.S. Army Corps of Engineers to come to his office for a chat. He asked what kind of ceremony I would like to have. "Do you want fireworks, a parade, the press, maybe speeches? Your wish is our desire! Honestly," he said, "we are plowing new ground here at the Topographic Command. You are the first ever to receive the Silver Star from our command, and we are all somewhat giddy about the ceremony!"

I was stunned. "Quite frankly, sergeant, I would like the smallest amount of fanfare possible."

"Your wish is our command! I will get right on top of this."

About two weeks later I learned the ceremony had been redirected to the top office of the Chief of Engineers. A small delegation of four station wagons traveled from the Topographic Command to the Chief of Engineers' office near Capitol Hill. This location was chosen because the Chief's office had a great view of the Capitol Building. The Chief of Engineers was assisted by the General of the Topographic Command with about a half dozen other witnesses including the press from the local TOPO-COM paper. A photographer took two photographs while I was pinned, and then we all went home. About a week later a large envelope appeared on my desk, containing two dozen glossy 8×10 photographs. I was very happy to have the event marked with the photographs. The next day I stuck the pics in an official TOPOCOM envelope and mailed them home with TOPOCOM paying the postage.

This was a very tumultuous season in Washington, D.C. for anti-Vietnam War and anti-military establishment protests. One weekend I attended an extremely large anti-military establishment protest on the Mall. There were probably over a million protesters in attendance. While standing there sporting a short military haircut in civilian clothes, several long-haired hippie types approached me about my dorky military haircut. To keep from getting mauled by the crowd, I told them I was a recent deserter from the military. They wanted to interview me and take my picture for their underground newspaper, but I told them I could not afford the publicity since I was on the wanted list of the military police. Then they let me in on their strategy for the following Monday. They planned to block all the major roads in D.C. to halt the military machine attending work. As soon as I had the opportunity, I eased out of sight and ran back to the base at Fort McNair and alerted everyone about the Monday surprise.

The following Monday our army olive-drab official business cruiser became one of the targets of the protesters. Our vehicle was hit by eggs and bricks as we traveled along the corridor to work. We were also cursed and flipped off about a hundred times along the way. All sorts of debris and garbage were dragged into the road in an unsuccessful effort to stop our vehicle. But the scariest incident was when some protesters rolled an old truck off a hill toward our automobile. The driver made some fancy swerving to avoid the truck missile. Luckily, we made it to work unscathed with only minor damage to the cruiser.

As the weather warmed, talk emerged about our office suite joining one of the city's recreational adult softball leagues. We signed up to play games two afternoons a week. We decided to name our team the Boone's Farm Apple Wine team. This was a popular inexpensive wine of the early seventies that cost a buck and some change for a fifth. In order to validate our team name, each player would have to consume a bottle of wine during the five-inning game. I don't recall winning very many games, but I do remember our team seemed to have the best time. I played first base because I had the longest stretch on the team, making me a perfect fit for the position. One afternoon during a scheduled game, an opposing player hit the ball down the third base line. Our player scooped up the ball and made an almost perfect pitch to me at first. The runner sensed he was not going to beat the throw to first base, so he chose to run over me in an effort to make me drop the ball. When he collided with my outstretched left hand, I felt a crunch and instant excruciating pain in my hand. The runner had successfully bent my wrist back into the opposite direction. All of the horrible pain of August 4, 1970, haunted me once again. An ambulance was called, and I was rushed to the nearest emergency room.

After remaining there on a stretcher for about four hours, I learned the hospital would not treat me because I was a member of the military. Around eight o'clock that evening an army ambulance transported me to Walter Reed for treatment. The best I recall, I arrived at the emergency room on a Friday evening, and most of the staff had gone home for the weekend. No one was present but a lowly intern and me. Swelling had already encompassed my wrist, making the possibility of setting the bones next to impossible. The intern suggested that because of the severity of the fracture, I should wait until Monday to be seen by an orthopedic surgeon. After spending the last six or so hours in excruciating pain, I was in no mood to wait two more days without medical treatment. I begged him to do the best he could. "If you have enough Novocain, we will straighten this sucker out," I retorted. "Okay," he replied, "but this is going to hurt!"

With that encouragement, he went to work. First, he hooked up some traction pulleys to the bed. Next, he loaded my wrist with about five shots of Novocain. Then he put my left hand into a Chinese finger-trap device and hooked it to the metal cables above the bed. For the next four hours we pulled with all our might, but the wrist would not straighten. The doctor stated he had done all he could, and it was a useless cause, and I would have to wait for a surgeon.

I encouraged him to pull one more time with all his might. The doctor climbed up in bed with me and straddled me, putting all his weight on my body. Slowly but surely, my wrist began to straighten. Using this method with a few more hefty tugs made the wrist look presentable. He quickly made an x-ray and placed a bent-arm cast that ran all around my hand to my left arm pit. After the cast was in place, he made one more x-ray to make sure nothing had not slipped out of place. One last adjustment was needed. Using a cast saw, he split the entire cast to allow for swelling.

Around two in the morning he rolled me into Orthopedic Ward 35 and by coincidence placed my bed in almost the exact position I had occupied some six months earlier.

On Monday morning when the regular doctors made their rounds, my old doctor and I were surprised to see each other once again. "James," he said, "I felt badly about the raw deal we handed you the last time you were here. This time I promise we will give you the care you deserve."

For the next two weeks I was flat on my back with the arm cast hooked up to traction. I must admit, it was the worst time of my life. My arm swelled twice the normal size, and my fingers protruding from the end of the cast turned black. Every beat of my heart caused the arm to pulsate with pain. I was very anxious for the upcoming progress report. A quick x-ray indicated the bones had slipped out of my wrist sockets once again. So, for the second time, I was loaded with Novocain, bones were set back in place, and I was fitted with my second arm cast.

After another week of being flat on my back in the bed, I was checked again. This time all looked well. My third cast was fitted. I took a much-needed shower and I was sent home once again for convalescent leave. After three months in a full arm cast followed by three months in a short cast, I was pronounced cured although it took another six full months for the normal feeling to resume in the arm and hand. Next my doctor ordered a third surgery on my right hand to correct the claw that had developed on two of my smaller fingers. After the surgery, I was sent home for sixty more days of convalescent leave.

The hand surgery did straighten the claw in my hand somewhat, but there was no doubt half of my hand would remain dead to sensation for the rest of my life. My second stay at Walter Reed had convinced the brass to release me from their command, and I was certain I would be going home this time for good with a medical discharge.

Once again, I was disappointed when someone else looking for a typist read my file. Within a week I was transferred to Fort Meade in Maryland to work as a company clerk. This was my eighth assignment in my twenty-eight months of active duty! When I arrived, I found a very unusual situation. Most of the enlisted men working for the company were college graduates with degrees in engineering. They worked during the day developing new night vision technology at the National Security Agency (NSA) that was located on the Fort Meade campus. It was a delightful change to be associated with intelligent people. The commanding officer and first sergeant I worked with were also class acts. I was happy to learn that not all army personnel were scumbags.

My job was much more relaxed than the TOPOCOM job. However, the first sergeant asked me to take the postal exam so that I could handle the men's mail. I studied the manual for about a week and took the test, becoming their official postal clerk. The company was much smaller than the infantry companies with only about seventy-five to eighty men total. Everyone worked a five-day, forty-hour week with no extra duty. I also was allowed to wear fatigues, making the workday more comfortable. I spent the weekends at a woodworking shop on campus and went to the movies two or three times a week. I could sleep as late as I wished on the weekends. I befriended a couple of guys with autos that would carry me with them to the steak houses on the weekend. A big steak dinner with all the trimmings including tip was about five bucks.

After a few months on the job, the first sergeant asked me if I would be interested in receiving a six-month early release of duty. This delighted me immensely. With Vietnam winding down, the army had too many personnel, and they were moving with all immediate speed to reduce numbers. The Christmas season was approaching and my new expiration term of service (ETS) would be December 26, 1971. About two weeks before the date, the first sergeant told me he appreciated my good work, and that he was going to promote me to E-5. I thanked him kindly for the gesture but declined the rank since it would only apply to the last ten days of my service. I am probably the only man on earth that ever turned down rank. Had I remained in an infantry unit after Walter Reed, the rank would have been represented by three stripes and the title of sergeant, but since I was working as a clerk, the rank would be represented as specialist fifth class. The whole idea of serving in Vietnam in the infantry and leaving the army as a clerk instead of a soldier left a bad taste in my mouth, adding to the overall resentment I felt toward my service.

As the last week of service approached, all I lacked was an exit physical examination and an orientation to civilian life. I had never witnessed such pandemonium than the day of my exit physical. It was held in an old gymnasium and there were over a thousand naked guys eagerly awaiting dismissal so they would be one step closer to going home. Other than the blood test of which I could not ascertain its accuracy, everything else was careless and slipshod. Everyone was moving at great haste. The main thing that happened was someone at each station would take our physical papers and scribble something, and we were moved on down the line. When it came to the hearing exam, we were divided into groups of about twenty-five and placed in an old dressing room adjacent to the gym floor. One guy said, "Everyone please stand up, turn around, and face the wall. After all conformed, he said, "Congratulations, gentlemen, you just passed your hearing test." After I was released from the exam with my exit papers, I realized there was no physician present during the physical, and my papers remained unsigned. No one seemed to care at that point.

On the morning of December 23, I attended the orientation to civilian life meeting. Once again, the meeting was held in an extra-large assembly hall that was packed with attendees. The crowd was rowdy, inattentive, and rude to the speaker. Toward the end of the critique the presenter called for questions. A black dude sitting in the window at the back of the room asked to be recognized. He yelled, "My buddy and I want to know when you are going to shut up so we can go home!" The crowd roared with laughter, embarrassing the presenter who quickly dismissed the crowd of hecklers and offered to remain for any others who had legitimate concerns. The most important point of the meeting was the importance of the DD 214, something I had already learned as a company clerk. I returned to my office and promptly made twenty-five copies of the form and made certain they were in my possession on my trip home. The next two days were terrible at the base. Everyone had gone home but me. I never understood why I had to wait around two more days to be cut loose. Everything on the base was closed including the mess hall. I fed myself out of snack machines as I watched the time slowly pass away.

With nothing to do but watch television, I picked up a pencil and began to compose a brown study about my army experiences. My superiors, including the President as Commander in Chief, had lied to me many times. I had sacrificed the very best of myself to a cause that America now considered shameful. I had just spent thirty months hurrying up and waiting to complete an impossible task that had no clear objective. I had coddiwompled toward an unknown destination, carrying out impossible orders for an ungrateful nation. I was weary from the many miles I had humped carrying too much weight. Still haunted by the atrocities I had witnessed, my nights were filled with images of barren wastelands carved from the terrible weapons of war. I had gazed into too many blazing suns searching for anyone who wanted to render harm to my comrades. I had wrestled with danger far too often. I had choked so much battle smoke into my lungs until the sickening aroma of war had become second nature. I had smelled too much death, witnessed too much destruction, and had consumed too much filth. The eternal roaring in my ears was a constant reminder of the noise of war. I had survived too many nights in holes filled with mud up to my neck. My reward was a broken, scarred body still writhing from the wounds of war. I bitterly realized this was my just recompense because my ability to serve had ended and my duty was done. Little did I realize that my tour of duty in Vietnam would be extended to the rest of the nights of my life since most of those nights would be spent reliving the horror. My injuries were indeed permanent.

That was the way it was. I came home from the army without an enthusiastic welcome from a grateful nation. Instead of celebration I faced contempt. No one said, "Thank you for your service." Many asked, "Why did you do it?" It was as if I had made a terrible mistake risking my life for a futile and unworthy cause. The scorn I faced cut me to the bone. I had prepared myself to be the best soldier possible. I prepared myself to be wounded and I prepared myself to make the ultimate sacrifice if my number was called. I wrote an ungrateful nation a blank check for my life and never disobeyed an order, no matter how ridiculous. However, when I came home, I was not prepared to be ridiculed and forgotten. Feeling badgered, betrayed, and belittled, Hanoi Jane's propaganda hit closer to the truth than the official war account told by the United States. A great cloud of shame now hung heavily over my very being.

Upon my arrival at home, my family surrounded me with love and affection. My brother, Jerry, was also home on Christmas leave from the air force. He would be reporting to Vietnam in the very near future. The first thing I did when I stepped down on the Elmer James property was grab a shotgun, throw my dress uniform hat up in the air, and blow it to smithereens. There was no way I could ever totally explain my utter exasperation to my family. Thankfully, I was safely home, and I wanted the nightmare of my life to be over.

AFTER THE ARMY

I spent the next two years trying to drown my anxiety in alcohol. While spending many long days at Walter Reed, I had spent my time playing pool. When I arrived back in Summertown, I spent most of my nights up on honkytonk hill shooting pool for a beer. My friend, Terry Pierce, and I could beat the socks off the lion's share of the challengers. As a result, we drank a lot of free beer. It was somewhat comical that Terry never developed an affinity for alcohol. Since beer was the prize for winning the game of pool, Terry always ordered Country Club Malt Liquor because, he said, "It was the smallest can of horse piss." The other irony of our friendship was Elmer James held great contempt for Terry Pierce. They had clashed in high school and Elmer was still carrying a grudge against Terry (and probably me as well since I had befriended Terry). Elmer had suspected I was carousing at night, so in order to make me come to my senses, he told me if I expected to sleep under the roof of his house, I would get up with him at 6:00 a.m. sharp. Ouch! That really hurt most mornings.

Summertown had made a great transformation during the

thirty months I had spent in the army. Stephen Gaskin, an often tie-dye-clad hippie philosopher, brought his clan of free thinkers from California to Summertown in 1971. The 320 original settlers pooled their money and decided through group consensus to purchase a 1,750-acre farm and experiment with communal living just like the early church as recorded in the New Testament. On a budget of $1 per person per day, the new settlers bought the land, erected buildings from salvaged wood, found water supplies, and became agriculturally self-sufficient in four years. That meant almost overnight, the unofficial population of Summertown almost doubled. The hippies were politically active and single-handedly reshaped Lewis County politics. All of the young men my age enjoyed seeing the young ladies from the farm because they dressed scantily and never wore bras. When they walked around, their breasts would jump up and down like two baby pigs in a toe sack. Very soon after their arrival in Summertown, the religious leaders from neighboring congregations thought they needed to rescue the hippies from their sinful ways. At one point a televised debate was held with Stephen Gaskin speaking for the Farm, and a minister from a large protestant congregation in Nashville. Stephen's loose interpretations of the scriptures made the minister squirm and became the talk of the town for weeks. The naysayers predicted the Farm would not last through the first winter. Much to everyone's surprise, the Farm flourished and by 1980 at its zenith, the population expanded to more than 1,200. In 1983 the residents took a vote and the communal life lost. In the once cashless society, members started to pay monthly dues. *(10-20-2020: The Farm is still in operation, but its operation is much different from the original experiment. Too many residents of the Farm became freeloaders and were not willing to pay for their fair share.)*

While I was in college and in the army, I had dated Linda Ayers, a Summertown hometown girl. After my army service, I found that she lacked a mutual affection for me. She let me know in a very curious manner, standing me up on our last two dates. The first time I thought it just a misunderstanding. The second time sent me a clear, painful signal. Being forsaken by what I considered a great friend, confidant, and soul mate shook me to my bones and contributed to my new life of self-medication with beer and darvon. I began casually dating a host of young ladies, trying to fill the void in my heart.

I continued on the darvon medication for about five years into civilian life. The VA hospital was happy to load me up with painkillers and periodically remove shrapnel that continued to work its way to the surface of my skin. As time marched on, I noticed I was taking more and more medication to free me from the pain I was experiencing in both legs. Giving into the pain, I began walking with a limp. I had seen several VA doctors about my condition, and all they wanted to do was increase my pain medication. The James family doctor lived across the street in Lawrenceburg from the Parkes family. One day Jim Parkes suggested I pay a visit to Dr. Taylor, who had been a physician during WWII.

Taking his advice, I scheduled an appointment with Dr. Taylor. He walked into the examination room, read my chart, and immediately diagnosed my problem. "You are addicted to the prescribed painkiller. Throw it away and you will get better," he gruffly retorted. "What about my pain?" I asked. "The pain is caused by the medication. It will take six months to get over it. But if you do what I say, you will be cured," he added. Dr. Taylor was exactly correct. I threw away the medication and I was almost completely pain free in six months.

One of my first objectives after returning home was to purchase an automobile. I found a cool 1959 Chevy hardtop with a 283 engine equipped with an automatic transmission. The paint was aquamarine and white, and it was still in relatively good condition. I laid down $500 for the wheels. I drove it almost fifty thousand miles in six months, and it was a really good deal for me. This was the first automobile I had owned in six years, being void of wheels through college and the army.

Needing something to occupy my mind, I decided to enroll in the trade school at Hohenwald and study machine shop. This would give me an income from the GI bill as well as an unemployment check. After three weeks' enrollment at the trade school, I received a call from the Lawrence County Board of Education to report to a teaching job at Ethridge Elementary School teaching English to students in grades six to eight. I really didn't want a real job at the time but decided to take it anyway. Although Elmer did not admit to putting in a word for me at the Lawrence County Central Office, I was confident he was instrumental in the teaching position. The transition to a full-time teaching job was difficult. The first few weeks slowly passed, but soon I managed to get with the program and really began enjoying myself. I worked at making my classes fun and soon found the students responded very well to my teaching methods. The principal thought I was doing a poor job because I did not make the students call me Mr. James. I explained that one very important lesson I learned in the army was titles did not necessarily bring respect. Respect was a two-way street that was earned by showing respect, in my opinion. I vowed that all the poor teachers I had would not be my mentors and set out plowing new ground using what some thought to be radical teaching methods. I spent class time playing games with the students, reinforcing the lesson objectives. If I gave a test and discovered many of the students had scored poorly, I would throw out the exam and reteach the subject, taking responsibility of poor grades being generated by poor teaching. To the principal's surprise, my students scored unusually high on the year-end achievement exams.

The achievement exams caught the attention of the central office, and at the end of my first six months of teaching, I was asked to consider teaching handicapped children at Summertown Elementary School. This appealed to me for a number of reasons. I had tallied a student loan under the National Defense Education Act for $2,500 for my undergraduate studies at Lipscomb. The loan would be reduced by 20 percent each year that I worked as a special education instructor. Secondly, I was given the opportunity to complete a master's degree in special education at no charge by attending summer schools at George Peabody College for Teachers (now Vanderbilt University) in Nashville. The very expensive tuition cost was paid by the Tennessee State Board of Education as an incentive for students to major in special education. I was able to attend graduate school for free since I was also taking advantage of the G.I. Bill, a perk offered to all veterans of the military.

My first purchase after returning to civilian life had been an IBM Selectric electric typewriter for $500. This was a considerable sum of money in 1972, but I knew I needed a very good typewriter since I would be returning to graduate school. It had been three years since I had been a college student and my reintroduction to the study grind was painful. My first class at Peabody required a two-page paper for each class period with a minimum of five sources not more than three years of age. The paper topics were broad, making it ever so difficult to use all the sources and cover the subject in a two-page typewritten paper. I soon discovered most of the classes had similar requirements, meaning writing papers was necessary for the Peabody graduate work. The labor-intensive class preparation soon paid dividends, forcing me to hone my communication skills. By the end of the second summer, I had learned how to play the Peabody game and could complete the multitude of required assignments easily.

I learned many new teaching techniques and I especially focused on learning everything I could learn about teaching elementary reading. I suppose one reason this fascinated me so much was because I was a poor reader in school. Most of the early referrals that were made to special education at Summertown Elementary were related to reading problems. After about a year, I discovered many of the students referred to me were behind in reading because of poor teaching instruction. After three years as a reading resource teacher, most of my students were scoring at or above grade level. Once again, the high test scores caught the attention of the central office. The following year I transferred to a system wide reading specialist position working with reading teachers in grades one through three. I was happy to make a move because I was bored sitting at the back of teachers' rooms and observing poor instruction. While I was a reading specialist, I decided to take a one-year sabbatical to complete a master's degree in administration and supervision at Tennessee State University so that I could be eligible for a principal's position.

Along the way while I was focusing on my teaching career, a curious thing happened. While attending in-service training one summer, I met a beautiful young lady, and immediately fell in love. When I first met her, I was astonished at how much she favored the nurse who tended my wounds while I was a patient at Cam Ranh Bay Hospital in Vietnam. She wore the same hairstyle and beautiful smile and had similar mannerisms as the nurse who I credited for saving my life. It was like a combination of déjà vu and good karma wrapped up in one big, beautiful present. That first afternoon after the training session, I asked her for a date. Her name was Carol Parkes. She had been teaching a couple of years longer than me, and she really enjoyed teaching the fourth grade at the Ingram Sowell Elementary School in Lawrenceburg. She accepted my invitation for a date, and after a whirlwind six-month relationship, we were engaged to be married.

After we began dating, I met her family, and really enjoyed my visits with them. Many afternoons after work I would end up at the Parkes home around suppertime. This was a convenient time for Carol and me, but I had an ulterior motive. Carol's mother was a swell cook, and she was always very gracious to extend an invitation for me to stay for supper which I readily accepted. While Carol and I were dating, I remembered some tips Elmer gave me about choosing a mate. He wisely pointed out that when I married someone, in a small part I was marrying the entire family. If I didn't like the mannerisms of the family, the new relationship would soon wear thin. He also said that I should take a good hard look at the young lady's mother because she would be very much like her mother in years to come. Carol's family was particularly kind and accepting of me from the very beginning.

One trait I especially admired about the Parkes household was the family discussions that allowed a free exchange of ideas and opinions without judgment. This was something I never experienced at home. Elmer either chose to bark orders or he sat stoically, rarely exchanging opinions with the family. Alice Lou was kinder and much easier to engage in conversation, but she would quickly add a short sermon if an alternative opinion was expressed that she did not support.

One opinion Elmer expressed quite frequently with me after I returned home from military service was that he expected me to get up out of bed when he got up. Elmer was an early riser and was up every morning by 6:00 a.m. This was especially difficult for me on weekends when I was dating and getting to bed at a late hour. My ear was trained to hear his footsteps coming up the hall in the mornings. If I did not immediately get out of bed, I was greeted with a quick glass of water to the face. I woke up swimming to what he called the water treatment. I became a quick study to water treatment and learned how to bail out of bed even in a sound sleep. Since I was allowed to live at Elmer's house, I knew I would abide by Elmer's rules.

Another Elmerism I heard many times over the course of my life was when I decided to marry, don't expect to live under his roof. "If you can't afford to keep up a wife and family, you have no business getting married. And don't come to me expecting to find sympathy and handouts!" This may sound somewhat harsh, but I agreed with what he said. Elmer James provided an excellent model of hard work and taking responsibility. I had never known anyone who could hold a candle to Elmer's work ethic. Many weekends as I was about to leave the house, he would say to me, "Remember who you are when you are away from home. You are a James. The James name is respected in this community, and make sure you do your part to see it stays respected, because Jameses are always on their best behavior."

Carol and I had a common interest in loving children. We talked endless hours about how to become more effective teachers by making learning for the students both fun and challenging. We would take long excursion drives throughout the back roads of Lawrence County just for discovery. We mailed each other love notes and talked endlessly so that we could understand each other better. After six months of dating, we were ready to get married. One Sunday afternoon we decided to share the news with our parents. Our first stop was to visit Elmer and Alice Lou. They were sitting in the den at home. Mom was knitting and Pop was reading the Sunday newspaper. After a brief moment of chitchat with Mom, I abruptly changed the subject. "Mom and Pop," I began, "we have an important announcement. After long and careful deliberation, Carol and I have decided to get married." Mom immediately had a pleasant expression on her face, beamed at the news, and offered us her congratulations. Pop never flinched, and stoically remained behind his newspaper. "And furthermore," I continued, "Carol and I have decided to move in with you." With that statement, Pop lowered the newspaper, and quickly entered the conversation. "You are mistaken about that," he countered. "I was just kidding, Pop. I wanted to make sure you were paying attention." "Oh, I have been paying very close attention for a good while! I predict this marriage won't last six months." Carol, Mom, and I just smiled. (*Carol and I recently celebrated our forty-sixth wedding anniversary. It was a fact that Elmer knew me very well. He had underestimated the good nature and golden qualities of a lady who was willing to take me at my worst, post-traumatic stress and all.*) Of course, I had no intention of moving in with Mom and Pop. I just felt it was a perfect opportunity to watch Elmer squirm.

After our short visit with Mom and Pop, Carol and I headed south to Lawrenceburg and deliver the news to Dot and James Franklin. When we arrived, Dot and Jim were in the den watching a baseball game on their portable nineteen-inch television. Carol and I sat down, and I waited for Carol to initiate the conversation about our marriage. We sat there until the baseball game was over, and we waited, and waited, and waited. Finally, Dot announced she was going to bed. We continued to sit, and I nodded to Carol to do something. So, Carol went to the bedroom and summoned Dot to come back to the den. Carol broke the news to her parents with Dot in her pajamas. Both Dot and

Jim seemed very pleased with the announcement. (*Phew! No doubt, I was the most pleased. I had begun to think Carol had changed her mind.*) From that moment forward they accepted, supported, and unconditionally loved me. (*They were the very best in-laws I could have ever imagined.*)

When Carol and I began planning our marriage ceremony, I assured Carol I would support her in all of her decisions about the wedding. Carol wanted a small family wedding at home and convinced her mother that the affair would be limited to close relatives only. Carol asked her sister, Marian, to be her maid of honor and I would invite a best man outside of the family. Elmer agreed to officiate the wedding (for free). Carol and I chose December 21 as the wedding day since it was the last day of school before Christmas vacation. Dot had plenty of experience on hosting parties, and she busied herself making casseroles and desserts to feed the party of 30. Mom, Dot's sister, Mary Kraus, and Jim's sister, Sarah Whitley, assisted in the cooking while my sisters, Becky and Deena, assisted in the serving. Carol invited one friend, Elaine Robertson, and my friend, Terry Pierce, served as my best man.

A few weeks before the wedding, I began shopping for a new suit. Suits in my size were difficult to find in 1973. Becky said she knew a seamstress who could tailor me a suit. One day before the wedding the lady brought the suit to me in Summertown. The suit fit perfectly, but the material reeked with cigarette smoke, and I did not have time to carry it to the cleaners. I call attention to the year once again. This was 1973—a period when fashion was being driven by bold stripes and colors. Carol and I have chuckled about my wedding suit many times. Others have laughed out loud.

Jim Parkes was absolutely delighted with Carol's plan for a small wedding. As a result, a few weeks before the wedding, he invited Carol and me to his garage where a surprise was waiting for us. Jim and Dot had been shopping with the Parkes Lumber Company wholesale supplier, Belknap. For our wedding gift, they had purchased a beautiful cherry bedroom suite made by the Cresent Furniture Company. Carol and I were both shocked and delighted with the expensive gift. Jim said for us not to worry because the furniture was much cheaper than a big church wedding.

On the morning of December 21, it began to snow and schools were closed early. It was a light snow, so Carol and I moved forward with the wedding plans. My brother, Jerry, had taken Christmas leave from the United States Air Force, and was in Summertown with his wife Joan to attend the wedding. Jerry had recently purchased a new single lens reflex camera while stationed in Vietnam, and he was anxious to make plenty of photos of the wedding. He arrived early at Jim and Dot's home and coaxed Carol to get ready quickly so that he could make plenty of photos of the bride. Jerry purchased ten rolls of 35mm film for the occasion, and he intended to finish off all of the ten rolls before the event concluded. Jerry made photos of everything imaginable. He recorded the cooking of the casseroles, the guests arriving, automobiles in the yard, and so on. He made sure the smallest details would live in perpetuity in his Kodak moments. Chris arrived with his camera and Jerry assured Chris this event would only require one professional photographer. Chris sulked, and carried his camera back to his automobile. A few moments later Deena arrived with her dinky Kodak Instamatic 110 camera. Once again Jerry admonished Deena to put her camera away. However, Deena favored her mother so much she would not listen to Jerry and continued snapping a few pics anyway. By the time the event was over, Jerry had finished making all ten rolls of film. The next day he mailed the film to be developed. About a week later we all received a surprise. None of the ten rolls Jerry made developed. He had failed to properly attach the flash to the camera body. Since Deena was a headstrong woman, a few Kodak moments were saved for posterity. (*About ten years later, the young couples at First United Methodist Church had a Valentine's party. Everyone was invited to bring photos of their wedding. Carol and I proudly displayed our 4×4-inch poorly focused Instamatic pics. Needless to say, our photos were the center of attention and won the prize, since we all laugh at the unusual and the unexpected!*)

Carol and I found a cottage to rent right outside of Lawrenceburg on Highway 64 East. The house had a very large yard bordering McLean Creek and the Beeler Fork of Shoal Creek. The house was not in a very good state of repair. A large, three-inch rusty ring encircled the bathtub. When we moved in, we discovered the water in the bath would not drain properly. I made it a priority to do something about the tub. After working with the drain a couple of hours, I finally hooked a pair of men's underwear that had clogged the drain. The following day I spent about four hours scrubbing off the rusty ring. Another problem that I did not address was the leaky roof. We could open a cabinet in the kitchen to reveal blue sky. We merely placed coffee cans in the cabinet to catch the rainwater. It was also my responsibility to mow the lawn. In the spring I went to the hardware store to select a lawn mower. The salesman convinced me the Lawn-Boy brand was the best, so I bought what I could afford—a nineteen-inch push mower. It would take me about four hours each week to mow the grass with the push mower.

While we were renting in Lawrenceburg, Pop was building a spec house in Summertown. Pop agreed to sell the spec house to us for $20,000 while it was under construction. Carol and I chose our paneling, color patterns, and floor covering. Pop also insisted on being our financier. We moved into the new home at the end of June in 1974. The house was located on Highway 20 directly across from the Summertown Baptist Church, and it sat upon a large one-and-a-half-acre lot. Since the house did not have central heat and air, it came equipped with electric wall heaters and a window air conditioner. Carol and I decided not to run the air conditioner the first evening in our new home since it was fairly comfortable with the windows open. After Carol went to the bathroom to prepare for bed, she abruptly ran out frightened to death. I wondered what could be the problem. "There is something making a scary horrible noise in our backyard! Come listen." I accepted her invitation while Carol continued to clinch my hand with fear. As we neared the window, I knew immediately what had frightened my new bride. Directly behind the house and across the fence in our neighbor's pasture was an old stock pond. For the first time, Carol had heard the mating calls of bullfrogs.

On the following Saturday morning, Carol and I were

awakened by what sounded like a tractor in the backyard. Sure enough, I spotted a tractor plowing up the backyard. Pop had decided our yard would make a delightful garden spot, so he had hired a gentleman to prepare a large plowed area behind and at side of our house. Of course, Pop and I had not discussed the wraparound garden. He naturally assumed that I would follow in his garden-tending footsteps. However, after spending most of my summers heeding his directions while working in the family vegetable garden, I had planned to take a break from the endless garden chores. Carol and I remained mum about how we really felt about being surrounded by a garden at our new home. A few weeks later we became aware of another disturbing development concerning our unwanted garden. The plow had decimated our septic line in the backyard, and raw sewage appeared at the top of the ground. All of my savings had been spent buying the new kitchen appliances, window air conditioner, and various household items. I did not have the money at the time to repair the septic line. Billy, the gentleman who did the initial work on the septic line, was a good friend of my brother, Chris. I called Billy to inspect the damage and see if he could find a cheap solution to the problem. After a thorough inspection, Billy said there was no hope in repairing the septic line, and a new one would have to be installed. I convinced Billy to run a temporary pipe that fed into the drainage ditch at the back of the house until I had the funds to make a proper repair. This *temporary* solution alleviated the problem for the time being. (*Carol and I lived there for twelve years, and it seemed I never had the money to properly repair the line. The overflow is probably still draining into the ditch behind the house.*)

WARMING BY THE FIRE

On the adjacent lot next to our house stood a three-room sawmill-type house that we used for storage. The house had a good tin roof and it was sealed well, so it provided room for overflow stuff from the house like canning jars and Christmas decorations. There was also a small barn behind the house and three mature June apple trees. The trees were about twenty-five feet tall, and the trees bore profusely. Of course, many of the apples were bug eaten and fell off the trees when they were immature. Pop and I gathered all of the apples that fell under the trees that were not fit for human consumption, and we carried them to Pop's house where we fed them to his cows and pigs. The pigs were particularly fond of the apples. They soon associated the truck making its way to their pen with apples, and they would celebrate with squeals of anticipation and excitement. Most people have probably observed a dog woofing down his chow. Please know that dogs can't hold a candle to lightning food consumption by pigs. Later in the season around the first of July, the trees would be full of good, mature apples. Mom froze several packages to use in her famous Sunday dinner apple pies. The apples had a naturally tart taste that Mom alleviated with plenty of sugar and butter. The apples also made excellent apple butter that Mom canned as well. Every meal that Mom prepared could be supplemented with something sweet on the side, whether it was jellies and jams of all sorts, apple butter, honey, and/or molasses.

Carol and I had a standing invitation to dine with Mom and Pop every Sunday after church. In the summertime, it was not unusual for Mom to serve half a dozen entrees, most of which were fresh vegetables from the garden. Occasionally we would ride to Lawrenceburg for a sampling of fried catfish or ribeye steak.

Pop owned a Dodge truck he had driven for several years. I was frequently borrowing the truck for various projects. One day Pop offered to give me his truck. "Thanks very much, Pop, for your kind offer, but I would rather you keep the truck," I explained. "Why is that?" Pop wondered. "When I borrow the truck, it is usually full of gas and in good repair," I continued. "Also, if I owned the truck, I would have to buy the insurance and keep up the maintenance," I teased. Elmer failed to see the humor in my explanation. A couple of weeks later, I came by to borrow Pop's truck to discover he had sold it. "How much did you get for the truck?" I asked. "Eighteen hundred dollars cash money," Pop replied with a smile on his face. "Let me get this straight. Since this is the same truck you offered to give me a couple of weeks ago, that would mean the $1800 is actually mine—right?" I reasoned. "You reasoned wrong," Pop continued. "Now, who has had the last laugh?" he asked.

The neighbor's old stock pond behind the house was perfectly located for a quick fishing trip. I could fish the pond in about five minutes. One day after a heavy rain I caught a five-pound bass. I released the fish to see if it could be caught again. I continued the practice of making a quick appearance at the pond after a quick rain. During the course of the next five years, I caught what appeared to be the same fish on several occasions.

Carol and I had come from slightly different religious backgrounds. Carol had been a lifelong member of First United Methodist Church in Lawrenceburg. Her mother's family had been members for many years. Both sets of her great grandparents on her mother's side were members, along with Carol's mother's family and her immediate family. Pop had been a part-time Church of Christ preacher since his graduation from David Lipscomb College, thus my family was entrenched in this religious dogma. I had begun attending Summertown Church of Christ with my family after my separation from the army. Since Carol and I were living in Summertown, we did not want to offend my parents by going to church somewhere other than with them. Carol agreed to join and be baptized into the church with our understanding she would also keep an active membership at First United Methodist Church which we occasionally attended. Carol and I felt this was the perfect arrangement for both of our families.

A couple of years after we had established residency in Summertown across from the Baptist Church on Highway 20, we noticed that a moving van was located at the Baptist parsonage. Carol decided to bake a batch of brownies and carry them to our new neighbors. Later in the afternoon after the moving van had departed, Carol and I walked across the street with brownies in hand to welcome our new neighbors to the community. We were greeted at the door by the new pastor. After exchanging introductions, the pastor inquired if we were members at the Baptist Church.

"No," I replied. "We just wanted to welcome you to the community."

"Do you attend church?" he asked.

"Oh yes," I answered. "We are members at the Summertown Church of Christ."

He looked bewildered. "You aren't Baptists, yet you were the first in the community to welcome us? I find that a little odd."

"Oh, that's not the oddest part," I continued. "In fact, Carol is a member in good standing with two congregations. She is a member of the First United Methodist Church in Lawrenceburg and also the Summertown Church of Christ."

Looking totally astonished, the pastor inquired, "She is?"

"Oh, yes," I added in a teasing manner. "We look at it as a double indemnity insurance policy."

At this point it was obvious our new neighbor was totally flabbergasted and was not amused by my comment. "Well, I'm not convinced that getting one's name on multiple church rolls is the quick route to heaven!" Then in the traditional Baptist fashion, he repeated the sentence again with pastoral diction for emphasis. We excused ourselves and said goodbye. On the way back home, I assured Carol we had just become the pastor's newest sermon illustration.

Our newest friends in Summertown were Leroy and Judy Voss. We had a standing date at our house with the Vosses every Sunday evening. Sometimes, we would grill on the side porch, but most evenings Carol would fix her famous grilled cheese sandwich with tomato soup. When the weather was fitting, Leroy and I would sit on the porch and drink beer while we left the hard work to Judy and Carol. On many occasions we would be sitting on the porch about the same time the Baptists were gathering for the Sunday evening service. One afternoon Leroy asked me what I thought Jesus would think about us drinking a beer about the time the Baptists were gathering for worship. "That's an easy question to answer, Leroy. I will answer your question with a question. Do you know why Jesus's first miracle was turning the water to wine?" Leroy shook his head knowing I would counter with a smart-aleck answer. "Light beer had not been invented yet." At the time Leroy and I were using a tiny hibachi-type charcoal grill somewhat larger than a loaf of bread. In bad weather, we simply placed the grill under the picnic table that sat on the porch. A piece of scrap cardboard would shield the grill from the wind. We usually grilled hamburgers or chicken breasts. Four servings of meat would fit perfectly on the tiny grill.

The following school term in 1976, I was appointed principal at Summertown Elementary School. Carol had transferred to Summertown and was teaching fourth grade there. I tirelessly spent the next six years focusing the teaching staff on classroom instruction and performance. I also initiated an intermural basketball program for boys and girls in grades four through six. It was enthusiastically embraced by the community, and before long the old gymnasium stayed open for extended hours every day of the week. The league began with six boys' teams and four girls' teams. The only expense requirement for the children was to wear a good pair of sneakers. Matching tee shirts were provided to teams, and kids who could not afford a shirt had the cost covered by the team, interested individuals, or the school. The only rule I insisted be added to the charter was that every member of the team was to play for at least one quarter each game. Expenses for the league were covered through profits of the concession stand that was manned by parents of the children participating in the league. (*I am writing this in 2020, and the basketball league is continuing to go strong.*)

The dilapidated gymnasium at the school had an interesting

and unique history. In the 1930s, community interest arose to provide an indoor gymnasium for basketball games. Pop was a student at Summertown High School at the time. Indoor basketball gymnasiums were scarce as hen's teeth at the time. Most of the gyms that did exist were small and the ceilings for the building were too low to shoot a basketball any great distance. Since local county funds were nonexistent during the depression, several community meetings resulted in a solution to building a gymnasium. A series of fundraisers were held and after a great community effort, $3000 was raised for the gym construction project. Trees were logged and milled locally to provide the lumber, and Will Black, a Summertown community leader, was appointed as overseer of the project. Free labor for the construction was provided through the local WPA office, and construction soon began. Another unique characteristic of this construction was that Will Black did not have any drawn plans for the facility. This building was literally a creation of Mr. Black's imagination. After the building was completed, leaders came from adjoining communities to study the facility and duplicate the building. The original gymnasium was heated with a freestanding coal stove that stood in the middle of the building on the north side. One night in the 1940s when Summertown was playing Loretto, a Loretto player (Kenneth Jones) slid into the stove and turned it over. There was a mad rush to pick up the hot coal bricks that had fallen onto the floor and reset the stove.

Another project I initiated as principal was to improve the physical education program. I spent a great deal of the profits from the school's annual fund drives on equipment for the PE program. For the first time, we had balls for all sports. Also, we had jump ropes so that every student had his own rope during PE. We wore out more ropes during those six years than anyone could imagine. In the spring, I held a special assembly program, allowing teams and individuals to show their rope jumping skills. Many of the teachers also participated to the delight of their children.

During my second year as principal, the Lawrenceburg Elementary Athletic Conference was formed of the four K-6 schools in Lawrenceburg and Summertown Elementary School. This gave our students an opportunity to compete in softball, basketball, and track. I approached the road superintendent at the time, Dave Curtis, to provide machinery and labor to build a quarter-mile track on the school grounds. The school raised the money for asphalt for the track activities by collecting scrap aluminum. I will never forget walking in the school during the aluminum drive and smelling the scent of stale beer.

My greatest emphasis for the academic program was to improve the students' reading comprehension skills. This was accomplished with longer reading classes along with stockpiling fun books in the school library. This was a very expensive undertaking, but well worth the investment. Special recognition was given to student improvement and academic excellence. Test scores improved dramatically.

After my second year as principal at Summertown Elementary School, the school board offered me the principal position at Summertown High School. I respectfully declined the offer for several reasons. I was enjoying my job at Summertown Elementary School, and I would not seriously consider the position because my Pop was still teaching there. I suppose the school board did not care about nepotism, but I could see many problems with the move. Summertown High School and Summertown Elementary School jointly shared a cafeteria that was placed in the middle of the adjoining campuses. The cafeteria staff had a county-wide reputation of providing the most excellent tasty meals. It was important that both schools stay on their allotted lunch times so that students at both schools could be fed in a timely manner. I would spend extra time in the cafeteria to ensure the classes were being served on the scheduled time. One day while I was in the cafeteria, Vivian Shields approached me. Vivian was a monument at Summertown High School. She had begun teaching right out of high school and continued to teach forty-five-plus years. In fact, she was teaching when Pop graduated from high school, and she was present while the six James children were students there. The high school principal position had not yet been filled and I am sure Vivian had heard the rumor the job had been offered to me. Vivian and I had little to talk about since neither of us had respected each other. Despite our differences, Vivian approached me anyway and asked, "Sid, why don't you move up with us?"

"Excuse me?" I asked.

Vivian stated again, "Sid, why don't you move up with us?"

"I do not consider the principal job at SHS a move upward."

I could tell immediately my response had galled her because she quickly turned around and sat down. About a week later, Vivian approached me in the cafeteria again, but with a new question. "Sid, your behavior has been especially disconcerting to me since you were in high school. I request that you now answer this question truthfully, because this has pained me for many years. Why did you glue all of the cards in the card catalog together with mucilage?"

Being surprised and confused by her accusation, I asked her to repeat the question.

"Oh, I know you did it. I just wanted to see if you had matured enough to admit to your mendacious behavior!"

"Let me speak clearly, Miss Vivian. I never glued your cards together, nor was I part of a group involved in this scandalous prank. However, your revelation explains why you treated me with vindictive contempt when I was your student. Had I known you had been harboring contempt for me these twelve years since my high school graduation, I would have gladly glued the cards together. It makes me regretful that I could not take credit for this misdeed." That was the last time the two of us ever spoke.

The majority of my days as principal at Summertown were absolutely delightful. However, major events that cause me heartache remain firmly etched in my mind. The single greatest mistake of my teaching career happened in 1977, the year Tennessee teachers were granted the right to collective bargaining with local boards of education. I was approached by the local teachers' union and asked if I would be willing to serve as the chief negotiating officer on the teachers' team. Without anticipating the challenges and future ramifications of the decision, I accepted. It took a total of five years to get the first teachers' contract agreed upon by the teachers and board of education. During the time of negotiation, I received numerous telephone threats at home and at school. I was visited by several members of the board who told me they planned to transfer me to Iron

City if I did not step down as negotiator. Other acts of intimidation followed that affected almost all the teachers.

The first thing the board did was hire a cocky, loudmouthed goon out of Chicago as their negotiator. Since this was unlawful, the teachers refused to recognize him at the negotiating table. The second form of intimidation was to dismiss all of the nontenured teachers. The teachers' union took the local board to court and forced them to change tactics. After that, the action by the board was more subtle. One night during a negotiating session, someone ran over my car with what appeared to be a farm truck. Ouch. That cost me $600 for an out-of-pocket repair bill. One of the northern Lawrence County Board members was particularly aggressive toward me and brazenly promised my next assignment would be teaching at Iron City. He was up for election the following summer, and I went door to door in the Northern District to campaign for a fair-minded candidate. There were five candidates in the race for two seats. To my delight, my agitator finished fifth in the race. I regretted many times accepting the negotiating position, because it painted a large target on my back by board members who abhorred the idea of collective bargaining. I knew some of the board members would not rest until they felt the score with me had been settled.

Another episode that caused me great personal pain occurred one day when I was visited by the supervisor of elementary education. She said a kindergarten parent had approached her and detailed a sexual episode that had allegedly occurred between her son and me in the school office. She claimed that I had pulled the boy's pants down in the bathroom and had jabbed a pencil up his rectum. An immediate investigation took place with the supervisor interviewing the student, the kindergarten teacher, and me. Fortunately, the child had made only one trip to the office, and that was with the entire class and the teacher to help orient the new students at the first of the school term. After the investigation, the supervisor reported the results with everyone involved, but the mother held firmly to the allegations. Soon the community became involved with rumors surrounding the incident. A few school board members discussed it publicly at a board meeting as well. Being surrounded by whispers was incredibly painful for Carol and me. The detail of the child's accusation left little doubt in my mind he had been molested by someone. After a few weeks, the event began to settle. That following summer while I was in summer school at MTSU, the supervisor called Carol to inform us the mother and family had dismissed the charges against me because they had found the real person who had sexually abused the boy. While I was home the following weekend, I received a visit from the mother. "I wish to apologize for the accusations I made toward you concerning my son. I now know this was a false accusation, and I am sorry for the pain I might have caused you. Is there anything else I could do to make this right?"

"Yes, please do this for me. Use your same energy and zeal to tell everyone you have talked to about me that you made a mistake. Especially talk to the school board members you called with your complaint and to the school superintendent." I continued, "I forgive you for your error. I recognize how hard it is to not act upon something your child told you with such detail. I do not plan to sue you for defamation of character, but please help me clear my name." Ouch, that was so painful!

Another incident living vividly in my mind involved a student who did not want to come to school. His attendance had been poor throughout school, but when he was in fourth grade his absence from school became excessive. He missed about forty-five days of school that term, causing him to repeat the grade. After two years in the fourth, he was socially promoted to the fifth. In fifth grade his absenteeism became worse and he missed over seventy days that year. After repeating the fifth, his absenteeism grew even worse. I called the attendance officer and asked him to intervene. Instead, the officer asked me to make a home visit. I was plowing new ground when I went to visit the young man at home. When I knocked on the door, the mother invited me in, and we had a very cordial conversation that seemed encouraging to me.

That afternoon I had to remain after school to catch up on some pressing paperwork due in the central office. About 4:30 p.m., I heard a knock on the front door. The boy's father was there and wanted to discuss his son's attendance with me. After inviting him in, I realized the man had been drinking, and he was quite inebriated at the time. He flew into a rage because his wife told him that I had broken into their home and I had made amorous gestures toward her. His wife told him that when she went to the kitchen, she was surprised to see me sitting at her table. Furthermore, the man said he had a pistol in his pocket, and he had come to school with the express purpose of shooting me dead. I began engaging in some of the fastest and most persuasive talk in my life. After about thirty minutes, the man had calmed down and he assured me he would personally bring his son to school the following day.

The next morning around 9:00 a.m., the man returned to my office to report his son was in the car, but he couldn't get him out of the car. He asked for my assistance. The two of us returned to his car and found his son in the front seat with the car doors locked. After about 15 minutes of coaxing, the boy agreed to open the door but remained frozen to his seat in the car. I reached into the front seat to pick him up out of the seat when his father said, "Don't you hurt him!" I quickly let go and went back to the office, leaving it to the father to deliver the child into the school. After about 15 minutes, they drove off together. The child did not return to school for the remainder of the school term. As a result, the boy was retained again for excessive absence.

Between terms the following summer while I was working at school, I was visited by the attendance officer and the high school principal. He had been assured by the child's parents he would indeed attend school regularly if we promoted him to the seventh grade. Everyone agreed to this novel approach since nothing else we had tried was working. The following term the absenteeism continued where it left off the year before. Finally, the attendance teacher and the juvenile judge sent the young man to the Tennessee Preparatory School (TPS) in Nashville.

Around Christmas, he was released from TPS with new transcripts that indicated he had been promoted to the ninth grade. In one semester the young man managed to move from the fifth to the ninth grade. Once again, his absenteeism began. Since he was nearing his seventeenth birthday, he was allowed to quit school. Within six months the young man was before the juvenile judge on grand larceny charges resulting in incarceration. I learned valuable lessons from this experience. Home visits and parent conferences would require two people so that another adult could back up events that took place at the conference. Secondly, I learned how important my memos and personal documentation became. Personal memos were a pain to record, but they were invaluable when an incident would be recalled in the future.

The worst mistake I ever made also occurred during my early years as principal. One cold February morning it began snowing after school had begun. After about forty-five minutes of heavy snow, approximately two inches had accumulated. The expected call from the central office concerning a shortened school day never came. Bus drivers were becoming unglued. Parents were in a panic. Out of desperation I called the central office and asked to speak with the superintendent. He was out of town at a meeting and could not be reached. After speaking to the person the super had left in charge, he informed me that it was not snowing very much in Lawrenceburg, and there was no snow south of Lawrenceburg. I reported the bedlam at Summertown and requested instruction. "Well, Sid," he began, "It looks like you are going to have to use your good judgment." I called the high school principal and we agreed it would be prudent to close school early.

Around noon, we dismissed both schools in the middle of a blowing snowstorm. Around 2:30 p.m., a curious phenomenon occurred. The sky cleared, the wind and snow ceased, and the sun began melting the snow. By 3:00 p.m. the roads were completely clear and only a small amount of snow clung to the shady areas. That afternoon I received a blistering call from the super reminding me of one of the famous lines from *Gone with the Wind*. "It's quitting time!" "You ain't the boss, I's the boss. I says when it's quitting time! It's quitting time!" I never made that mistake again! As payback, the coal-fired furnace at school petered out one cold winter day. The superintendent dismissed the students from school the following day while the boiler was repaired, but he ordered all of the teachers to be present. The faculty hovered closely around two small electric heaters in the library. The temperature inside the library remained below forty degrees the entire day. At 3:00 p.m. the superintendent called to make certain none of the teachers had made an early exit.

In 1978, after Carol and I had been married five years, our first child, Lara, was born. I celebrated at school by passing out Tootsie Roll Pops to faculty, staff, and student body. Carol began an extended leave of absence to help raise the family. In 1981, Carol and I celebrated the birth of our second child, Leslie. Once again, I had the honor of inviting everyone at Summertown Elementary School to the celebration with Tootsie Roll Pops. Carol was a fabulous mother to the children. She made certain the children received a variety of early childhood instruction before they started to school.

It was two weeks before Lara's third birthday celebration when Leslie was born. In 1981 children were not allowed to enter the maternity ward of the hospital. On the second afternoon after Leslie's birth, I carried Lara around to the outside window of Carol and Leslie's room. When Carol neared the window holding the sleeping Leslie who was tightly wrapped in a new blanket, she opened the window to allow Lara close inspection. Lara exclaimed, "Weswee, Weswee, wake up. I am your sister, Wawa.

Weswee, speak to me." Leslie was an unusually quiet infant in the hospital. In fact, Leslie didn't cry when Dr. Qualls gave her a pat on the bottom at her birth. For the first week of life, Leslie did not utter a cry. Unexpectedly the following evening when Carol was changing her diaper, Leslie let out a bloodcurdling scream reminiscent of the eerie sound of a female bobcat in heat. At the moment of the scream, Lara came running into the bedroom inquiring, "What's that noise! What's that noise!"

Our children have always been the crowning moment of our life. Luckily, both children received a lion's share of their DNA from their mother. Carol and I could not have programmed sweeter, kinder, thoughtful, articulate, intelligent, beautiful children. At the moment of their birth, they became the center of our lives. They rarely left our side until they were old enough to realize their parents were actually dorks. The kids had the advantage of living close to both sets of grandparents who were eager to participate in their everyday lives. Mom shared her appreciation of nature and Carol's mom shared her appreciation of cooking. Carol's dad enjoyed teasing the kids, and even Pop showed an unusual fondness toward the kids as well. Pop introduced the kids to the livestock and his beautiful garden. He would allow them to help gather apples and grapes from the orchard. Carol's dad enjoyed taking the kids to his woodworking shop in the backyard where he allowed them to help drive nails in boards and build toys.

When Lara was nearly two years old, we were visiting the Parkes grandparents. Carol's dad invited Lara to sit in his recliner, and accidently pinched Lara's finger in the seat shift. As Lara was being consoled about her boo-boo she announced,

"I'm telling Santa Claus not to bring Big Daddy any presents this year." I purchased a La-Z-Boy recliner soon after we married that was especially designed for big and tall people. I was impressed at how well it matched my lanky body, and I was further impressed the chair carried a lifetime warranty. Also, the chair was covered in the exotic hide of a Nauga! (*I have owned the chair since 1974. It has lived through two upholsteries, and it remains one of my favorite possessions. I figure that the warranty has not expired because I'm not dead yet.*) One day after work I noticed five toothpicks had been neatly inserted in the seat cushion. "Lara, do you know anything about these toothpicks in my recliner?" "Uh huh," she replied. "Do you know who did this?" I asked. Quite sheepishly Lara answered, "It was my imaginary friend, Charlie Brown."

Leroy and Judy Voss adopted our children as their own. They shared in all of the firsts of the girl's lives. They were there for the first teeth, the first steps, the first words, and most certainly all of their birthday and Christmas celebrations. When Lara was about two years old, Judy and Leroy had come over for the usual Sunday afternoon social. As they walked through the door, Lara gave Leroy this familiar greeting: "Hello, Leroy! Do you want a beer?" A few weeks later Leroy introduced us to a new restaurant. After we ordered from the menu, we noticed that the service was unusually slow. After about forty minutes and no food, a waitress came by our table. To everyone's surprise, Lara stopped the waitress and asked, "Excuse me, where is our food?" One summer afternoon when Leslie was about two years old, Leroy and I took the children fishing at a neighbor's stock pond. The small fish provided abundant entertainment for the girls. It was a full-time job keeping the hooks baited and the little fish removed. Lara kept a tally of the number of fish she caught. When the fishing trip was over, Lara announced to Carol and Judy that she had caught the most fish. Since Leslie had not learned to count, she chimed in, "Yes, but I caught the biggest fish."

From infancy through childhood both children inherited my early childhood illnesses. Almost every weekend we ran to Dr. Qualls's office. He prescribed many bottles of pink medicine (amoxicillin) to treat strep throat, croup, ear infections, and tonsillitis. No doubt, Leslie was the queen of tonsillitis. She was having constant problems until she had her tonsils removed when she was in the fourth grade.

During our morning routine with the children when Leslie was a baby, I would feed and entertain Leslie while Carol took her morning shower. I would place Leslie in an infant seat on the dryer in the utility room where I would shave in the mornings. This arrangement worked satisfactorily until Leslie grew larger. One morning while I was shaving, Leslie did a head plant off the dryer onto the floor. Carol and I immediately carried her to the doctor's office. Dr. Qualls did not find any serious damage from the fall, but he assured us she would have a shiner the following morning. Sure enough, Leslie's eye was swollen shut the next day. I made a photo progression of Leslie's black eye. When Leslie was kindergarten age, she fell off a counter in the office at Coffman and broke one of her front teeth. I felt awful that both of her boo-boos had occurred under my less-than-watchful eye.

Another curious quirk about the kids as infants: Lara loved milk, and Carol and I wondered if we were ever going to fill her up. From the day we brought Leslie home from the hospital, she would not take a bottle. The first time Chris visited us at home after Leslie's birth, he recognized Leslie's hunger cry. He showed us how to create a thin mixture of formula and rice cereal. Eventually Leslie began swallowing the pabulum and became satisfied. We continued her on the regimen until she was old enough to eat solid food. Carol and I worried about Leslie not drinking any milk until she was old enough to swallow liquid. At that moment, Leslie became the milk drinker, requesting a glass of milk before she went to bed every night. On the other hand, Lara abruptly ceased drinking milk when she was about two years old.

Our house in Summertown contained 1,300 square feet. It felt really large until the children were born. All of a sudden, our spacious home seemed cramped. The kids' toys required a large portion of the floor space. The problem was partially solved by carrying the excess of toys to the empty house next door we called Wal-Mart. Soon after we adopted the practice, the kids began missing certain toys. In order for them to retrieve a toy from Wal-Mart, they had to temporarily exchange it with a toy from the house. Lara had no problem with this arrangement, but it was very difficult for Leslie to make the exchange. One day after an exchange, with a sad face Leslie exclaimed, "I feel like I just lost my best friend."

When the kids came along, I was fearful the children would develop the early reading problems that plagued me as a child. Carol and I were determined the kids would be good readers. We began reading to the children from the very beginning. When the children were old enough to sleep in a regular bed, I would read them to sleep every night. Leslie had no problem falling to sleep, but it was difficult for Lara to become comfortable. The reading routine seemed to help Lara relax. Most evenings I would lay down with them and read at least three books. The Disney *Little Golden Books* were their favorites, and *The Haunted House* was their number one requested book. Sometimes I would attempt to speed up the nightly ritual by paraphrasing the words on the page. It didn't take long for the kids to protest. "That's not what it says, Daddy." This gave me a wonderful opportunity to allow them to correct me. Using my finger to point to the words, they soon could pick out frequently used words. I would also allow them to finish the words at the end of the sentence. One day at school I discovered a set of the old primers that were used to teach me to read when I attended first grade. Lara was very eager to learn to read the books since they were part of my childhood. Very soon, she mastered the first book in the series called *Tip*. She proudly read it to the grandparents and Judy and Leroy. The children especially loved sitting in Leroy's lap in the oversized rocking chair in the kitchen. His avuncular charm earned him the title of "Uncle Leroy." He read to them constantly when they were toddlers. The kid's most requested book was *The Diggingest Dog*. The book was eventually in tatters after years of loving use.

About twice daily Carol taught Lara and Leslie to watch *Sesame Street* on television. By shaping the kid's behavior, she was able to teach them to watch the program by themselves. This freed Carol to complete household chores while the kids were entertained by the *Sesame Street* characters. As the children's reading skills progressed, Carol taped index cards with names of all the objects in the house. Words like refrigerator, washer, dryer, cabinet, table, telephone, etc. soon became etched into the children's memory. We played a multitude of games using sets of flash cards about word families like rhyming words and words from the Dolch Sight Word list. As a result, both children have no recollection of learning to read. Reading was just a natural part of their childhood development like walking and talking.

As the cold winter months passed and the weather warmed, the kids would beg to play outdoors. They loved playing on the swing set and in the little doll cottage that Jim Parkes had built for their cousin, Emily. Adjacent to the doll cottage was a sand bed that included homemade excavation equipment. We would play for hours at a time. In the spring we would take adventures in the yard to search for birds' nests and seek insects crawling about the yard. I encouraged them to focus on the flowers, collect and identify tree leaves, and learn the call of the birds, toads, and frogs.

A favorite summer pastime was to take the kids minnow trapping. During their afternoon nap, I would set the minnow traps in streams nearby. As soon as they had awakened, we made a mad dash to the streams to check the traps for minnows, snail darters, crayfish, and the like. The children soon became inured to all of the inhabitants of the stream and were not afraid to handle the mixture of unusual critters. It took them a little extra time to warm up to the crawdads (crayfish) because they would pinch if they were given an opportunity.

Another fun adventure was to check all the bird boxes for new nests. We would mark the weekly progress of the clutches that had hatched. Occasionally we discovered flying squirrels building nests in the bluebird boxes. The kits had sharp claws used to grasp the kids' shirts. As the kits began to mature, they would run up the kids' necks and eventually park in their hair.

I bought a martin box a few years after we married, and we had great success attracting purple martins to the yard and nesting box. One Sunday afternoon in March while Leroy and Judy were visiting, we decided it was time to take the martin box out of the barn and erect it for the new brooding season. As Leroy and I began to push the box into the prepared hole, a martin landed on the box even before the pole was attached to the ground. We raised a bumper crop of martins every year while we lived in Summertown. (However, I never had any luck attracting them to our home on Quail Drive in Lawrenceburg.)

On especially warm days the back porch would be equipped with a small swimming pool. Oh yay! This provided endless entertainment because the porch was shielded from the westerly sun. When Lara was kindergarten age, Carol and I enrolled the children in beginning swim lessons at Mount Pleasant. Building upon their comfort in the water, the following year we enrolled them in swim lessons at Rotary Park in Lawrenceburg. Both girls soon became water dogs and loved the visits to the swimming pool.

While Carol was home raising the children, money was always tight. I picked up a little extra money by working as a homebound teacher after regular school hours. I would meet with homebound students for two, one-and-a-half-hour sessions each week. Homebound students were diagnosed by a medical doctor as being too sick to attend school. I worked with kids with broken bones and other childhood diseases, but occasionally I would work with children with behavior disorders. One snowy winter, one of the fourth grade boys decided he didn't want to come to school any more. I met with the student and the mother one afternoon to see if we could find a solution to the boy's excessive absence. During the meeting, the boy suggested that he needed to be placed on the homebound roster. He promised to be cooperative, but he understood if he became uncooperative, he would be placed in regular school again. I had my doubts this would actually work, but he and his mother seemed to be motivated to give it a whirl. As fate would have it, I was chosen by the central office to serve as his homebound teacher. I received the assignment on a day that it had snowed six inches and regular school was dismissed. I phoned the mother to report I was going to begin his homebound classes that afternoon. The house was located on a rural road that had not been treated for the snow. The mother feared I could not make it to her house. "Did your husband go to work this morning?" I asked. "If he did, I think I won't have much trouble getting there." I loved the challenge of driving on slick roads anyway. When I arrived at the house, the boy was befuddled about having school on a snow day. However, he kept his promise and reluctantly participated in the first session. At the end of the lessons, I made assignments which would be checked at the next session in two days. "But schools are closed! Why do I have to continue to work on my assignments?" he asked. "Because you are a homebound student," I replied.

Upon my return to the home the back roads were still covered in snow. It appeared schools would remain closed for a few more days. As I arrived at the house, I sat down at the kitchen table waiting for the boy to join me. "My son is in his bedroom, and he said he was not going to participate anymore," the mother reported. Since I was already there, I asked the mother to retrieve her child from the bedroom. As I sat waiting the altercation between the mother and child escalated into a howling, screaming crescendo! The knock-down, drag-out fight continued for about five minutes. The mother returned with her hair mussed and her clothing in tatters. "He just about broke my arm in his bedroom door, and I could not make him come to the kitchen! Mr. James, if you will allow him to return to school, he will be there the first day after the snow breaks," the weeping mother declared. I agreed. The boy was miraculously cured, and his truancy problem ceased.

I also made extra money in the summer selling World Book Encyclopedias. I had great success in selling the books for several summers. (Oh, how the times have changed. Hardly anyone consults the opinion of an encyclopedia since the invention of personal computers and the World Wide Web.) I recall one afternoon I stopped by to see a friend of mine from Summertown High School. He and his wife were very polite and social. They invited me in and respectfully listened to my sales pitch. One of my selling points was there was a strong correlation between using World Book at home and achievement in school. When I asked for feedback my friend quickly dismissed the need for the books because he thought they would create more harm than good. I had never heard someone refuse to buy because of the harm the books might cause, so I asked him to explain further. "Sid, I want my children to go through school and be just a little bit dumb. I have noticed that high achieving students go to college and many never return home to live close to their parents. I would rather my kids be just a little bit dumb and remain close to my wife and me." I couldn't argue, because I knew he was right. The good-paying jobs were not in Summertown, Tennessee.

When the girls were old enough for potty training, Carol and I bought a special gift that we wrapped in beautiful paper. The gift was placed on top of the refrigerator out of their reach. Lara's gift was a Fisher-Price Cash Register, and Leslie's gift was a walking doll called Baby Skates. We explained the gift could not be opened until they had success in the potty. It was a red-letter day that required abundant enthusiasm on our part when the successful day arrived. When the children retired for a nap or bedtime, the toy was placed back on top of the fridge, and another successful potty performance was required to retrieve the special gift. As a result, special toys that required performance on the girls' part soon became among their all-time favorite gifts.

When Lara was a little over two years old, she accompanied me in the yard to retrieve rocks that had been dug up over the septic line. I encouraged Lara by giving her 25 cents for every five-gallon bucket she would gather, and I would allow her to spend her own money on a toy that met her budget. With my encouragement and to my utter surprise, she picked up twenty five-gallon buckets! We made a special trip to Lawrenceburg so that Lara could shop. Lara studied all of the toys with great deliberation, and she eventually decided on a cute rodeo truck that included a horse, saddle, and driver/horse rider. The truck combo remained one of Lara's most precious possessions.

After six years as principal at Summertown Elementary, the student body doubled their reading and comprehension scores and made substantial gains in the other test areas. I had really enjoyed my role as principal at Summertown, but I was about to embark upon a new journey that I expected to be challenging. I secretly hoped I would measure up to the task.

LAWRENCEBURG

In 1984 when Leslie was three years old, Carol decided to return to work so we would have enough collective money to build a house on our new lot in Lawrenceburg. Lara would enter first grade at Lawrenceburg Public School and Leslie would enter extended care at First Presbyterian Preschool. I had accepted a new position as principal at Coffman Middle School, and Carol had accepted a position as a Title 1 reading teacher at Five Points Elementary School. The whole family was plowing new ground, and Carol and I wondered if we were putting too much stress on the children. Our daily school routine became much more complicated. Our day began at 4:30 a.m. Carol and I would shave and shower, carry the sleeping children to the auto and drive to 620 First Street in Lawrenceburg. Carol's mother would fix our breakfast while Carol and I dressed the children for school. At 6:50 a.m. Carol would depart for her sixteen-mile journey to the Five Points school. I would depart with the children at 7:00 a.m. and drop the children off at their schools. Poor little Leslie clocked a long nine-hour day each school day at the preschool. Lara would walk two blocks from the old Public School to Coffman each afternoon and would remain in the office with me until I finished my work. The change was hard on everyone. According to the kids, the one positive that came out of our disruptive lives was we had the privilege of dining at McDonalds every school day. In fact, both Lara and Leslie wanted their birthday party to be at McDonalds. We would make it back to Summertown just in time for bed.

I was appointed as principal at Coffman one week before the beginning of the school term. When I drove up to the campus, I was flabbergasted at the poor condition of the school campus. I counted eight dead trees, noted a large erosion gully by the gym, and could not believe the grass had not been mowed all summer. The grass on the football field was waist high. Large potholes filled the parking areas around the school, and there were no sidewalks adjacent to the city streets. More surprises were in store as I entered the building. All of the floors were dirty, and the restrooms reeked with the odor of urine. When I walked into the office, mail was piled three feet high on an old counter. I walked into the teachers' lounge to discover the residue of a going-away party with a half-eaten cake infested with flies. On my first tour of the classrooms, I found one janitor fast asleep on top of a library table. The other janitor was AWOL. In a quandary I hurriedly backed my car out of the parking lot and smashed the fender of the cafeteria manager's car for good measure. What was I thinking? I left a school in excellent shape after six years of improvements to inherit the largest mess in the county. The school had a poor reputation in the community, and I certainly understood why from my first brief visit.

On my first official day at work, I began looking for a

secretary. I hired a lady the next day who I felt would do an adequate job. We worked tirelessly sorting the mail and straightening the office. The phone was ringing off the hook. On the day before the opening of school, she quit. (*Oh, how I wished I could also walk away from the mess!*) Although I did not feel the next secretary was up to the job, at least she was punctual, willing to learn, and could begin work immediately.

My first meeting with the faculty was also a surprise. During the meeting, a few of the ladies excused themselves to a back table in the library and lit up cigarettes and chatted among themselves during the meeting. I was schooled by several of the teachers to not make any fast changes. They assured me the poor reputation of the school in the community was undeserved, and the teachers knew how to run a good school without the interference from the principal. I agreed to hold off on changes until I had adequate time to observe. I would wait until the end of the school term before I would make any major changes. After all, I was the new guy on the block, and the teachers were not familiar with my leadership style.

The first week of school was horrible. School continued for everyone even though the school plant was under major reconstruction. After student registration, it was obvious there were not enough classrooms to house the students. When I brought this to the attention of the superintendent, he replied, "Sid, you are a smart fellow. Just figure something out."

"How am I going to come up with another classroom out of thin air?" I retorted.

"It's your job to get it done. Come hell or high water, I order you to take care of the problem!" I had not been given an impossible order like this since my days in Vietnam, but I was determined to think outside the box to arrive at a solution. I called the local National Guard unit and asked if I could borrow a large tent. After a long laugh, they agreed to erect a tent on the front lawn of the school campus. My next call was to the newspapers. I invited them to report on the less than adequate accommodations made for our incoming students. Class was held in the army tent for almost all of the first semester. Classroom accommodations were being made in the old alumni gymnasium. Although less than adequate because of the constant noise in the gym, it was much better than spending the colder days of the school year in a tent.

My next large logistical problem was student desks. I reported to central office that I needed thirty additional student desks. The supervisor laughed, stating there were no extra desks. That afternoon I drove to the school bus shop and noticed a shed full of broken desks. I began sifting through the desks and by borrowing and sharing pieces from the discards I was able to come up with enough junk desks to adequately serve. Then I borrowed a truck from Parkes Lumber Company and hauled them back to the Coffman campus. The next morning, I received a call from the superintendent. "Who gave you permission to retrieve desks from the bus shop?" he asked. "No one, sir," I replied. "I was a smart man and just figured it out." That ended the conversation.

About a week later, the superintendent paid me a visit. He wanted to conduct a walk-through building inspection. The last place he wanted to visit was the basement of the gymnasium. I had not been in any area of the gym basement but the football dressing rooms. He wanted to explore the old woodshop area from the LCHS days before 1970. Among the scattered junk were a few items that I considered valuable. The Superintendent looked at me and said, "I want this basement cleaned out. Get rid of everything down here."

"What would you like me to do with this stuff?" I asked.

"I don't care what you do with it, just get rid of it," he snapped! Shazam! Just like that, I became the owner of several very nice woodworking tools that included a large Delta band saw and several wood vises. There was also a giant 1000 amp electrical can among the goodies. My friend, Terry Pierce, was in the process of building electrical hookups for campers at the family's bluegrass music park in Summertown. He was delighted to take the expensive electrical can off my hands. (*As a result, the kids received free passes to the bluegrass events for many years, and I continue to use the band saw and wood vises in my shop here at home.*)

During the course of my first year at Coffman, the superintendent and I locked horns over the ongoing building program at the school. Although approved by the board, the superintendent slashed the building program at every opportunity. For starters, he reduced the architect's hall width dimensions by four feet. It was total bedlam when the bell rang for classes to change because there was not enough room for the kids to navigate. We were forced to reroute some of the classes to the outside walks. When we moved into the school, no accommodations were made for a telephone or intercom system in the office. The school quickly raised $5,000 to pay for these needed items. Furthermore, the superintendent omitted the cost for the new dining room floor covering stating the current covering was adequate. The current covering was installed in 1948, and many of the floor tiles were missing or loose. The superintendent was going to attend an open house for the new facility, and the parents were invited to assemble in the dining room. In preparation for the meeting, I wielded a hoe to remove the loose tiles in a large 20×20-foot area right in front of the doorway. When the superintendent arrived, the parents began to question him about the floor covering in the dining room. He reluctantly conceded to place the flooring back into the plan.

"Same song, second verse, it can't get better, so it's going to get worse." Among the factors in our major family upheaval, we were also in the midst of building a new house. We broke ground on September 15, 1984. The goal was to have the roof on the house before Thanksgiving. Trusting the wise counsel of Carol's dad, we trudged forward. Unfortunately, two factors disrupted our plans: deer season and the use of unusual materials in the house framing. Jim had on hand at the lumber company a great deal of pine shiplap siding which we could purchase at a fraction of the cost of plywood sheeting and decking. He theorized we could turn the siding inside out and use the material for sheeting and decking, and it would make a good strong frame. He was right on both accounts. However, we did not consider how labor-intensive the project would be. Many beautiful dry days of October were wasted on hunting deer instead of house framing by the carpenters. Soon the cold windy days of November and December came, and the house frame was incomplete. I would visit the job site many days at lunch to make a quick inspection on the progress to find the workers huddled around burning barrels trying to stay warm. This ate at the very fabric of my soul. Eventually, the new roof was in place to shield the house from the weather. Unfortunately, substandard shingles created a twelve-year nightmare for me as I constantly attempted to reseal the flopping shingles. Finally, we moved into the new house in September of 1985. Jim had done a great job keeping the materials cost as low as possible. Unfortunately, we underestimated the labor cost by $25,000.

Elmer was happy to lend Carol and me the money to build our new house. We borrowed $65,000 at the going rate of 12 percent interest, and we would not have to make payments during the months of June and July, but the interest clock continued to run. Pop simply said, "You do the paperwork and keep up with the loan." The plan was to sell our home in Summertown in two lots during the summer of 1985. I figured I could easily sell the house and lot for $34,000, and the adjacent lot for $6,000. We knew the cost of our new home would run close to the $100,000 mark, and it seemed to be a logical plan. As summer wore on, it appeared we were not going to be able to sell our home. Finally, on September 1, 1985, we found a buyer for the house. Pop could sense my frustration and cheerfully offered to buy the adjacent lot for $6,000. Phew! We were so happy to be able to move forward, and Pop was happy as well. He resold the lot for $10,000 a month later.

One Saturday afternoon while the house was under construction, Mom and Pop visited the project. The builders were putting the finishing touches on the fireplace. "How many bricks did you use in building the fireplace?" Pop inquired. "Ten thousand not counting the 1,500 antique bricks on the fireplace façade," I said. "Wow, what a waste," Pop countered.

"Ten thousand bricks will complete the entire outside covering on one of my houses." Once again, Elmer marveled at my apparent stupidity. During the winter of 1985, Mom and Pop often frequented our new home for a meal and a visit. I would prepare a roaring fire in the fireplace. Pop surprised himself as to how much he enjoyed the fire. "Tell me again how many bricks are in that fireplace," he would teasingly ask. After my response, he repetitiously would state, "Wow! That's a huge pile of bricks, but I am really enjoying the fireplace!"

When we moved into the house, we really were not ready to move. Without warning, Darrell and Deena showed up to our home in Summertown and said they had come to move us into the new house. Ouch! We were patiently waiting for the polyurethane to harden on the oak floors and really wanted at least another week before we moved. Also, the air conditioning was not complete, which meant we would be living there the hottest part of the year. We trudged forward with Deena's plan. We had not packed a single item in boxes when we began. We haphazardly stuffed items in boxes and forged ahead. By the end of the day, we had moved. We thanked Deena and Darrell for their help and lived the next two weeks with Carol's parents while we waited for the house to be finished. During the move we misplaced the sugar bowl. As a result, I learned to get by without sugar in my coffee and my dry cereal. *(We found the sugar bowl stuck in a box in the linen closet five years later.)*

In the beginning Carol and I wondered if we would ever be able to afford the utility bill for our new house. In an effort to lower the use of electricity, I installed ample ceiling fans, and a whole house fan in the attic. The first time we ran the attic fan

Leslie was sickened by the flow of the outside air coming into the house. I also learned Carol did not want to use the overhead fans. I still gaze upon those fans as monuments to my stupidity. For heat, I mounted a large whole-house wood furnace in the basement and filled the basement full of firewood to burn in the winter. However, there was a problem. If I built a fire in the furnace before going to work, and the outside temperature rose, the furnace would smolder and build up creosote. Yuck! I soon sold the large wood furnace at a half-price special. One of the happiest days of my life came in 1990 when natural gas became available to customers on our street.

Money was especially tight the first years after we built our house. The garage was unfinished on the inside, the driveway needed gravel, and the yard needed landscaping. Slowly but surely, we chipped away at the remaining jobs necessary to complete our construction project. *(The garage and the attic wood shop were finally completed in 2005, thirty years after we moved in, and the last phase of the sidewalks was completed in 2017.)*

Carol and I owned only the basic furniture when we moved in 1985. We found that much of the new furniture was expensive and of an inferior quality. We began exploring other furniture options, and we were delighted at the selection available at the Flea Market on the Lawrenceburg Square. Most of their furniture was purchased in England and shipped to Lawrenceburg. The owners called the furniture antiques even though most of what they sold was fifty-plus years old. Carol and I liked her antediluvian selection of the sturdy English oak furniture, and during the next fifteen years we purchased a variety of pieces to fill our house.

I plunged heart and soul into the principal position at Coffman. I was bound and determined to make the school a success. I made several personnel changes and embarked upon a program of positive reinforcement for the students. I printed a multitude of success cards that were to be given to the students to positively reinforce behavior. Unfortunately, some of the teachers refused to be trained in operant conditioning. At one meeting after I initiated the program one teacher blurted, "The only thing I am positive about is how much I hate playing this stupid positive reinforcement game." Her ignorance and arrogance caused her public embarrassment as she felt the stares of the faculty upon her. Other teachers would invite students to take all the success cards they wanted from a box on their desk. In the long haul most teachers who were not hindered by bad attitudes were happy to resolve student conduct in a positive manner.

Another program I initiated was the exploratory program for all students. One hour each day, students would rotate between physical education and exploratory classes. The cornerstone of the exploratory was drama class. During the school year, every student could be involved in a dramatic production. When the production was ready, the kids would perform at the Old Crockett Theatre. While most of the students loved the program, some of the teachers became bored with the program and bickered about having to help watch the kids during the large drama classes. I understood that it required work to provide an excellent program. I would not compromise on this effort.

However, I did make several changes all of the teachers appreciated. I solicited only volunteers to help with after-school activities like ball games. Bus duty was reduced to normal school hours. Faculty meetings and team meetings were held from 7:45 to 8:00 a.m., which meant teachers were not obligated to spend extra time after school. I also made the teachers' flower fund part of the general expenses of the school so that they were not required to support the program out of their pockets. Finally, I gave the teachers two parties a year which was funded out of my pocket. I also encouraged teachers to take advantage of the Master Teacher program and tutored teachers on how to pass the performance exams and collect the extra pay.

It did not take long for our new house to feel like home. The children enjoyed the large yard during the warm days and especially enjoyed playing in the basement on cold days. The basement was an excellent place to roller skate, play on the trapeze bar hanging from the ceiling, and complete art projects. I set up a table with paint, brushes, and wood objects for the kids to create their art masterpieces. Some winter days our children would only come out of the basement to eat and use the restroom. At the end of the day, I would gather all the paint brushes and give them a thorough cleaning so that they would be ready for the next project.

One afternoon early in the school year Lara came into the office wearing a lugubrious expression. When I questioned Lara about what was troubling her, wiping away a tear, she gave this report: "The sheriff's department came to school today to fingerprint the first graders. I noticed the deputy who took my fingerprints gave me an F in sex. That is the first F I have ever made in school!"

The first year in Lawrenceburg, Leslie took a ballet class. For the recital we purchased her a pink tutu that had a beautiful waist sash. Leslie liked to wear the tutu on weekends when she was playing around the house. One Saturday morning Leslie shrilled out a bloodcurdling scream. Carol and I ran upstairs to see what had happened. While Leslie was using the commode and finishing her business, the beautiful obi from her costume accidently flushed itself down the commode. Leslie was distraught! Carol and I concealed our amusement as we consoled her.

After we settled into our new home, Carol's mother announced a surprise for the girls. Nana said she wanted to pay for private piano lessons for the girls, and she would also provide the Parkes family piano. Lara was very excited about taking the lessons. She worked hard at practicing for several years. When she began to tire of the lessons, Carol would tell Lara she just couldn't let Nana down. The Parkes grandparents attended every one of the children's piano recitals. Lara continued her lessons until she was in high school. When Leslie became old enough, she also took piano lessons funded out of Nana's generosity. Leslie continued her lessons through the first two semesters of college. Both children joined the band in middle school and continued in the band as percussionists through high school. Lara participated in the MTSU marching band her freshman year.

In the summer, the kids enjoyed playing with box turtles. We would pick them up on the road after a rain during the summer. I built a turtle house and a corral to keep the turtles. The children would feed them strawberries, lettuce, watermelon, and earth worms. One day, Leslie discovered one aggressive male turtle she had named Rambo loved Chicken McNuggets. To everyone's surprise, the turtle would allow Leslie to hand-feed him! On the back terrace the kids had a small kiddie-type swimming pool. One of their favorite pastimes was taking the turtles swimming with them. In the fall of the year the girls would paint the turtles' names in fingernail polish before releasing them into the wild. To our surprise some of the turtles stayed in close proximity to the yard. Many years later, especially rainy days, Carol and I would see a box turtle amble across the back patio.

A few summers later when Leslie was entering second grade, a small half-grown whitetail deer showed up in backyard where the girls were playing. To their delight, the deer allowed them to approach and pet her. After they fed the deer, she became a regular playmate the entire summer. The girls promptly named the deer Baby. One afternoon the girls were feeding Baby apples off the back porch. I caught a blue-tailed skink that was scurrying across the porch. While I was holding the skink, Baby curiously approached the skink. As she sniffed the skink, the little skink clamped its mouth onto Baby's nose. I have often regretted that the episode was not caught on camera, because the deer danced a cute little jig on her hind legs as she was furiously shaking her head in an effort to make the skink release her nose.

Later one summer morning we noticed that Baby had attracted a boyfriend to the yard. The two deer courted together in the back of the yard the rest of summer vacation. When school resumed, the deer followed us to school one day, and spent most of the day on the football field at Coffman. Deer actually became too plentiful in the yard for a time after that. One night when Carol and I came in from choir practice, we counted three bucks and nine does bedded down in the yard. The following Thanksgiving, a hunter knocked on our door one afternoon. "There's a ten-point buck in your backyard," he excitedly reported. "Is it okay if I shoot it?" I was amused and also somewhat annoyed. There were too many houses adjoining our backyard to allow for a safe shot. "Just be patient," I replied. "The deer will soon be back in the woods where you can hunt them safely."

In 1988 I decided to undergo evaluation for the Master Teacher program. I worked many late nights at school in an effort to become more organized so that I could ace the evaluation. After the four-month evaluation program, I scored well enough to make the highest level for Tennessee principals. For my effort, I was given a $2000 annual raise, and the opportunity to earn $2000 more in a two-week summer program. Carol and I decided to spend some of the extra cash on weekly maid service. Having someone taking care of the house and bathroom cleaning was a wonderful luxury the whole family enjoyed.

After I aced the evaluation program, I began to encourage teachers on the Coffman staff to join in. My first protégé was Wayne Richardson. Wayne responded to my instructional pointers, and that made him a quick study for the program. Wayne was an earth science teacher who really enjoyed teaching environmental science. We began planning school-wide science fair projects that were fun for the students. Wayne and I both enjoyed environmental science, so we decided to build an outdoor classroom nature trail at David Crockett State Park. For the following five summers we worked at the park on building the elaborate one-mile trail that included an observation pavilion large enough to seat a classroom of students under the open shelter. The pavilion, mounted ninety feet above Shoal Creek on a rocky ledge, provided a breathtaking view. The trail meandered around the side of a large hill and crossed a branch that filled the fish pond. For five years, Wayne and I talked fast and furiously concerning the project. Over $250,000 was raised from the private sector to fund the construction of the project. Wayne and I spent the following twenty summers teaching summer classes on the outdoor classroom. In preparation for the summer environmental classes, I brushed up on bird calls, frog and toad calls, and insect identification. On my trips to and from school, I would listen to *Tennessee Toad and Frog Calls*. I must admit, this was not a favorite hit with the kids. They would groan and roll their eyes as the tape played.

There was also an unfortunate spinoff concerning the Master Teaching program. After three of the male teachers on the staff aced the evaluation, there were a few teachers who thought too much of their teaching ability to be willing to adapt for the evaluation. I continued to encourage them to play the game. If the evaluators did not see effective classroom management and instruction, they could not give them an adequate score. A few teachers resented the fact they did not ace the evaluation and accused me of not helping them enough.

I recall this particularly humorous moment at Coffman many years ago. One winter day the faculty and staff were hit exceptionally hard by a stomach bug. The secretary and I were frantically calling everyone available on a newly adopted substitute list. At the same time, we were in the middle of the band's annual citrus fruit sale. Two truckloads of fruit had been delivered to the office, and we were overwhelmed with trying to prepare for the school day without sufficient staff to cover the classrooms while dealing with the massive band fund drive. A few minutes after 8:00 a.m., a very well-dressed elderly lady appeared in the office for the first time. "Are you here to help us out during our crisis?" I asked. She pleasantly smiled. "Oh yes! Just tell me what I need to do." I kindly thanked her for coming on such short notice and escorted her to a classroom full of rowdy seventh graders that was adjacent to the office. After everyone settled down, I made the students a quick assignment and assured the elderly lady that I would be back in just a few minutes. In the meantime, more teachers had gotten sick and were checking out of school as we tried to get the school day started. During the confusion, I forgot about the new substitute I had dropped off at her new teaching assignment. At 9:00 a.m., the class bell rang, and students began transferring to their second period class. After the traffic settled, the elderly lady reappeared in the office. "Excuse me," she politely said in a sweet, soft-spoken voice. "I think we have had a misunderstanding. I left my automobile running in the parking lot, and I must leave. Have I come on the wrong day to pick up my fruit?" Hark! It was just one of those days!

My biggest problem at Coffman was dealing with the misanthropes—the teachers who didn't like their students. I never understood why someone would pretend to teach school if they hated the students. One particular teacher had been a thorn in the side of every principal in the schools in which she had been assigned to teach. This particular case got so bad that I began documenting charges against her. In the beginning I was cheered on by one of the supervisors. In a twist of fate, when the charges came before the board, the supervisor began supporting the teacher. I presented three years of teacher evaluations, improvement plans, and a ton of anecdotal notes on the teacher to prove the teacher's neglect of duty, but the board took no action on the charges. The following year, no student would agree to be in the teacher's classroom. The teacher was moved to the central office and given a desk but was not assigned any teaching duties. The Peter Principle had been raised to its highest degree of incompetence.

No doubt, the most colorful teacher I ever dealt with was Elmer Brown. Elmer was the physical education teacher, and he regularly committed off-the-wall antics that caused him to receive undue attention. Elmer was a smooth talker. He could twist the truth in such a way to become almost believable. As we were wrapping up a school term, the teachers were required to bring the student permanent records up to date and turn them into the office for inspection. When Elmer turned his records in, he had misplaced two of his students' records. I sent Elmer back to his room to search, but to no avail. Elmer swore he had never had all of the records. I proceeded to his gymnasium office and began looking through his desk. While searching for the records, I found four boxes of Skoal snuff and the two missing records. I had chastised Elmer on numerous occasions about using snuff, and he had promised me he had quit dipping at school. In a rage, I turned his desk over and emptied all the contents out on the floor. "I will give you until tomorrow morning to straighten up this mess or we will have problems, Elmer." Elmer had a knack to look like a whipped puppy when he received a scolding, and he would be most apologetic about the whole ordeal.

Since the PE classes were large an extra teacher was required to supervise the classes. One day the resource teacher assigned to help Elmer called in sick. I was still somewhat miffed at Elmer about the Skoal fiasco, when a brand-new substitute showed up at school to help Elmer. I informed the sub that Elmer was losing his hearing. I further explained a person had to holler in his left ear in order to be heard. "Please don't mention this to Elmer," I revealed. "He is very sensitive about his hearing." The sub did as he was instructed. When the school day was over, I asked Elmer how the new substitute fared. "Don't hire him again," Elmer retorted. "He yelled into my ear the whole day."

One afternoon two school board members paid me a visit. They wanted to have a private discussion with Elmer. I arranged to get an assistant to cover his class and Elmer came to the office. One of the board members had heard that Elmer was talking unpleasantly about him at school. After about a thirty-minute private conference between the two of them, Elmer had smoothed everything over so well he managed to sell the board member a new rod and reel from his bait store.

After the gym renovation, a huge box of keys made their way to the office. Every door in the gymnasium took a separate key, and there was no master key. I arranged to change the locks on the front entrance doors, but everything else required its own key. Elmer would come to the office for an hour at lunch while I was in the cafeteria with the kids. He would leave his keys on the desk in the office. Just for fun one of the teachers began to slip an extra key on Elmer's key ring. After a few weeks, Elmer was carrying around a massive conglomeration of useless keys. Elmer's redeeming quality was he knew how to relate to his students. The kids really liked Elmer. As a result, I received very few complaints about Elmer's teaching performance.

It was not unusual for the police to call me in the wee hours of the morning. One morning at three o'clock I was beckoned to school because the officers had found a window unlocked. Upon arrival the police and I made a quick search of the school plant and found a young man hiding in one of the classrooms. He had broken into the coach's office and his pockets were stuffed with cash. He was quickly arrested and carried to jail. Early the next morning a friend of mine had checked out some of the trusted jail prisoners to help clean up debris from a recent storm on the campus. I agreed to feed the prisoners in exchange for their morning work on campus. At lunchtime I was surprised that one of the trusted prisoners was the same young man who had broken into the school during the wee hours of the morning. When I inquired what had brought him back to campus so soon, he said, "Mr. James, I was really sorry for breaking into the school. I saw this as an opportunity to make up for my evil deeds." I marveled at the speed this young man became a trusted prisoner.

Around 6:30 each morning I would briefly meet with some of the early-rising teachers in the teacher's lounge. Quite often the two male janitors would also meet with us. One of the distinguished custodians gave the teachers a morning weather report. One of the morning radio DJs began calling him each morning for the weather news. The custodian became a regular radio celebrity for more than a year. One Friday morning one of the coaches caught a raccoon that had trapped himself inside the football locker room. He brought the live raccoon to the teachers' lounge and presented it to the custodian as a gift. The following Monday morning we inquired what the gentleman did with his gift raccoon. "I cooked it, and I ate it," he replied.

The coach inquired, "How did you cook a raccoon?"

"Well, the same way you cook a possum."

I really enjoyed working with the adolescents at school. The students were at an awkward age that was combined with hormones and rapid body growth. Quite suddenly many of the students had the body of an adult and the mind of a child. Many of the students wore their emotions on their sleeves which led to occasional inappropriate behavior. Halloween was always interesting during my tenure as Coffman principal. The large yard on Quail Drive was the site of many yard rolling activities by the students. Just for fun, I purchased several motion lights that I would set up in the yard prior to the Halloween rituals. The lights frightened most of the Coffman students away. However, some of the older Coffman students were not as easily deterred. One evening, we heard a clamor in the yard and saw several older kids rolling the yard. I slipped out the back door and sneaked to the edge of the yard where I found their car. The keys to the car had been left in the ignition so the boys could make a quick get-away. I retrieved the keys and waited for the boys to return to their ride. They were surprised to meet me by the car. They were much more surprised when they realized I had taken the keys from the vehicle. I bargained with the boys to return their car keys in exchange for help with picking up the toilet paper. When Lara and Leslie entered high school, occasionally some of their friends would roll our yard as well. The boys would usually volunteer to help pick up the paper the following morning.

In the summer of 1989 Jerry invited our family to Rockville, Maryland, to spend the week at their home so that the kids could take in the attractions at nearby Washington, D.C. On the way to Rockville, Carol and I took a side trip to visit the homes of Thomas Jefferson and James Monroe. Of course, we made bathroom stops along the way, visiting several McDonald's and ordering ice cream for the kids at almost every stop. Jerry and Joan owned a beautiful home conveniently located about two blocks from the D.C. Metro. It was really easy to take the train into the city and conveniently stop near D.C.'s national treasures. We spent the first four days exploring the Smithsonian exhibits and the presidential memorials. I had the opportunity to visit the Wall (the Vietnam Veterans Memorial) which was funded by small donations from Vietnam veterans from all over the United States. I also took a short trip from the Mall to visit Fort McNair (where I was stationed after my release from Walter Reed Army Medical Center). Jerry and Joan treated us like royalty, serving us delicious meals every evening. On Saturday our two families took a tour to Mt. Vernon and a nice ride down one of the refurbished canals. The trip was especially meaningful for the children, who would soon be studying our destinations in school. Of course, we stopped for several Kodak moments to preserve the memories of our trip.

In the summer of 1990, we carried the kids to Walt Disney World. We flew down to Orlando, Florida, and rented a car to drive on to WDW. While I was making arrangements for the rental vehicle, Leslie requested that we upgrade and rent a van. This was the trip that I decided I would cater to every whim of our children, so Leslie's wish was granted. A few minutes later a large fifteen-passenger van pulled up in front of the rental office. It was about a thirty-minute drive to WDW so both of the kids stretched out on the long benches of the van. Our reservations were for the Dolphin Hotel which had opened only a few weeks earlier. As we entered our room, Leslie spotted a small refrigerator. Her eyes lit up when she saw the vast assortment of candy and soda pop. We allowed the kids to indulge in the fine refrigerator cuisine every afternoon. In the mornings we ate a continental breakfast prepared by the hotel. In the evenings, the girls spotted a hamburger joint that served burgers and shakes. They both voted for the soda shop every evening for supper. During the day, we ate off the numerous snack wagons located throughout the park. Carol and I were impressed at how nice the WDW staff was to their guests. The park was immaculately clean and free of debris. I took about four rolls of film to properly document the highlights of the trip with Kodak moments.

The following five summer vacations were spent in Gatlinburg, Tennessee. The Tennessee State Middle School conference was held at the Park Vista Hotel. While I was attending the conference, Carol and the girls were exploring the attractions downtown. After a couple of years, the girls were very comfortable on exploring the attractions with some of the other teachers' children. The middle school conferences were an excellent source for exploring innovative teaching strategies—many of which I invited the Coffman faculty to incorporate into their classrooms. While many of the teachers made an effort to improve their instruction, some were determined to accomplish nothing but to continue to feed their negative attitudes about teaching. One exciting idea used to enhance student motivation I picked up from the conference was called Learn Ball. Dividing the students in two competing teams, the focus of the game was on reviewing lesson objectives and shooting hoops through a small basketball goal with a nerf ball. Review questions were divided into three categories—easy, medium, and challenging, earning ten, twenty, or thirty points depending upon the difficulty of the question chosen. Making hoops were given the same credit of ten to thirty points depending on the distance the shots were made from the goal. Review questions and basketball shots were alternated each inning, with every student participating in both events. The great attraction for the game was for the slower students who were better at shooting basketballs than answering questions. The last round of the game allowed students to shoot a desperation shot from the back of the room for seventy-five points. When the occasional shot was successful bedlam would erupt in the classroom with students from both teams cheering! When I found none of the Coffman teachers willing to incorporate Learn Ball into their teaching strategy, I convinced Carol to try it out on her fourth grade class. The game became an instant sensation with everyone in school enthused about the progress of the game. Carol continued playing Learn Ball for the final ten years of her teaching career. (*In 2020, Carol's former students continue to approach her in her fifteenth year of retirement, to thank her for being their most favorite teacher of all time because of the excitement of Learn Ball.*)

In 1997 after Pop passed away, my post-traumatic stress disorder from my days in Vietnam came roaring back at me. My battle with nightmares about the war began to spill over in my work as principal. I decided to resign my position as principal and ask for a teaching position at Coffman. Much to my surprise, when I tendered my resignation letter to the superintendent, he refused to accept it. "I am giving you a few days to reconsider, and I strongly encourage you to remain in your current position." When I announced my resignation plans to the faculty, several teachers immediately came to the office to beg me to remain as Coffman principal. I was surprised at the outpouring of well-wishers who encouraged me to stay. I returned to the superintendent's office and requested the resignation letter which he gladly returned. However, the cat was out of the bag. Several of my nemeses camped out at the superintendent's office and began accusing me of all sorts of unbecoming behavior that included sexual harassment of some of the women teachers.

A so-called investigation about my unbecoming conduct was launched where each staff member was privately interviewed about my unbecoming behavior. While it was true, the PTSD had caused me to offer terse explanations, I had not consciously debased any of the women during my tenure. The investigation was concluded without providing me with the nature of the charges against me, or due process to defend myself to the charges; both rights were guaranteed in the teachers' contract. With my brother Joe's assistance, I saddled up with a Nashville attorney to fight the charges.

During the discovery period, my attorney learned more specific information about the sexual harassment charge. One female teacher I had considered a very dear friend of the family was behind the charge. She told the investigation panel I had told her sexual jokes that made her very uncomfortable. This friend and I had swapped dirty jokes for twenty years. She would relate jokes to me on direction from her husband, and I would do the same. This was a huge shock to me. Not only were her accusations painful, I felt I had been betrayed by a close family friend. I knew this person had been sore at me because she had not made the highest level on the Master Teacher evaluation, but I was hurt she would use this against me.

That spring the superintendent told me the board had decided to transfer me to the high school alternative school. Secretly, I was very pleased with the transfer, but since I had not been given due process, I stayed mum about the transfer. A few weeks later, I received a letter signed by the superintendent stating I would be assigned as principal at Coffman Middle School the following school term. I signed the letter that I accepted the position and returned it to the Central Office. It was obvious the superintendent had made a clerical error, but I recognized the letter would aid in my lawsuit against the board. A few weeks later I arrived unannounced to the Central Office and requested to see my personnel file. The teachers' contract was very clear that my request could not be denied. To the superintendent's surprise, I carried the file to the copy machine and made duplicate copies of everything in the file. Since the superintendent had been sloppy with my file, I received the notes on all of the unfounded allegations that were made against me, and the file revealed which board member was leading the charge to have me transferred. If these accusations became public, the superintendent would be embarrassed because he had promised the remarks made to the group would be held in confidence. After I revealed the new information to my attorney, he was ready to file our court suit. Immediately, the attorney for the board called my attorney and asked for an out-of-court settlement and further asked the results of the settlement be protected by a non-disclosure agreement. I was very happy when this chapter of my life was in the rearview mirror. I was pleased with my out-of-court settlement, and I was relieved to be out of the administrative saddle at Coffman Middle School. Since I had won the suit (without going to court), my liability insurance paid all of my attorney fees. The board could have saved themselves a great deal of extra money had they engaged in genial conduct. I would now receive pay for untendered administrative service.

At the high school alternative school, I was assigned a maximum of twelve students in grades seven through twelve. The alternative school had been moved to the old West Highland Elementary school building. My first job was to repaint the classroom and wash and wax the floor since no janitorial staff had been assigned to the building. At the beginning of school, no students had been assigned to my care, so I helped other teachers prepare their rooms. I soon tired of my unofficial janitor status and began to explore new options to occupy my time. This position was an abrupt change from my role as principal at the middle school. I never had the luxury of free time in the principal role. I decided to train myself to work crossword puzzles. In the beginning the crossword puzzle of little-known facts was difficult, but I soon learned most puzzles had a recurring theme making them easier to solve with daily practice. The supervisor in charge of the building was an old friend of mine, and he was easygoing. The supervisor of the alternative school did not have a clue about the role of an alternative school teacher. As a result, I was given free rein to set priorities and write my own program.

Most of the students were assigned to alternative school because of their poor behavior. Therefore, the centerpiece of my pedagogy was based on behavior. I developed a token economy based on a point system whereby students were required to earn a certain amount of points in order to be released to their respective schools. Students earned points completing assignments in their textbooks and by displaying appropriate behavior during the day. Students could also lose points for behavior infractions. In the beginning I had to brush up on practically the entire high school curriculum since students assigned to me were taking a large variety of classes at school. After my first year, it was a much easier task to check student work, making sure they remained correctly on task. Every day after lunch I taught a group behavior class based on Stephen Covey's *Seven Habits of Effective People*. The longer I taught the class, the easier it became for me to adapt Covey's book to practical applications for my students. Students who paid attention during class and could answer the questions on a short quiz were dismissed to enjoy a break while I continued to teach mastery until all of the students passed the quiz. The break was a tremendous motivator for the students to listen up because they learned the class would not be over for them until everyone reached proficiency.

I was assigned one female teacher assistant. She had been kicked around in the system for several years because she lacked the skills required for adequate performance. I required very little of my assistant. I asked her to accompany me to the hall when I was talking individually to a student, and to accompany students to the restroom if they asked to be excused outside of regular break time. I also asked her to stay with the students for ten minutes daily when I would step out of the room for a coffee break. All hell would usually break loose during my ten-minute break, but with time she became better at managing the kids while I was away. If I ever was called away from school because of a doctor's appointment, bedlam would wreak havoc in my classroom. The kids took advantage of the holiday when I was away. Boys generally reacted positively to my teaching methods. They understood my no-nonsense approach, and they enjoyed playing basketball with me during the breaks. The girls were the most challenging. I was assaulted several times by the girls, and quite often they would accuse me of inappropriate sexual behavior. That made the teacher assistant's second set of eyes very important so that she could vouch for my behavior.

When Jerry was in Vietnam, he bought a small refrigerator from the Post Exchange for $25. Upon returning home, Jerry gifted the refrigerator to me. I used the refrigerator at every teaching assignment, and when I retired, it became a backup fridge at home. One day while I was away, a student picked up the little refrigerator and threw it through the classroom window. It scratched it up a bit, but to everyone's surprise it continued to operate. (*The refrigerator has now been in service for 50 continuous years.*)

My workday began at 7:45 a.m., almost an hour later than my role as principal, and it ended at 1:30 p.m., more than two hours earlier than my role as principal. In just a few weeks I became accustomed to the easy life my new position afforded me. Also, I soon discovered my paycheck would go much further in my new role. Until that revelation I had no idea I was spending so much of my own money on school projects as principal. I did not have to fund teacher parties, and no one was appearing in my office asking for a donation.

One day on the way to work, I passed a jon boat in someone's yard for sale. At the time no students had been assigned to me. I spent the next two weeks with the boat parked under a shade tree at alternative school customizing the boat the way I had watched Jim Parkes play with his. Owning a boat was on my bucket list. Carol and I carried the boat to Laurel Hill Lake quite regularly. After a couple of years, my boat bug had been sated, and I was ready to pass it forward to my son-in-law, Daniel Hunt.

Another bucket list came to fruition while I was working at alternative school. One day my barber was talking about a cabin he was tweaking on a three-acre lot on the edge of Giles County. He said several springs were on the property as well. When I inquired about the property being compatible for a spring-fed pond, I was assured the property would be excellent for such a project. I had dreamed of building a beautiful pond for years. In just a few weeks, he deeded the property to me, and I began working on the pond. The small quaint cabin had only two rooms, but it also came with a beautiful front porch and a covered patio. The adjoining patio was an ideal location for a swing. One of my first projects was to improve the cabin roof and screen in the porch. The cabin had a small bathroom and kitchen. I purchased a small LP gas stove and an air conditioner to heat and cool the cabin. I also built three corner cabinets in the front room for storage. The quaint rustic appearance of the cabin was well suited to the majestic landscape. Before the pond could be built, several trees would have to be removed. I called a friend who removed the trees and burned the debris in about a week. Next, I located a highly recommended dozer man to build the pond. He completed the work in just a few days.

Then I added a concrete spillway for the pond. The pond was only about a third of an acre in size, but it was a beauty. To my delight it soon filled with water, and there was no doubt about it holding water.

I financed the project by selling eleven of the seventeen acres of our homeplace in Lawrenceburg. I received $45,000 for the sale of the property, and very soon I had invested all of the money into the project. The pond property was located off Muckle Branch. Carol and I named the pond property Blessings, but soon everyone was referring to it as Muckle Branch. At the top of the hill and across the street lived the Amos Gingrich family. Amos was an Amish gentleman who had several children afflicted with cerebral palsy. Two of the teenage children had difficulty walking. Amos owned about a third of an acre at the top of the hill where the drive to the cabin was located. He agreed to sell me the small parcel of land if I would allow his children and him the opportunity to fish in the pond. I had made up my mind that I would never turn down anyone who wanted to fish, because I knew how it felt to have my request rejected so many times when I asked permission to fish.

Amos and his family soon became our very dear friends. In just a few weeks Carol and I learned the names of Amos's children, and we invited them to help themselves to the cold sodas we kept stashed in the small kitchen refrigerator. My barber warned me about locking the cabin doors. He said thieves would break the door down to get in, but if it remained open no damage would occur. We owned the property for ten years, and we never missed a single item in the cabin. In the early spring of the year the valley along the driveway was covered in an assortment of beautiful wild ferns. There was also a spring house and a small shed on the property which I used to store equipment for the pond. I installed outside running water and electric lights in the shed, making it an ideal location to clean fish. I also installed a small dock on one end of the pond where I attached a battery powered fish feeder. I stocked the pond with catfish and bream the first spring the pond was filled with water. In a very short time, the fish grew to eating size. It was amazing how eager the fish were to bite a hook. I invited a gathering of youngsters from church to fish and also invited my family and friends to enjoy the pond.

My most frequent visitors besides Amos and his family were my brother, Joe, and his boys. His boys were preteens at the time, and they came to fish and swim. Often, they fished from an inner tube while paddling around in the pond. The first summer, someone pitched in several nice sized bass. Also, the bass were not bashful about biting a line. Joe and the boys spent several extended stays at the cabin property. They fondly speak of the Muckle Branch adventures as some of their favorite childhood memories.

As the pond and property manager, every ten days I would dedicate the day to the Muckle Branch project, keeping the grass mowed and the sticks picked up around the pond. I bought a five-foot aluminum rake I attached on a rope I used to clean the excess algae and weeds from the pond. In the fall it came in handy pulling the leaves and sticks from around the pond spillway. In the beginning I really enjoyed myself keeping the place in pristine condition. Ten years after completing all the cabin accoutrements and property improvements, I found that building the pond of my dreams was more rewarding than maintaining the property. Amos and his children began to fish so regularly that the fish did not have a chance to mature. I placed the pond property on the real estate market with an asking price of $90,000. Several of the local neighbors tried to buy it with a lowball offer which I would not accept. As Elmer would say, they became a nuisance bothering me with a lowball price. After about six months on the market, I informed the realtor I was changing the price of the property to $110,000. It sold in two weeks at the new price. The pond was a highlight of bucket list accomplishments. I enjoyed the project very much until I had nothing to improve. Photographs and memories of the Muckle Branch adventure remain dear to my heart.

After I had worked at the alternative school job for eight years, the Central Office informed me they had hired a guidance counselor to help with the students. They hired the young lady even though I complained that I did not need help. The lady came down and observed for about two weeks. I sensed she was very uncomfortable about working in the alternative class with the older students. I did not rush her to commence her guidance program. In about three months the guidance supervisor came by to see how the new help was working for me. The supervisor was appalled the new help had not begun a program. The next week the supervisor and the counselor came by to spend an hour with my students. I excused myself from the classroom and drove down to Ledbetter Drug Company (about two blocks away) for a ten-cent cup of coffee. The class was in a terrible uproar when I returned. The supervisor said it would be necessary for me to remain in the classroom with the new counselor in the future. "Let me get this straight," I began. "You both are licensed personnel, but neither of you are capable of keeping a small class of twelve students on task?" They complained it was much harder than it looked. "If I were you, I would keep it a secret that your teaching license and experience does not equate to student performance." Embarrassed and offended, the two ladies exited my classroom and never returned while I was the teacher. The alternative school guidance counselor was given an office and a desk with no responsibilities. During my ninth year at alternative school, a new superintendent insisted on assisting me with my class. He hired five certified personnel to teach the two alternative school classes. I insisted I did not need or want any help. The superintendent had already hired the new personnel for the following school term.

I was informed the countywide homebound teaching position was open. I applied for a transfer, and I was accepted into the position. The special education supervisor was having trouble finding someone with global special education certification that could handle difficult students. I informed the supervisor I would be happy to work with her most difficult cases. We shook hands on the agreement, and I was transferred to the position.

I was only one school term away from retirement. I was waiting on Carol to finish her thirty years so that she could retire with full benefits, and I was excited about my new job placement. I had been told war stories for years about how difficult this teaching assignment would be. However, I had a vast knowledge of successful teaching strategies, and I had been heckled by experts during the thirty-five-plus years I had served the Lawrence County School System. I was confident I could also meet this challenge. The homebound teacher was responsible for a caseload of twelve students weekly. I was required to give each student two, one-and-a-half-hour classes each week, make assignments, and complete a learning assessment. As I began to schedule the classes, I found it possible to complete all the teaching in four school days. The fifth school day each week was for teacher planning. I found this was the job of my dreams. I could easily manage teaching and planning in four days weekly. To keep from receiving complaints from other teachers, I gladly claimed sick leave every Friday for the entire school term. During my tenure as a school board employee, I had amassed over 280 sick leave days because I rarely took sick leave. The new school superintendent said he wanted to help me, and indeed his help far exceeded my wildest dreams.

Meanwhile back at alternative school, the new personnel needed help. The new alternative school supervisor approached me and asked if I would be willing to train the new teachers the program I had assembled while at the school. I offered to give them all of my information and engage in a five-day in-service training program for $20,000. "We thought you would consider helping for free," they replied. "You must have forgotten that I am no longer recognized as a principal/supervisor by the board," I mused. Twenty thousand dollars was a very fair price, because I had firsthand knowledge the board had paid much more to consultants who were hired for similar in-service training sessions. I was relieved they did not accept my offer.

One case that was given me in the homebound program was a seventeen-year-old special education student who had been dismissed from high school because he failed to obey any of the teachers. During the summer he burned down a local grocery store near his home in West Point. Everyone who had worked with this young man became totally flabbergasted with his misbehavior. Upon my first meeting with this student, he told me he did not intend to look at any of the textbooks I had brought for his assignments. "I'm okay with that. Just tell me what you like to do," I stated. With a big smile on his face he began, "I like to walk the roads and go to the creek."

"Good," I added. "I like to walk the roads and go to the creek as well. I will make you a deal. We won't bother with your textbooks, if you will listen to me as we walk."

With a blank look on his face, he asked, "Is that all? You have yourself a deal, partner," he added. From that moment forward, I had no problems with this young man. The supervisor was worried that when the young man turned eighteen, he would end up in jail. Therefore, I taught him the alternative school behavior class as we walked the streets one-and-a-half hours each session, constantly reminding him this knowledge would keep him out of jail. At the end of the school term, the student told me I was his all-time favorite teacher. I ran into him several times at Wal-Mart after I had retired. With a smile on his face he would report, "Hey, Sid! I have managed to stay out of jail. Thanks!"

In June of 2005, Carol and I retired from the Lawrence County School System. Carol clocked thirty years teaching fourth and sixth grades and driving her 1971 Volkswagen Super Beetle to work almost the entire time. My thirty-seven years had offered me a very unique experience. I served as an elementary school teacher, an elementary reading supervisor, an elementary principal, a middle school principal, a secondary alternative school facilitator, and as a global special education homebound teacher. During my tenure I had the opportunity to work with students in grades K-12 teaching every subject in the curriculum with the exception of foreign language and advanced mathematics. I suppose the most unusual class I taught was cosmetology.

Planning my work and working my plan paid huge dividends for me. I knew almost immediately when entering college that I wanted to work with children. I was only seventeen and the youngest student in my class when I graduated from high school. My young age disqualified me for summer employment and going to summer school was a logical choice for me. Jerry had embarked upon a three-year path to college graduation, and he encouraged me to do likewise. Jerry also showed me how to study the college catalog and choose the right courses to stay on the three-year path. I graduated from Lipscomb in May of 1969 in twelve consecutive quarters. My next decision was to volunteer to the service of the United States, and I joined the army partially knowing if I did not join I would soon be drafted anyway. After 30 months in the army, I came home to a teaching job waiting for me in the Lawrence County School System. I worked thirty-three consecutive school terms, and earned additional retirement credit for my army service and accumulated sick leave. I could have retired at the minimum age of fifty-five, but Carol was still working and Leslie had not finished her schooling.

When Carol and I decided to build a house in Lawrenceburg, I figured the cost of the house and loan interest and calculated I could pay off the mortgage in twelve years. The following nine years Carol and I worked diligently to provide our girls with the Sid & Carol James college endowment so that both children could finish their college work debt free. Lara graduated from MTSU with double certification in elementary education with an emphasis in communication and with a BSN nursing degree. Leslie graduated from MTSU with a degree in communication disorders and from Western Kentucky University with a master's degree in speech pathology. As fate would have it, planning our work and working our plan worked perfectly.

The perfect plan mentioned above would not have been possible without the loving encouragement and support from my beautiful wife and our parents. Carol's sweet personality and easygoing demeanor made the task of raising the children and making the correct financial decisions along the way much easier. I have considered myself very lucky to be a part of two loving and supportive families that modeled Christian living and a strong work ethic. Our parents offered help and sound advice without hesitation anytime we needed them. But the most critical factor in making the stars align for the master plan was the contribution of our gorgeous and talented children. Fortunately, both Lara and Leslie inherited most of the best genes Carol and I had to offer. Since I struggled with reading in elementary school, I was bound and determined our children would not experience the same fate.

Lara was blessed with the grit and determination to achieve academic success. She was also gifted with creativity and an intuitive nature, and she began carving her niche as a resourceful communicator early in her education. With our reinforcement and reassurance, Lara developed into a headstrong young lady with a tool bag full of confidence and ingenuity that would make her successful in her future endeavors.

Leslie benefited greatly from Lara's strong resolve and encouragement. When Lara was in kindergarten, I restored two old student desks I had retrieved from the junk pile at the school bus shop. With a little elbow grease and a new paint job, the desks looked good as new. In the afternoons after school, Lara would present her daily work pages to Leslie and teach her the kindergarten lesson of the day. As a result, one could say Leslie repeated kindergarten. Lara was a good mentor for Leslie. Occasionally they would have a sister squabble, but Carol and I quickly reminded them their sister would be the best friend they would ever have. With Lara's tutelage Leslie had very little difficulty in school and easily made high marks for her classes. One challenge Leslie faced later in school was making decisions. She had always followed Lara's example. When Leslie entered college, Lara was not as handy for Leslie to lean on. Eventually, Leslie learned to make excellent decisions, but the first years in college were challenging for her.

Both of our children were blessed with poise and kind hearts. I attribute this to the tremendous influence of their mother. Both children were musically inclined and earned outstanding personal awards throughout high school. This is due in a large measure to Dot Parkes who provided them a piano and paid for their private piano lessons through their high school years. Their Nana and Big Daddy were present for all of their annual recitals. As each child entered the seventh grade, they joined the Lawrence County Big Gold Machine marching band. Both girls were recognized and regularly rewarded as outstanding percussionists. For nine consecutive years I sold programs at the LCHS football games and became the official popcorn popper at the

LCHS basketball games. In the last week of the first semester, I would load my truck with citrus fruit to be delivered to all of our friends who supported the band. Carol and I also attended nine straight spring concerts at the Old Crockett Theatre, nine straight gatherings for the Lawrenceburg Christmas Parade, and nine straight midnight season rendezvous with the band bus as it returned from trips. Our effort was richly rewarded as we watched our kids perform on the field. Both girls agree participating in the Big Gold Machine was the most rewarding accomplishment of their high school experience.

I suppose both children inherited a portion of my grit and perseverance which I learned from watching my parents. Leslie was challenged by a friend in fourth grade to read the most books in a school year. Leslie's nemesis was often a bragger and arrogant. Leslie was bound and determined to arise triumphant to this challenge. As a result, she spent almost all of her free time in the afternoons and on weekends reading. Leslie shattered the fourth grade accelerated reading record which also hushed the bragging. The two girls continued to compete at knowledge bowls throughout their elementary years. When Lara joined 4-H club in the fourth grade, she wanted to participate in the public speaking contests. Lara won the contests for three consecutive years. When Lara was in seventh grade, she began to prepare herself for the Presidential Physical Fitness Award, a program initiated by President Kennedy in the 1960s. Much to our surprise she scored high enough to win the award. Later while in nursing school, Lara volunteered to participate in the ROTC Basic Training one summer. Before she left for boot camp, I instructed her on how to properly aim and fire a rifle.

Much to the surprise of the drill sergeants, Lara received the expert rifle award, a feat accomplished by less than 4 percent of cadets. Lara was in elite company, being one of a handful of females who had successfully completed the officer boot camp. Lara now serves as an oncology nurse supervisor at a large hospital in Oklahoma City, and Leslie is a certified speech pathologist who is currently employed at an elementary school near her home in Summertown.

Now that Lara and Leslie are married and have families of their own, Carol and I continue showering our children with our love and support. Prioritizing our simple lifestyle has continued to pay enormous dividends. Our children communicate regularly with us and shower us with their love. As time marches onward our lives have been enriched by three fabulous grandchildren who we constantly spoil.

RETIREMENT

I recall how much Pop enjoyed his retirement. He commented very frequently about how much he enjoyed going by Summertown High School and not entering the building. He didn't miss the bell, the students, and especially the parents. As Carol and I were approaching retirement age we wondered if we had prepared sufficiently to live a comfortable life without pinching pennies. Much to our surprise we ended up with more money than we could spend. The house note had been paid off for several years, and through frugal spending we had successfully paid for our children's higher education degrees without borrowing money. Our retirement came the summer after Leslie finished her college work in speech pathology at Western Kentucky University. Chris alluded that every time one of his children finished their schooling or were married it was like getting a big pay raise. Pop's retirement aphorism hit the nail on the head. Finally, Carol and I had found something that we could accomplish equally well! Retirement was indeed an abundant blessing of life.

My first retirement project was to complete the wood shop

above the garage. After the wood shop was completed, I bought a variety of woodworking tools. Although I had limited space, the shop has been a constant source of satisfaction. The grandchildren are always excited to work on projects in the shop when they stop by for a visit. I have made hundreds of bluebird boxes over the years. I have around 30 boxes in the neighborhood that I frequently monitor.

As school began in August of 2005, Carol and I were very happy to find new jobs to occupy our retirement time. On August 29, 2005, the massive F-5 Hurricane Katrina hit New Orleans and the surrounding eighty-plus miles of the Gulf Coast. Katrina was the largest and most devastating hurricane ever to hit the United States. The storm surge was recorded at ten to twenty-eight feet, and 80 percent of New Orleans had flooded. More than 1,800 people were killed and millions were left homeless in New Orleans and along the Gulf Coast. In the following days as the disaster played out, we saw a mass of humanity crying out and begging for help. The Outreach Committee at First United Methodist Church called an emergency meeting and began planning a response team to travel to New Orleans offering help. Our first hurdle was to find a family or church in New Orleans that would serve as our base camp. In just a few weeks we were teamed with Mickey and Susan Crumb who were living in Luling, Louisiana, a southwest suburb of New Orleans. Mickey was business manager for Metals USA. He agreed for his house to be used as our base camp while we worked in New Orleans.

Over the course of the next few weeks our church family began collecting bedding linens and other household goods, and a large assortment of clothing for children and adults. Ron Cato owned a huge forty-foot horse trailer, and he agreed for the church members to pack the materials into his trailer. By the middle of October, we were contacted by United Methodist Committee on Relief, who was working in New Orleans, and they gave us a green light to come help. This was the earliest that volunteers could be established since it took several weeks for the flood waters to recede.

On Wednesday, October 26, 2005, our team left for New Orleans. Volunteers included Beverly and Sonny Duke, Gracie Henson, Mary Ellen Douglas, Dean Erwin, Jerry Gibbs, Ken Nelson, Ron Cato, and Carol and me. We arrived at New Orleans around 4:30 p.m. and saw horrible devastation for miles. We received a rather cool reception from Mickey Crumb because he lacked confidence in our sincere wishes to help. However, over the next three days, he changed his mind about the workers, and was very impressed with our work. During the following days, we distributed all of the linens and clothing to the needy, tore out and replaced drywall, and cleaned debris from yards. On Friday, we completely gutted one house that was in the Lower Ninth Ward of New Orleans, where devastation was the worst. Water had been standing in all the houses there for about six weeks. The house we were assigned was under four to five feet of water, and all the household furnishings and appliances had to be removed and piled toward the street. The house belonged to the grandmother of one of Mickey's employees at his business. We began early in the morning, working in the rankest grime imaginable. When we entered the kitchen, the job became even more terrible as we attempted to move all of the rotted meats out of the freezers. After an exhausting day of work, we quickly found the showers at Mickey's home. On Saturday morning, we put the finishing touches on four of the jobs we had begun. That afternoon, Mickey announced that his company would like to take the response team out to dinner. He carried us to the New Orleans French Quarter to the Red Fish Grille where we were treated to a great meal that included appetizers, mixed drinks, and dessert. By the time we packed up and prepared to leave on Monday morning, Mickey had a newfound appreciation for the team because he had doubted anyone would tackle the work we had accomplished.

In 2011 after Mom died, the children agreed to sell the two Bud James farms that Pop eventually inherited in Summertown. Mom was very disappointed that none of her children wanted to make the homeplace on Monument Drive their permanent residence, but all of the children had already put down roots in other communities. When the property survey was completed, new lots were created, and the auction was held. We had a large task of distributing the personal property among the siblings. When we sold the homeplace, all of the stuff in the Ketchum House that later became Pop's shop had to be disposed of and distributed. Chris carried home many of the tools that were his and also some of which belonged to Bud James, Paul James, and Pop. Paul James worked several years as a mechanic, and during that time he accumulated an odd assortment of washers. Pop added to the collection as well. The washers found a new home in my shop. I placed all of the washers in a wooden five-pound cheese box for safekeeping. When I saw an odd washer, I brought them home to add to the washer collection. I also inherited a wide assortment of fasteners, nails, bolts, and nuts. I decided to organize them into metal assortment bins like the ones at Parkes Lumber Company. The two bins cost me around $300. I spent weeks neatly assorting all of the miscellaneous doodads in the neat compartments. After the job was complete, I stood back to admire my exceptional work. I spent $300 to organize an estimated $17 in junk. Pop would have been so proud!

I was finally in the position to finish the interior of the rest of the garage, replace the windows throughout the house, build the rest of the sidewalks, and update the exterior of the house by removing the plastic siding and replacing it with brick veneer and hardy plank siding. The finishing touches to the exterior of the house were finished in 2017, thirty-three years after we began building the house in 1984. The delay in project details reminded me of the tediously long process Thomas Jefferson endured building his beautiful Monticello.

With extra time on our hands, Carol and I involved ourselves in the work of helping the needy and the homeless which yielded us new learning experiences. I once helped a young man who was picking up aluminum cans outside our home. I invited him to the garage where I had been saving my cans for someone whom I considered industrious. That began a five-year relationship with him and his family. During that time, I encouraged him to make goals for himself and imagine a better life. He told me how he had dreamed of becoming a transport truck driver. I showed him a six-week program that would help him obtain a commercial driver's license. Of course, there were hidden snags along the way. He left his home state of Michigan owing the state $1800 in unpaid drivers' fines. During this time, he chalked up another $500 in unpaid Tennessee drivers' fines. It seemed every time I helped him get to a point to work toward his goal, he would find other ways to spend the money I was helping him earn. It finally dawned on me I was more interested in pursuing his goals than he was. I finally cut him loose and wished him well. About ten years later he showed up at church as Carol and I were going home from choir practice. The county jail just happened to be located across the street, and he was being released. He was incarcerated because he had failed to pay the court-ordered child support to his children. I gave him a ride outside of town and wished him well again, but I did not offer any more support. Ben Franklin correctly defined many of my protégées when he mused, "You can't teach an old dog new tricks."

On another occasion we invested heavily in helping four Amish ladies who had been shunned from the tribe. After five years of getting them in a position of independence, they refused to do the simple things like securing a photo ID. The supplemental funds I had pledged the ladies ended up doing more harm than good. Instead of saving it to pay their property taxes, they spent the money frivolously, and became jealous of each other causing two of the sisters to move away from the premises.

When Jesus told his disciples, "You will have the poor with you always," I observed many poor people make poor decisions for themselves, and no matter how much help they receive, they remain in the poor rut and fail to explore other options while others are imploring them to do so.

One afternoon I passed a fellow walking down the road carrying a backpack. I asked him if I could give him a lift. As he entered the truck, I asked him his destination. "Nowhere in particular," he replied. "I am homeless." I brought him home, fed him a hot meal and offered him work in the yard where he could earn some needed cash. That afternoon, I offered him the opportunity to sleep in the barn and take a quick outdoor shower. "Why would I want to do that?" he replied. "If you will give me a ride to the public square, I am supposed to meet with my friends." Then it dawned on me he was homeless because that is what he chose to be. After that experience I encountered numerous homeless people in the Wal-Mart parking lot holding up their desperation signs. I have offered many of them work in my yard in exchange for some quick money. No one has ever taken me up on my offer. One more peculiarity I have observed is people only seem to be desperate on beautiful days. No beggars appear when the weather is bad.

Our church family at First United Methodist Church in Lawrenceburg has supported a sister church in Nicaragua for more than 30 years with educational scholarships. This has been a worthwhile mission that has yielded tremendous success over the years. I have observed our brothers and sisters have a wonderful work ethic and a positive attitude toward life, even though most of them live in poverty. With the support of others, the people in the tiny hamlet of Amatitan, Nicaragua, has built a school, offering an opportunity of a better life. Our investment in their school and community has reaped huge dividends, and I was happy to be part of their supporting team.

Retirement has also offered me an opportunity to fight the demons of post-traumatic stress that have regularly tormented me since my days in Vietnam. While working with a shrink at the VA hospital in Nashville for over twenty years, she suggested that I write down my feelings and experiences in Vietnam. Much to my surprise, the exercise yielded positive results which encouraged me to record my life experiences for my family. I remain vigilant and carefully avoid triggers during the day that lead to restlessness and nightmares. These coping mechanisms give me some semblance of normalcy. The downside means my beautiful and always supporting wife has also been locked away with me in my personal prison while I have remained on the qui vive. I remain entertained at home with my woodworking shop, my flower garden, and my rambling yard. However, I sometimes sense that Carol is bored with her daily routine and the reading of novels. I have encouraged her on many occasions to explore social opportunities on her own, but her steadfast devotion to me will not allow her to consider the invitation.

Of course, the best part of retirement means we have had more opportunities to communicate with our children and grandchildren. Lara and Leslie are now enjoying beautiful families of their own, and they are most eager to share the many intimate details of their lives with us through visits, phone calls, and messages and photos over the internet. Playing with the grandchildren remains our most favorite activity. After they have briefly visited us, I quickly find my favorite recliner where I can recuperate from the rambunctious activities.

During the first few years of retirement, Carol and I made several trips to the Oklahoma City area to visit with Lara and family. During that time Lara had moved into a nurse supervisor position at Mercy Hospital. As her children became school age, it was more difficult for Lara to find a good opportunity for us to visit her. Instead, she and her family came to visit us, which delighted Carol and me.

In 2020, the one-hundredth anniversary of women's suffrage in America was celebrated. It reminds me of an interesting story told to me by Grandmother Emmons. She said my mother was just a baby that year, and there was great excitement in the community about women participating in the political process for the first time. "Mr. Emmons (that's what Grandmother called her husband) drove me to the polls, lecturing me all the while about who I needed to support with my vote. When we arrived, I was surprised when Mr. Emmons entered the voting booth with me to make certain he controlled every vote I cast. I was totally irked with Mr. Emmons's interference with my right to vote. On the way home I assured Mr. Emmons that this would be my first and only trip to the polls. I never intended to be publicly humiliated by him again."

My yard has been a constant source of satisfaction during my retirement years. I have enjoyed the large flower bed that joins the patio at the rear of the house. Every year, I plan something different. The flower bed is always in a state of transition as I experiment with different species of flowers. However, I seem to always go back to the flowers that attract the butterflies and the hummingbirds of late summer. Mom used to call butterflies jeweled flowers with wings. Little by little I removed the saw briers, poison ivy, multiflora rose, and privet from the wooded lot that joins the yard on the six-and-a-half-acre lot. As the undergrowth was removed, Mother Nature covered the ground in beautiful green moss. Finding shade plants that could survive the dry spells of late summer has been a continual challenge, but the surviving specimens have been especially beautiful. Unfortunately, many of the large red oaks in the yard have been struck with blight and they are slowly dying. As the dead trees are removed, more sunlight sneaks through the tree canopy to offer an opportunity to plant new sun-loving flowers.

DENOUEMENT

In 1969 I was a senior at David Lipscomb College completing my student teaching in elementary education. The instructors stressed the importance of teaching through a series of unit studies. At the conclusion of a unit, a culminating activity was planned so that student learning could be driven home using higher order thinking skills and multidisciplinary activities. For example, when I finished the sixth-grade social studies unit on United States geography, I planned a series of companion lessons in the other disciplines of mathematics, language arts, spelling, and reading. The final week the students celebrated their learning with a denouement. The philosophy was based on the notion that a holistic teaching approach perfectly mirrors how we live our everyday lives. To the casual observer from outside the classroom, it would appear from the noise and excitement generated by this teaching method that the teacher had lost control of the students. However, nothing could be further from the truth. As a school principal for twenty years, I quickly learned that classrooms that were quiet as a mouse day in and day out revealed a great number of students bored to death.

Ben Franklin said this about pedagogy: "Tell me, I forget; show me, I remember; involve me, I understand." A teacher's most useful asset is not a head full of knowledge, but a heart full of love, an ear ready to listen, and a hand willing to help others. Kids need the opportunity to share their learning with their peers through drama, learning fairs, debate, and art and music. These are the moments students develop an enthusiasm for learning that spreads throughout the classroom. Children have always been at the center of my universe. I spent my life being paid doing what I have enjoyed the most: playing with kids.

Denouement (day-new-'mah) is a fancy French word that literally means culmination of a series of events. It would be unfair to my reading audience if I concluded this book without sharing how the stories of my life shaped my character. Hearing Mom's call to "Be something, do something, and leave something," I wish to leave a series of parting thoughts that I have learned from others about life itself.

I am certain that I was not the smartest kid of the Elmer and Alice clan, but I am rather confident my average ability did not make me timid. What my physical body has lacked in strength, I compensated with endurance. My achievement in life was not due to intelligence, but I could hold my own against anyone because I developed tenacity and mule-headed pervicacity. When I was twenty-one, Vietnam rewarded me with a permanent handicap of a withered right hand. Losing the feeling and strength because of the permanent nerve damage meant I had to learn to reprogram simple tasks I normally assigned to my dominant hand so that the disability would not make me a quitter. Former President Teddy Roosevelt delivered this bully pulpit speech in two terribly long sentences in 1910 which I found also described many of my life's challenges: "It is not the critic that counts; not the man who points out how the strong man stumbles, or where the doer of deeds could have done them better. The credit belongs to the man who is actually in the arena, whose face is marred by dust and sweat and blood; who strives valiantly; who errs, who comes up short again and again, because there is no effort without error and shortcoming; but who does actually strive to do the deeds; who knows great enthusiasms, the great devotions; who sends himself in a worthy cause; who at the best knows in the end the triumph of high achievement, and who at worst, if he fails, at least fails while daring greatly, so that his place shall never be with those cold and timid souls who neither know victory of defeat." Winston Churchill added this familiar quote: "When you are going through hell, keep going. Never, never, never give up!"

Grandmother Emmons taught me many great lessons on how to live life to its fullest. She was nine years old when her mother died. The following year she lost an older brother who had become her surrogate parent. Although she was an excellent student, poverty forced her to drop out of school and go to work when she was a teenager. While growing up poor she never allowed negative thoughts of desperation cloud her thinking. When all seemed hopeless, she said she would sew beautiful dresses in her mind. She imagined the dresses adorned with intricate needlework that would draw large groups of admirers of her handiwork. She trained her mind to see the good in every situation. Accordingly, her chipper and jovial personality attracted many friends, and it opened doors to employment opportunity. Her powerful dreams eventually became reality when she was recognized as an accomplished and talented artist with needle and thread. Her imaginative skill incorporated with her Singer treadle sewing machine rescued her from starvation several times during her life. She encouraged me to dream powerful dreams as well. Dreams that I chose to act positively upon also became my reality.

FRIENDS

Choosing one's friends is one of life's most important assignments. Pop's Elmerism said it well: "One can't run with the goats without smelling like them." While serving as a school principal for twenty years I observed that whiners loved to hang out together. Instead of being proactive and taking care of classroom management strategies in a timely manner, some teachers preferred to whine about their situation. They blamed their classroom chaos on their students. In order to legitimize their whining, they found other whiners to whine with them at their combined pity party. Likewise, those teachers who set high standards for themselves were more confident and independent. High-achieving teachers did not have time to whine and put other people down; rather they lifted others up. My greatest decision in life was choosing Carol Griffith Parkes to be my soul mate. All of my success has been anchored in her unconditional love. I was seriously wounded when I returned from Vietnam. Fighting demons became a nightly ordeal when all of the horror I had vividly experienced on the battlefield returned in nightmares. Carol woke me many nights when she could obviously tell I was asleep but fighting for my life. I am certain that most women would not have tolerated the rage I felt in the morning that followed my dramatic fits at night. Thankfully, with Carol's enduring love and emotional support, I have learned to avoid triggers during the day that become my evening's nightmares. Carol has been my steady date for almost fifty years. She is the center of my universe and the anchor holding my sanity. Relationships last not because they were destined to last. Relationships last long because two people made a choice to keep it, fight for it, and work for it. Choosing one's friends definitely shapes one's character.

LOVE

Nothing in life is fiercer than formidable, unconditional love! I have often observed that our own selfishness becomes our greatest stumbling block in our quest to find love. Everything we have is a gift from God and yet we view our blessings wearing selfish blinders. We all fall short when it comes to coveting. We protect our stuff with titles, deeds, locks, alarms, and guns. As Pop often said in a famous Elmerism, "What difference will all of this stuff make a hundred years from now?" We can easily discover how rich we are by inventorying our treasures that money can't buy. The greatest examples about love are found in the Bible. The last commandment Jesus gave his disciples on the night he was betrayed was for them to love each other. Jesus had modeled perfect love to his disciples for almost three years, and yet he felt compelled to spell out the purpose of life a final time. The United States of America often calls itself a Christian nation. A Christian nation feeds the poor, houses the homeless, freely educates the masses, heals the sick, and helps all people to work together for the greater good of all creatures on planet Earth. "The metamorphosis of Jesus Christ from a humble servant of the abject poor to a symbol that stands for gun rights, prosperity theology, anti-science, limited government (that neglects the destitute) and fierce nationalism is truly the strangest transformation in human history." (Rainn Wilson,

2020) "We cannot pray in love and live in hate and still think we are worshipping God." (A.W. Tozer) It baffles me that when Jesus talks about feeding the poor, it's Christianity, but when a politician does it, it's socialism. In the 1960s, the Youngbloods turned these lyrics into a hit song: "Come on, people now, smile on your brother, everybody get together, try to love one another right now!" Quotes from Dr. Martin Luther King Jr.: "We need leaders not in love with money but in love with justice; not in love with publicity but in love with humanity... Returning hate for hate multiplies hate, adding deeper darkness to a night already devoid of stars. Darkness cannot drive out darkness; only light can do that. Hate cannot drive out hate; only love can do that." We could live in an amazing world if we could spread love as quickly as we spread hate and negativity. I have often heard people say they cannot give anything because they are not wealthy. Anne Frank added, "No one has ever become poor by giving." The most generous people I have encountered had very little money; some of the wisest persons I have known had little formal education, and some of the kindest people had been hurt the most.

LISTEN

Greek philosopher and scholar, Epictetus, is credited with this quote in 60 A.D.: "God gave us two ears and only one mouth so that we should spend twice as much time listening than we do talking." My master's degree thesis at Tennessee State University was based on listening. Often body language speaks louder than words. A good listener makes the speaker feel he is genuinely interested in the speaker's conversation. A good listener maintains eye contact with the speaker and focuses on the speaker's emotions. To engage in active listening is an art form rarely practiced because our emotions interfere with our ability to hear what the other person is saying. When we see someone is broken, don't try to fix them. (We can't.) When someone is hurting, don't attempt to take away their pain. (We can't.) Instead love them by walking beside them in their hurt. (We can.) Sometimes people simply need to know they aren't alone. A hug is worth a thousand words. I am also certain that no one has ever listened themselves out of a job. I consider it good advice to speak only when one feels his words are better than his silence, but before one speaks let his words pass through these three gates: Is it true? Is it necessary? Is it kind? In my haste to reply, I have often wished I could have retrieved many of my comments. Kindness is the universal language that softens any conversation because it is a language the deaf can hear, the blind can see, and the act most appreciated by our human psyche. I gratefully revere the special people in my life (most especially my mother) who have listened without judgment, helped without conditions, understood with empathy and loved me no matter what! "It is easy to judge, but it is more difficult to understand. Understanding requires compassion, patience, and a willingness to believe that good hearts sometimes make poor choices. Through judging, we separate. Through understanding, we grow." (Doe Zantamata)

LAUGH

I have learned to never take myself too seriously. It is far better to laugh at one's mistakes than to ridicule the one who points them out. One day while Carol and I were shopping, I noticed several beautiful women smiling at me. I asked Carol if she had noticed the smiles. "Absolutely," she said. "What you didn't know is that after you passed them, I also noticed they were laughing out loud!" I didn't know if that should have been attributed to being too tall for my height or being smarter that I look. My Emmons grandparents were famous for their great sense of humor and being the life of the party. I have been told my grandfather, Jack Emmons, had a booming rotund laugh that would shake the windows of the house. He was a "joke-a-minute," and connected with a large audience through his good nature and personal charm. Life is hard, and if one doesn't laugh, it's even harder! Our happiness depends upon our personal ability to lighten up and start each day with a smile on our face. "This is the day the Lord has made; let us rejoice and be glad in it."

My following brand of humor is designed to lighten one's heart: "The most functional English word is 'shit.' You can smoke shit, get shit-faced, buy shit, lose shit, find shit, tell people to eat shit, forget shit." George Carlin continues in this vein for every imaginable turn of phrase regarding excrement.

"I Have Outlived My Pecker" by Willie Nelson: "My nookie days are over, my pilot light is out. What used to be my sex appeal is now my water spout. Time was when on its own accord from my trousers it would spring. But now I have a full-time job to find the gosh darn thing. It used to be embarrassing the way it would behave. For every single morning it would stand and watch me shave. Now as old age approaches it sure gives me the blues. To see it hang its little head and watch me tie my shoes."

"If my Nose was Running Money," one of Mike Snider's greatest hits:

"You say that I don't love you. You say my love is untrue. Well darlin' if I was a rich man I'd prove my love to you. I'd buy you a diamond ring and a new fur coat or two. If my nose was running money honey I'd blow it all on you.

If my nose was running money, I'd blow it all on you. I'd buy you a Cadillac and a new Mercedes too. I'd build you that mansion on the mountaintop. If my nose was running money honey but it's snot."

Spoonerisms are quite humorous, as Matthew Goldman relates in his tale of Rindercella and her prandsom hince: "Once upon a time, in a coreign fountry, there lived a very geautiful birl; her name was Rindercella. Now, Rindercella lived with her mugly other and her two sad bisters. And in that same coreign fountry, there lived a very prandsom hince." Will they "live everly hafter happward"?

Here are some of Pop's favorite humorous Elmerisms: "When I was born my ears were so large, it was six months before my parents knew if I would walk or fly." "One can't find a dancing foot and a praying knee on the same leg." "One can't drink oneself sober any better than one can borrow oneself rich." "A man too busy to fish is just too busy." "Anybody that gets up after 6:30 a.m. won't be worth killing." "Close the door! You weren't raised in the barn!" "He that doth not toot his own horn doth not get it tooted." "Life is fun when we don't take ourselves too seriously."

"Professor Twist" by Ogden Nash: "I give you now Professor Twist, the conscientious scientist. Trustees exclaimed, He never bungles, and sent him off to distant jungles. Camped on a tropic riverside, one day he missed his lovely bride. She had, the guide informed him later, been eaten by an alligator. Professor Twist could not but smile. You mean, he said, a crocodile."

One particular Sunday morning the pastor was delivering a heated hellfire sermon. When he cited the quote from the Bible concerning weeping and gnashing of teeth, an elderly lady sitting on the front pew with a friend loudly blurted to her friend she was really happy all of her teeth had been pulled. The pastor was not amused. He quickly retorted, "Madam, teeth will be provided in hell!"

An elderly lady was walking her dog when a young man grabbed her purse and ran away. I asked if she was okay, and she smiled and said that it's really no big deal because she carries her old purse to put the dog's poop in it until she gets home to dispose of it.

In Mark Twain's classic *The Adventures of Tom Sawyer*, Aunt Polly was lecturing Tom about heaven and hell. "What's so good about heaven?" Tom wondered. Polly explained how everyone sat on clouds and played harp music. "Do you think my friend, Huck, will go to heaven?" Tom asked. "OoooH, no!" Polly exclaimed. "Huck never goes to church, he says ugly words, and he rarely takes a bath." Right then and there, Tom decided he preferred to be in hell in the company of his friend, Huck, because he never felt he could take a licking to sitting on a cloud and playing a harp.

In 1969 upon successfully completing my BS degree, I had already learned years earlier what BS stood for. I completed an MS degree from Tennessee State University in 1976. MS stands for more of the same. The professors at TSU encouraged me to enter their PhD program, but I decided against it, because PhD stands for piled higher and deeper. I learned in graduate school the pursuit of a degree meant learning more and more about less and less until a feller knows everything there is to know about nothing.

One day a young boy was conducting a yard sale when his preacher came by to see what was for sale. "Is that lawn mower for sale?" the preacher asked. "Oh yes," the boy quickly responded, "and only for $25." The preacher began inspecting the mower and pulled the cord a couple of times to see if the mower would start. "You have to cuss it to get it started," the boy chimed in. "I don't cuss," replied the preacher. "Keep pulling the cord, and it will come back to you," the boy answered.

"Knock knock!" "Who's there?" "Banana." "Banana who?" "Knock knock!" "Who's there?" "Banana." "Banana who?" "Knock knock!" "Who's there?" "Banana who?" "Knock knock!" "Who's there?" "Orange." "Orange who?" "Orange you glad I didn't say banana again?"

"Knock knock!" "Who's there?" "Who." "Who Who?" "I didn't know you were an owl!"

"Knock knock!" "Who's there?" "Boo." "Boo who?" "Just because you are an owl, you don't have to cry about it."

How many elephants can one get in a Volkswagen? Five. Two in the front seat, two in the back seat, and one in the glove compartment.

What did Tarzan say when he saw the elephants coming? "Here come the elephants!"

What did Tarzan say when he saw the elephants coming wearing sunglasses? He didn't say anything; he didn't recognize them.

How did Tarzan stop a herd of stampeding elephants? He cut off their stampeters.

Strive to be the person who laughs a little louder and smiles a little bigger. Humor makes us have more friends and causes us to live longer and adds to our happiness! Dolly Parton said, "If you see someone without a smile, give them one of yours." I indeed hope my corny jokes brought a smile to your face.

COMMONALITY

While completing my graduate studies at Peabody, I was required to study phenomenological research. Phenomenology is an approach to qualitative research that focuses on the commonality of a lived experience within a particular group. While this sounds complicated, it really isn't. Living through the Great Depression and WWII garnered shared experiences for my parents, grandparents, and their neighbors. The common threads of poverty, grief, uncertainty, and death were the influential paradigms that would bind a family and a community together working toward a common goal. I often heard my parents talk about the hardship and sacrifice they endured through those epic eras of American history. Common idioms emerged and were often repeated by people of the Greatest Generation: "Measure twice, cut once"; "Is this trip necessary?"; "Don't put all of your eggs in one basket"; "Learn to get by with less"; "There is nothing glorious about war." Franklin D. Roosevelt took advantage of this phenomenon and become a great national leader, elected as president for four consecutive terms. The middle class of America was formed primarily due to his unique leadership style. President Roosevelt said this in 1937, and these words apply today more than ever: "The test of our progress is not whether we add more to the abundance of those who have much. It is whether we provide enough for those who have too little." The tie that bound America then has largely disappeared. Commonality can be found, but in smaller subgroups. In the fifties and sixties, the majority of Americans received their news via television through three network channels. The internet and the multitude of cable news programs that broadcast continuous news had not been conceived. Today a host of multimedia outlets compete for larger viewing audiences by sensationalizing the news, and by airing stories, interviews, and commentaries based on the common paradigm of their viewing audience. News agencies on opposite ends of the continuum often skew perceptions about the truth and endorse conspiracy theories in order to pander to their audience. Audience share and ratings have become more important than truth.

SYNERGY

Pop grew up on the Buffalo River on a farm directly in front of Leslie and Daniel's (Hunt) house in Summertown. He spent many of his summer days plowing a team of mules on that river bottom land. Pop said we could learn good lessons from his mules. They always pulled harder when he turned the team around at the end of a long row and the mules faced the direction of the barn. "You see," he said, "mules always worked harder when they were working toward a goal. When they faced the barn, their goal of going to the barn was planted firmly in their mind. When his mother rang the dinner bell, the mules would race to the barn in breakneck speed, because they knew the bell also meant a rest period and feed for them also. Another curious phenomenon about mules was they could pull much harder working as a team. Pop said two mules could pull three or four times as much as a mule pulling in single harness because he said they received strength from one another. "Synergy" is a word used by Stephen Covey to describe the bonus groups receive when they work together. He said, "Synergy is better than my way or your way. It's our way." He added, "The main thing is to keep the main thing the main thing." In the book of Acts the early church grew by leaps and bounds because they were bound together by a common purpose. Pop often said he wished the congregations he worked with over his fifty-plus years as a minister and elder had as much sense as the mules he plowed with as a boy. When division arose in those congregations, members would often swarm like a hive of bees. Observing this as a child I once asked Pop why so many of the members left. He answered with one of his favorite Elmerisms: "Too many chiefs, and not enough Indians." The Gaithers sang a gospel song years ago that concisely spoke to the problem when synergy wanes: "We tend to make it harder. Build steeples out of stone; Fill books with explanations of 'The Way.' But if we'd stop and listen and break a little bread, we could hear the Master say: 'Loving God; loving each other; making music with my friends. Loving God; loving each other; and the story never ends." We need to embrace synergy and keep "the main thing the main thing."

THE JAMES CODE OF CONDUCT

I was a grown man before I realized I was born a privileged child. Other than an occasional Elmerism, Pop had little to say to the children. However, he left an excellent legacy of modeling hard work and integrity. "Your name is the most important gift you have ever been given. Never do anything that will tarnish the James name in the community." Pop said to be vigilant in one's encounters with others. He continued, "I am often surprised how cheaply someone will sell their integrity. Integrity is a very expensive gift. Don't expect it from cheap people." I grew up with the James code of integrity firmly planted within my heart. The James code meant if it's not yours, don't take it; if it's not true, don't say it; if it's not right, don't do it, and forgive and forget! A grudge can eat at the very fabric of a person's inward being. The Bible teaches if we want to be forgiven of our many sins, we must first forgive others. I have learned that offering forgiveness helps the forgiver more than the perpetrator. Jesus taught there is great reward for those willing to forgive. We simply cannot hold grudges and do ugly things to people and expect to live a beautiful life! By chance I was born free in America to loving parents who modeled hard work, kindness, integrity, and Christian ethics. They managed to stay married when money was scarce and times were hard, and their great examples propelled all six children to graduate from college with honor and live beautiful lives, never tarnishing the James name.

ENCOURAGEMENT

On report card day I always sensed that Pop was annoyed by my performance, but rarely did he offer encouragement. I suppose Pop felt that was Mom's job. Pop was totally baffled and pleased when I made the dean's list at Lipscomb. He carried my grades and the letter from the dean to Summertown High School for show and tell. Mom's nonjudgmental encouragement kept me working at becoming a better student. She once told me she had named me David after the great king of Israel who was a man after God's own heart. She gave me a name that stood for goodness, strength, and integrity. When I began college, she could sense I was struggling to keep my head above water. Her words of love and encouragement gave me the stamina to keep plugging and to never give up. It was during one of those pep sessions she confided to me that Pop also struggled the first year he was in college. Mom composed and typed many of Pop's papers that were due because he was working a second job at H.G. Hills grocery store, and he did not have time to finish all of his assignments. Mom's smiling face always met me at the door when I returned home from school and the military service. Her powerful unconditional love gave me the strength to keep working and to never give in or give up. When I was in Vietnam, she wrote me a letter every day. She often mentioned she was also praying for me daily. The other guys in my platoon were jealous about the amount of mail I was receiving from home. Mom saved every letter I wrote home while in the military service and surprised me by returning them to me one special Christmas. Mom's cheery disposition lightened the burden I was facing in my life. Mom encouraged me to never doubt myself even when others were putting me down. "No matter what others say or do, don't you dare doubt your worth or the beauty of your character. Just keep smiling, and never allow an adversary to control your emotions." Mom's character exuded goodness and mercy daily. She always pretended to be in a good mood even when she was going through a rough patch. A few weeks before Mom died, she was battling cervical cancer, and it was becoming more obvious by each passing day that her life on earth was evaporating. The nurses and staff were totally amazed how Mom continued to be chipper and happy in her final days. Everyone at the nursing facility wanted to have Mom as a patient on their rotation because Mom was an exceptionally kind patient who continued to spread joy to everyone until her last breath.

BUILD THE FORT TODAY

In the summer of 1990, I was attending the Tennessee Middle School Convention in Gatlinburg. The keynote speaker for the banquet was Jim Kern. Jim was a delightful speaker and I remember a few things he discussed that evening. Jim told the story of a seven-year-old boy who asked his father to help him build a fort. Daddy began making excuses to the boy about how busy he was at work, and that he came home exhausted every evening. When the boy asked again, Daddy's explanation was that he and Mom were going to a party, and he still didn't have time. The fourth time the boy asked, Daddy promised to help the following Saturday, but something happened unexpectedly at work and Daddy put his son off again. Finally, the promised day to build the fort had come. The boy dashed out of school at the closing school bell and decided to run the seven blocks to get home as soon as possible. With a head full of dreams and happiness, the boy ran as fast as he could, not aware of the too familiar world passing by. As he entered the busy road, he forgot to look both ways. A truck appeared out of nowhere and the small boy was hit. At the emergency room the first evaluation contained only one word, "Coma!" When Dad received the call, he drove recklessly at full speed, finally standing by his son's bed. Daddy watched two little eyes open, a little smile appeared, and a voice too weak uttered the boy's last words, "Daddy, we won't have to build that fort tonight after all." The child died, and I believe the child was okay, but Dad was not okay. Oh, how Dad wished he had taken the time to build the fort! Things could have been much different if Dad had asked, "How long will it take to build your fort?" The child's idea would have been much simpler than the adult's perception of a fort. Maybe it was only a bedspread thrown over the backs of two chairs. The fleeting moments we can spend playing with our children are very important in building lifelong relationships. If we are too busy when the children are young, they will eventually stop asking us to be the center of their universe, and they will find someone else to fill their great need to be loved and belong. Children notice a father or a mother who doesn't want to be involved in their lives. Stop the nonsense of always thinking that your spouse has turned your kids against you. Your absence is the biggest problem. Human beings are priceless and precious. Unfortunately, many think this only applies to adults. Kids are people too! Too often when Carol and I are grocery shopping, we witness adults publicly badgering and humiliating their children. Orders and threats begin to accumulate at such a rapid speed, these parents feel they have to shout louder with more drama as they continue to raise the bar to obtain their children's correct behavior. The kids become so insulated to the constant nagging and threatening until the parents' intervention has no effect whatsoever. Unfortunately, I have also observed licensed teachers who were trained to know better continue changing acceptable limits for their students, and all the while lose control of managing their classrooms. During my thirty-seven-year tenure as an educator, I spent a great deal of time with handicapped children. Of course, handicapped children can be quite a handful, and many times progress is recorded at a much slower pace. "Sometimes angels are disguised as kids with special needs to teach us how to be better people." (Kelly's Treehouse) When I began teaching special needs children, I mistakenly believed they all could learn just as well as regular kids if I broke the learning down in small enough steps. On one occasion I was tutoring a young fifth grader with his multiplication tables. I showed him how we were going to break the task down to smaller tasks where we would only be learning just a few tables a day. Everything worked surprisingly well on the tables through the fives. When the sixes were added we began hitting a few snags, but I was confident we would be successful. As the days passed, my student became reluctant to work on the tables. In a few days, he began missing school quite regularly. I became concerned and decided to make a home visit one day after school. His father ran a country grocery store in town and I knew the family quite well. I stopped by the store first and asked his father if it would be okay for me to pay his son a visit. "Of course," he said, "but on your way back, please stop by the store again." I found the child to be in perfect health, but I sensed the mother was annoyed with my visit. When I stopped by the store the second time, the father said, "I have a question. How much is 365 × 853?" "Give me a pencil and a paper and I will give you the answer," I replied. "No need," he said. "I have the answer right here for you." With a quick couple of calculator strokes, he did indeed have the correct answer. Handing me the paper receipt he continued, "I don't know my multiplication tables either, but it has never stopped me from making a good living in this little store. Ease up on those useless multiplication tables and my son will come back to school." Shazam! I learned the greatest lesson of my career that afternoon. Neither the state's curriculum nor my daily lesson plans was the agenda of the student or the parents, and I learned I had been majoring in minors. I had failed in earning the respect of the most important people—my students and their parents. From that day forward I allowed my students to address me as Sid. Some kids were uncomfortable with this in the beginning. When they insisted on calling me Mr. James, I also insisted on calling them as Mr. or Miss as well. There is more than one way to skin a cat. The young man never learned his multiplication tables, but in the scheme of things it didn't make a rat's ass difference. He became a very talented diesel engine mechanic earning himself handsome wages that far exceeded what I was making as a teacher. The time we spend playing with our children is one of our greatest investments. "I find myself worrying most that when we hand our children phones we steal their boredom from them. As a result we are raising a generation of writers who will never start writing, artists who will never start doodling, chefs who will never make a mess of the kitchen, athletes who will never kick a ball against a wall, musicians who will never pick up their aunt's guitar and start strumming." (Glennon Doyle, *Untamed*) A parting thought from Mother Teresa on raising your children: "You will teach them to fly, but they will not fly your flight. You will teach them to dream, but they will not dream your dream.

You will teach them to live, but they will not live your life. Nevertheless, in every flight, in every life, in every dream, the print of the way you taught them will remain."

POLITICS

Will Rogers said, "I am not a member of any organized political party; I'm a Democrat." As I grew older, I stopped taking everything at face value and began seriously planning my own path based upon what I felt was in the best interest of our American society. Occasionally I have been chided for not voting for what was in my best personal interest. Now that I have retired and I am not struggling financially, many of the Republican ideals actually put more money in my pocket. After all I have lived in America as a privileged white guy where most government laws are written to favor my well-being. The opposite political side tells me that liberal Democrats are socialists and baby killers. Most Americans wouldn't know what socialism is even if it directly deposited a Social Security check in their FDIC-insured bank accounts. A Democratic Socialist is not a Marxist Socialist or a Communist. A Democratic Socialist is still a capitalist; but just one who seeks to restrain the self-destructive excesses of capitalism, and to channel government's use of our tax money into creating opportunities for everyone. I believe that both economy and society should be run democratically to meet human needs, not simply to profit a greedy few. One of the shocking lessons learned from Vietnam was to witness an entire society that lived in abject poverty. Almost every American family enjoys a higher income than the world median annual income of $10,000, and yet our middle class has continued to shrink since 1980. The upper class in America continues to get richer as the poor in America become poorer. I am certain this is due to our government making policies that benefit the rich mistakenly believing these policies will pay for themselves, should last forever, and they are good for all Americans. However, if government policies benefit the poor, many Americans mistakenly feel our government cannot afford it and the policies should be ended as soon as possible or it will destroy our nation. I also believe that being open to data, facts, and science doesn't make me a liberal. On the issue of pro-life, I really don't feel qualified to discuss it in detail because I don't have a uterus. I can hardly imagine what it means to be a woman. Men can have sex with a woman and walk away (which they often do). Unfortunately, the woman is often stuck with pregnancy, childbirth, and usually poverty as a result. I strongly believe in human rights. I agree with Sister Joan Chittister: "I do not believe that just because you're opposed to abortion that makes you pro-life. In fact, I think in many cases your morality is deeply lacking if all you want is a child born but not a child fed, not a child educated, not a child housed. And why would I think you don't? Because you don't want any tax money to go there. That's not pro-life. That's pro-birth. We need a much broader conversation on what the morality of pro-life is." I have observed that most pro-lifers are in favor of capital punishment—the death penalty. I have also observed the people who don't want to help refugees because "we have our own poor" also don't want to help our poor. The pandemic of 2020 also made me realize that many pro-lifers joined the #mybodymychoice movement over wearing masks to slow the spread of Covid-19 but keep fighting the pro-choice movement. While this baffles me, it makes perfect sense to many conservatives who are pro-life and pro-choice simultaneously. It is ironic the left is referred to as radical. It's the right running around with their assault weapons, denying science, spewing conspiracy theories, and not accepting the results of the 2020 presidential election. The only way our United States democracy will survive is for us to do a better job preparing an educated electorate. Winston Churchill said, "A nation that forgets its past has no future." Mark Twain added, "No amount of evidence will ever persuade an idiot!" We need to remain teachable because we are not always right.

PATRIOTISM

"The American's Creed" by William Tyler Page: "I believe in the United States of America as a government of the people, by the people, for the people; whose just powers are derived from the consent of the governed, a democracy in a republic, a sovereign nation of many sovereign states; a perfect union, one and inseparable; established upon those principles of freedom, equality, justice, and humanity for which American patriots sacrificed their lives and fortunes. I therefore believe it is my duty to my country to love it, to support its Constitution, to obey its laws, to respect its flag, and to defend it against all enemies." The creed was written in 1917 when the world was embroiled in the Great War (WWI) and many Americans thought that we dwelled on our privileges and had forgotten to consider the duties and obligations of being citizens of the United States of America. New York State Commissioner of Education, Henry Chapin, conceived the idea to promote a countywide contest to achieve the briefest possible summary of American political faith, founded upon fundamentals most distinctive in American history and tradition. While teaching at the alternative school, we began each school day reciting this creed and the Pledge of Allegiance. I was inspired by President John F. Kennedy during his inaugural address when he beckoned children and adults to civic action and public service with his historic words: "Ask not what your country can do for you—ask what you can do for your country." I grew up during the fifties and sixties where every able-bodied male citizen of the United States enrolled in the selective service program, i.e., the draft. The Vietnam War did away with the program because the draft was overused to find a solution to a failed diplomatic mission. Vietnam was a war fought without a clear mission and a belief that might makes right. As a result, our nation was robbed of the idea that every abled person, male and female, should be required to SERVE their country for a period of time, and that war is the worst solution to solve disagreement between nations. Our volunteer army of the United States has insulated the American people from the great sacrifice American veterans took on with their oath of allegiance: …"I will support and defend the Constitution of the United States against all enemies, foreign and domestic; that I will bear true faith and allegiance to the same; and that I will obey the orders of the President of the United States and the orders of the officers appointed over me, according to regulations and the Uniform Code of Military Justice. So help me God." When I took the oath of allegiance, took up arms, and fought what I thought was the enemy of foreign soil, I did so as a combat infantryman in the United States Army. I was given an automatic M16 rife that held a twenty-round magazine and was also schooled on the M60 machine gun, the M40 LAW, the M79 grenade launcher, and a variety of other small arms weapons all of which were designed to maim and/or kill the enemy. My tour of duty in Vietnam made me see human carnage my eyes will never quit seeing. I answered my nation's call to duty because I thought it was the honorable thing to do. My generation grew up standing for the flag and saying the pledge each morning at school. I grew up playing with toy guns, and the favorite backyard games were Cowboys and Indians, Cops and Robbers, and Kick the Can. I spent most of my free time playing outside and inventing new games to play without adult supervision. When I was a teenager, I hitchhiked to Lawrenceburg and played pool on Saturdays. I drank from a water hose and only had dessert on Sunday afternoons. I was taught to respect my elders and got spanked when I didn't toe the line. I grew up fighting with my brothers, but we rarely drew blood in the scuffles. Duty, honor, and country was drilled into my character in the Boy Scouts. Because of this I never considered avoiding a call to the service of my country. I have often wondered how different my life would have been if President Eisenhower had been willing to sit down with Ho Chi Minh and discuss business without being influenced by American colonialism, and if the following presidents had cared more about forging a lasting peace than building a legacy for themselves. While I kept my oath to defend the Constitution, I have sadly watched many of our presidents violate their oath and duty to America in exchange for personal wealth or glory. Those North Vietnamese and Viet Cong soldiers I fought on the battlefield could have been just as gentle and understanding as the South Vietnamese I worked with daily. I am confident I could have been friends with those my government trained me to hate and kill as my enemy. Today our government has cultivated a segment of society who believes that owning personal assault weapons is their God-given right which carries no real sense of patriotism. Owning the assault weapon bears no personal responsibility to defend America. The Constitution has been manipulated to mean anyone can possess and carry weapons designed for the purpose of human carnage. I encourage anyone who holds that belief to join the militia also mentioned in the Second Amendment. They can take their oath of allegiance and serve their country in the National Guard or one of the branches of the armed services and become a real American patriot instead of feeding an ego by holding an assault weapon. I know for a fact one can easily tire of combat. If every citizen was required to serve, I am confident we would not be having this discussion about assault weapons in the hands of private citizens today.

THE PRIVILEGE OF GROWING OLD

An older man and woman sat on the senior center porch and they argued. She challenged him with, "I'll bet I can tell you how old you are."

He came back with, "I'll bet you can't." They carried on like little kids, "…bet I can," "…bet you can't." In exasperation he said, "All right, do it!"

"Stand up over there," she directed, "and take off all of your clothes." He did just as she instructed. After she carefully looked him up and down, she stated confidently, "You're ninety-four!"

"How did you do that?" he demanded.

"You told me yesterday," she answered.

In 2017 country music star Toby Keith and mega silver screen star Clint Eastwood were sharing a golf cart at Eastwood's charity golf tournament in Pebble Beach, California. Out on the green, Eastwood shared he would be starting work on a new movie, *The Mule*, in two days, which also happened to be his eighty-eighth birthday. Struck by Eastwood's relentless energy when many of us are content to sit and reflect, Keith asked how he keeps going. Eastwood responded, "I just get up every morning and go out. I don't let the old man in." Keith recounts, "I'm writing that down." In a few weeks Keith had penned these lyrics that became a hit record:

> *"Don't let the old man in, I wanna leave this alone*
> *Can't leave it up to him, he's knocking on my door*
> *And I knew all of my life, that someday it would end*
> *Get up and go outside, don't let the old man in."*

Being in poor health King Hezekiah prayed to God and asked him to extend his life for fifteen more years. God answered Hezekiah's prayer and Hezekiah lived for fifteen more years. We know that it is unusual for God to answer prayers directly and give the petitioner exactly what was asked. Many times, we ask for healing and receive death unaware in God's eyes this is the perfect healing. When God intervenes directly and immediately, we tend to think we have witnessed a miracle. I believe in miracles because I am one. When I was on the battlefield in Vietnam wounded and abandoned, hiding in a giant prickly pear cactus, and within inches from the enemy, I prayed the hardest prayer of my life. I recall the prayer I prayed was not very eloquent, and I know I also had not been righteous in Vietnam, but I guarantee it was the most fervent prayer I had ever prayed because my life depended on it. I asked God to grant me an impossible miracle. I wanted to live through the terrible conundrum of imagining my life being cut short because of war! Fifty years later I am still living, and I praise God daily for the undeserved extension of my life. I am confident I am not the only person who asked God to extend their life when all possible options are exhausted. I have had the opportunity to find the love of my life, and in marriage raise two beautiful children. I have never been unemployed, hungry, or cold. My wonderful life has been better than I ever imagined, and my grandchildren are the icing on my chocolate cake.

When Carol and I attended my fiftieth class reunion of Summertown High School back in 2006, I was astonished at how many of my classmates looked old. I never noticed that maybe I had aged as well. I have considered myself young at heart my entire life. Pop and many of my teachers called my condition immaturity when I was in school. I never minded the tag because I have always loved being the biggest kid when playing with my students at school or with my children and grandchildren. Being old doesn't seem so old now that I am old, because I still like to play. I characterize all of my yard and woodworking projects as play although aching muscles remind me otherwise. I have had to rethink playing a little bit when my grandson, Ezra, comes to visit. He likes to gather up the tools and go to work in the yard. After 72 years of living, I find myself in a comfortable place—a place where peace is priority and negativity cannot exist. I have forgiven everyone who took advantage of me through deceit or the usurping of authority. It feels good to be unburdened by those who have attempted to control my behavior. I have reached what William Wordsworth called self-actualization, and what Dr. Martin Luther King Jr. called being on the mountaintop. That freedom is indeed exhilarating! "I have fought the fight; I have finished the race; I have kept the faith." (2 Timothy 4:7) Yet, "It ain't over till it's over" (Yogi Berra) or until the fat lady sings.

FAITH

My life is not just about me. It is more about the God I serve and the manifested faith that have been a constant in my life. "I believe in God the Father, infinite in wisdom, power, and love, whose mercy is over all his works, and whose will is ever directed to his children's good. I believe in Jesus Christ, Son of God and Son of man, the gift of the Father's unfailing grace, the ground of my HOPE, and the promise of our deliverance from sin and death. I believe in the Holy Spirit as the divine presence in our lives, whereby we are kept in perpetual remembrance of the truth in Christ and find strength and help in time of need. I believe that this FAITH should manifest itself in the service of love as set forth in the example of our blessed Lord, to the end that the kingdom of God may come upon the earth. Amen." (A Modern Affirmation, United Methodist Hymnal, p. 885) I believe that Christianity should manifest itself in service to others. Jesus gave us the perfect example to emulate. When I look at his example, I marvel at his kindness. Even when Jesus was completely exhausted, he continued to be a suffering servant who modeled beautiful acts of kindness. The kindness Jesus modeled was not limited to his friends. It was not limited to members of his Jewish religion. It was not limited to those who could return the favor of kindness. For Jesus, life itself was about service to others. Jesus said the blessed people who will inherit the earth are the humble, the meek, and the lowly. Those who were always kind to their fellow man, especially to the poor, the marginalized, and the immigrants, would be the greatest in his kingdom of heaven.

My Christian faith has been the anchor that has guided me through the valley and the shadow of death. I am most certainly a Christian because of my heritage and my ZIP code. Had I grown up in the Middle East, I would probably be a devout Muslim. A South American home would probably have made me a Catholic. An Indian neighborhood would probably have made me a Hindu. A Far East hamlet would probably have made me Buddhist. I thank especially God, but also fate and my lucky stars for my Christian heritage which has served as my moral compass throughout my life.

BEING A GOOD STEWARD TO MOTHER EARTH

As a usual summer practice, I was helping Pop frame a house. Pop built or remodeled more than thirty houses during his career. Pop discovered very soon after college that he would need to work a second job to make ends meet to provide for his growing family. We usually quit our carpenter work around 3:00 p.m. One afternoon after I had gathered all of the tools and placed them in the back of the car, I noticed Pop working out in front of the house with a pick and a garden rake. "What are you doing?" I curiously inquired. Never breaking his stride while swinging the pick Pop responded, "I'm going to dig up these saw briers in the front yard."

"Why?" I asked.

"Because I always want to improve upon a property before I offer it for sale. I intend to be a good steward of Mother Earth." I really did not understand Pop's answer until years later when I found myself digging up saw briers on my property as well. Mom wanted to continue to improve her beautiful flower garden every year. Almost every November she directed me to the flower bed to plant daffodil bulbs. I asked Mom why she wanted more even though she had a very large garden filled with spring bulbs. "Honey," she said, "you can't have too many buttercups." While serving as principal of Coffman Middle School for 14 years, I became very interested in ecology. Wayne Richardson, an enthusiastic science teacher at Coffman, understood how important student involvement was to successfully applying higher order thinking skills. Wayne and I began planning annual science fairs that involved all of the Coffman students. We adopted a stretch of U.S. Highway 64 to remove litter. Occasionally we incorporated the help of the exploratory teachers to plan special ecology musicals. Our largest and most successful project was the Outdoor Classroom at David Crockett State Park. The earth is revered by our Native Americans. Mourning Dove of the Salish tribe said, "Everything on earth has a purpose, every disease an herb to cure it, and every person a mission. This is the Indian theory of existence." Once as a child I carelessly threw a pop bottle out of the car. Pop immediately stopped the car and beckoned me to retrieve the bottle. As I reentered the car he said, "We are not slobs. If you are tempted to litter again when you are confident no one is watching and pitch it out anyway, you just sold a part of your integrity. The most important person will always be watching because integrity means being true to oneself." Booker T. Washington said, "Everyone's life is measured by the power that individual has to make the world better."

LEGACY

My family circle is a large part of my story because I did not grow up in solitude. Mealtime at the Elmer James household meant nine family members dined at one large table, and there was always extra room for unannounced guests. I deeply love my brothers and sisters, my charming wife, my extended family, my children and grandchildren, my church family, and my stalwart friends. When I have been on the mountain of delight in the height of stellar celebration or in the valley of despair knocked to my knees by the bitter pills of life, family and friends have always been there helping me rejoice or comforting me in my sorrow. I remind myself I am a product formed by my father and my father's father and mother. Likewise, I am my mother and my mother's mother and father. They have had a tremendous influence in who I am and how I have formed my character. Life's most important treasure has always been my family and friends. The greatest of all of life's celebrations has been spent with family: grandparents, parents, brothers, sisters, cousins, uncles, aunts, my soul mate, Carol, our wonderful children, their extended families and especially our grandchildren, and true-blue friends. Furthermore, in that classic Gaither hymn, *Child of a King*, we hear, "Oh yes, oh yes, I'm a child of the King. His royal blood now flows in my veins. And I who was wretched and poor now can sing: Praise God, praise God, I'm a child of the King!" I am and always will be a child of God and a member of his Kingdom.

Pop used to say at funerals, "We all have an appointment with death." When life brings me to my knees a final time and I cannot find the strength and perseverance to stand back up, my life will not end in death. I remind all of my descendants, I will always be part of my surviving family's story because I am a part of you, and you are my story! I will become part of the great cloud of witnesses that continue to surround all those kindred spirits whose lives continue to move forward. Whether we call them Chinese Watchmen, Guardian Angels, or Christian Saints, I will be cheering you on to "run the race that lies before us while keeping our eyes fixed on Jesus, the leader and perfecter of our faith (KJV, Hebrews 12:2)." So family, never give in or give up until you find a way to love ALL of your family. Search for those precious souls on earth that make you laugh a little louder, smile a little bigger, and live in blessed Christian love! Living in love caused me to discover heaven while I am still living. I beckon you to join me in living the good life.

ABOUT THE AUTHOR

Meet Sid, an accomplished storyteller and king of one-liners. He admits eagerly that his ears are only for decoration, he is taller standing than he is sitting, and does his best fishing for salmon at Kroger. He is a man of faith, a product of a devout family who raised a faithful family of his own. He loves his neighbor through acts of service and would much rather trim branches or plant buttercup bulbs in your yard than sit and talk for hours.

His compassion for people in need led him to focus his career on children with special learning needs. As the principal of the middle school, he focused on the wild idea that every child could be successful, and every student had the opportunity to participate in the extra-curricular activity of their choice. Students were given business-sided "Success Cards" for good deeds or good work in class, which could be converted to candy or prizes.

Being genetically positive with a dirt gene on his green thumb, he encouraged programming that would expose students to earth sciences, culminating in a school-wide Earth Day science fair and musical opportunities. This extended beyond the walls of the school with his friend and teacher, Wayne Richardson, with their work on the Outdoor Classroom in Davy Crockett State Park. This project, available to anyone in the community, was not only curriculum they wrote to be used with any age level, but also included dragging railroad ties, clearing saw briars, and building the trail for classrooms to use as they learned.

Sid has sung bass in the church choir for 36 consecutive years and has graced several barbershop quartets along the way. Perhaps he is most known for using these musical talents to serenade every middle school student during their lunch on their birthday in front of their peers. Despite the humiliation of being singled-out in the lunchroom by the towering principal wearing suspenders and plaid pants, this is remembered fondly as a time when every student knew they mattered. He did not have to make everyone feel special, but he did (intentionally out of tune).

Although his brothers were valedictorians and graduated Summa Cum Laude, he will tell you he graduated Lordy How Come. Studying and school success did not come easily to him, but his natural work ethic consistently superseded his natural intelligence. This work ethic inspired many fatherly pep talks to his children, and they would come to know him as their biggest cheerleader when faced with adversity. He taught determination by modeling this behavior in every task he undertook.

His career with the school system ended sweetly with the opportunity for him to work one-on-one with many kids facing the greatest obstacles, greatest risk, and greatest need. This included students with no verbal skills, when he would take his ukulele and sing them songs and read them and their younger siblings stories with great theater and animation; students who were so physically sick they could not attend school, when he would sit and teach and tell stories so they knew they were still connected; teenage moms who were recovering from childbirth and learning how to be parents while juggling their classwork, when he would encourage them that their lives were not over and their futures were still full of hope; even a student he would take fishing and they would talk about how to stay out of jail.

He has encouraged every Sunday School class he has taught to memorize Psalm 23, and rewarded the children who could recite it back to him with a silver dollar. This psalm was especially important to him during his drafted service in Vietnam, where he would recite it at the hand-dug graves of fallen soldiers. When asked once why it was him who recited the scripture, he answered, "Because I was the only one who had it memorized." Though he walked through the valley of the shadow of death, he allowed God to lead him and bring him comfort. He knows that the building blocks of faith profoundly impacted his survival and his life, and this motivated his service to help with so many vacation Bible schools and Sunday school classes.

A gregarious introvert, Sid is happiest at home and entertaining family in front of a roaring fire. Even as a child, he knew that hospitality did not require linen napkins and a fancy meal and could easily be achieved through peanut-butter-cracker-sandwiches. As an adult, he is happy to serve grilled fish and grilled veggies in season. After the meal, he is eager to sit in his recliner and sip cabernet cardboardaux and nibble on whatever his bride can find in the kitchen. He will stretch his legs as the fire pops and listen eagerly to the stories of those around him and join with stories that become more grandiose every time he shares them.

The family goal has always been to keep our dysfunction to ourselves, but Sid insists on letting it get air long enough for you to read and enjoy. The intent of this autobiography is to capture the stories of one grunt's point of view despite the hardships he faced. Any offense to the reader is unintended.

He and his saintly, patient wife, Carol, are always eager to entertain. If you let them know you can visit, they will keep the light on for you. If you give them enough warning, he will go through his holding bed to see what plants you can take back with you, too.

Sid's snippet written by Lara Parkes James Gaston.

www.ingramcontent.com/pod-product-compliance
Lightning Source LLC
Chambersburg PA
CBHW021437070526
44577CB00002B/202